SOMPO GUIDE
TOKYO
Have a safe trip

CONTENTS

Top report

The 8 keywords for enjoying Tokyo 12

Area report

The hot areas of Tokyo 35

Venture a little further!

Interview

TOKYO TOPICS

BASIC INFORMATION for your journey 181

Please make sure to read the following points before reading this magazine.

About the data

Address ... Indicates the address of listed properties
TEL ... Indicates contact information of each facility
Opening hours ... Indicates business hours. If there is a time of last order or last admission, it is stated in parentheses. *Not available unless you order or enter by the indicated time, so please be careful.
Closed ... As a general rule, indicates public holidays not including special holidays, such as the year-end and New Year holidays, Golden Week (from end of April to early May), Obon holidays (August 13 to 15), temporary closures, etc.
Fee・Price・Charge ... Indicates standard budget for restaurant, and admission fee for facilities. Facility admission fee indicates the price per adult.
Access ... Indicates the time required from the closest station. 60 meters is converted into 1min.
URL ... Indicates the web address.

How to read the map

MAP P.38 A-3
A-3 — Indicates location on the map
P.38 — Published on page 38 of this magazine

"dori", "kaido": words for streets and roads
"zaka": the word for slope
A1: ground exit of the subway

About PICT

... Foreign language-speaking staff available
... Foreign language menu available
... Facility guidance or brochures in foreign language available
... Wi-Fi available *Password may be required depending on the store
... Reservation required
... Credit cards accepted *Cards accepted may vary depending on the store
... Smoking allowed *Sometimes with limited hours or separate smoking depending on the store
... Vegetarian menu available
HP ... Website available in foreign language
... With dress code
... Tax-free available
... PICT color is grey when not available

About published content

The content published on this magazine dates from June 2016 to January 2017. Please check in advance before using the facilities listed here, as there might be changes due to various circumstances. Prices may change following reconsideration of consumption tax. For this reason, prices are sometimes shown without tax. Understand that our company cannot pay compensation for any trouble or damage that may arise from use of the information contained in this magazine.

About QR codes

In this magazine, we have inserted the QR codes of sites for foreign visitors to Japan "Live Japan" and Japan National Tourism Organization. They are packed with useful information for your journey, so do not hesitate to contact them. The URLs are as follows.

Live Japan URL
URL:https://livejapan.com

Japan National Tourism Organization
URL:http://www.jnto.go.jp/eng

TOKYO AREA MAP

A B 1 2 3 4

Toshima-ku · IKEBUKURO · Seibu Ikebukuro Line · Otsuk · Mejiro · JR Yamanote Line · Takadanobaba · Seibu Shinjuku Line · Nakano-ku · Ghibli Museum,Mitaka(p.174) · Kichijoji · Nishi-Ogikubo · Ogikubo · Asagaya · Koenji · Nakano · Higashi-Nakano · JR Chuo Line · Inokashira Park · Suginami-ku · Shinjuku-ku · Okubo · Shin-Okubo · SHINJUKU · Shinjuku Gyoen · Yoyogi · Sendagaya · Meiji Jingu · Shinanomachi · Shibuya-ku · Meijijingu Gaien · Keio Line · HARAJUKU · Odakyu Odawara Line · OMOTESANDO · Keio Inokashira Line · SHIBUYA · HIROO (p.7) · EBISU(p.7) · Tokyu Denentoshi Line · SHIROKANEDAI(p.6) · Meguro-ku · Meguro · Gotanda · Tokyu Toyoko Line · Osaki · Tokyu Meguro Line · Tokyu Oimachi Line · Nishi-Oi · Tokyu Ikegami Line · Omori · Kamata · Keikyu Line

IKEBUKURO

→ P.162

Plenty of commercial and entertainment facilities centered on Sunshine-dori!

SHINJUKU

→ P.36

Have fun from morning till night! A huge, convenient terminal that offers everything

HARAJUKU/ OMOTESANDO

→ P.100

Harajuku, the driving force behind "Kawaii" culture. Omotesando, where the "newest" things gather

SHIBUYA

→ P.86

Super crowded at all times! An energetic epicenter of trends

ROPPONGI/AZABU/ SHIBA-KOEN

→ P.114

A sophisticated cosmopolitan area, home to the symbol of Tokyo

©TOKYO TOWER

GINZA

→ P.50

Lined with historic restaurants and department stores, a district that fuses traditions and trends together

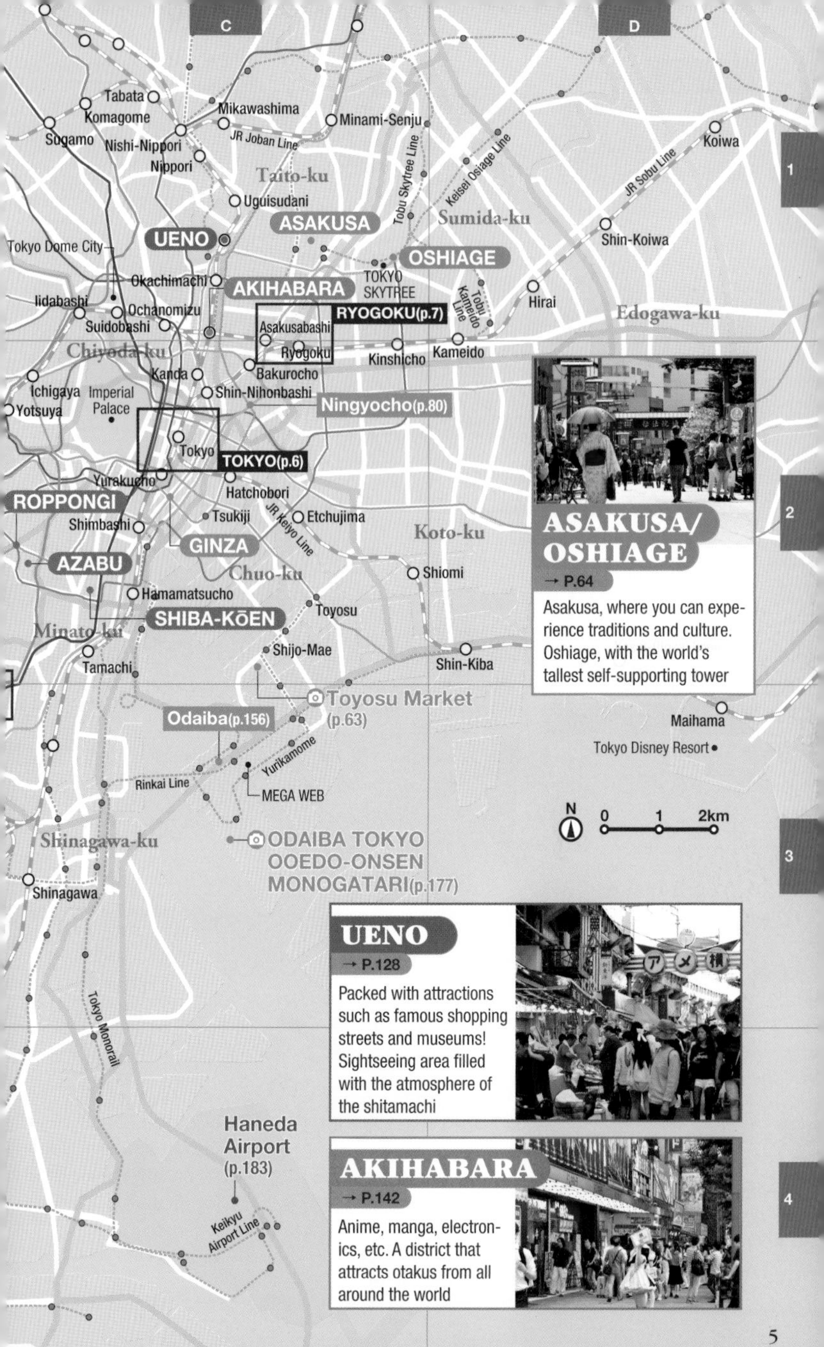

C
D
1
2
3
4

Tabata
Komagome
Sugamo
Nishi-Nippori
Nippori
Mikawashima
JR Joban Line
Minami-Senju
Tobu Skytree Line
Keisei Osiage Line
Koiwa
JR Sobu Line
Taito-ku
Uguisudani
ASAKUSA
Sumida-ku
Shin-Koiwa
UENO
Tokyo Dome City
OSHIAGE
Okachimachi
AKIHABARA
TOKYO SKYTREE
Tobu Kameido Line
Hirai
Iidabashi
Ochanomizu
Suidobashi
RYOGOKU(p.7)
Asakusabashi
Ryogoku
Edogawa-ku
Chiyoda-ku
Kinshicho
Kameido
Kanda
Bakurocho
Ichigaya
Imperial Palace
Shin-Nihonbashi
Yotsuya
Ningyocho(p.80)
Tokyo
TOKYO(p.6)
Yurakucho
Hatchobori
ROPPONGI
Tsukiji
JR Keiyo Line
Etchujima
Shimbashi
Koto-ku
GINZA
AZABU
Chuo-ku
Shiomi
Hamamatsucho
SHIBA-KŌEN
Toyosu
Minato-ku
Shijo-Mae
Shin-Kiba
Tamachi
Toyosu Market (p.63)
Odaiba(p.156)
Maihama
Tokyo Disney Resort
Yurikamome
Rinkai Line
MEGA WEB
N
0 1 2km
Shinagawa-ku
ODAIBA TOKYO OOEDO-ONSEN MONOGATARI(p.177)
Shinagawa
Tokyo Monorail
Haneda Airport (p.183)
Keikyu Airport Line

ASAKUSA/ OSHIAGE

→ P.64

Asakusa, where you can experience traditions and culture. Oshiage, with the world's tallest self-supporting tower

UENO

→ P.128

Packed with attractions such as famous shopping streets and museums! Sightseeing area filled with the atmosphere of the shitamachi

AKIHABARA

→ P.142

Anime, manga, electronics, etc. A district that attracts otakus from all around the world

A B

1 2 3 4

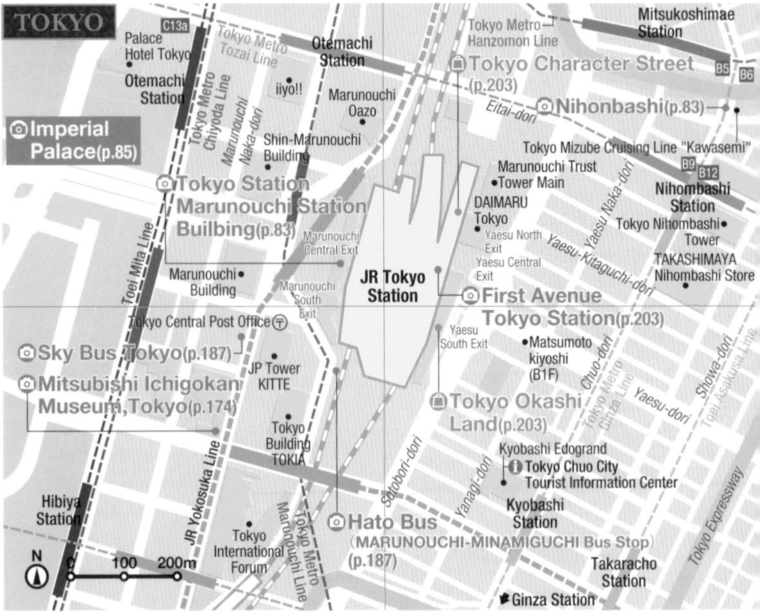

TOKYO

C13a
Palace Hotel Tokyo
Otemachi Station
Tokyo Metro Tozai Line
Otemachi Station
Tokyo Metro Chiyoda Line
Marunouchi Naka-dori
iiyo!!
Marunouchi Oazo
Tokyo Metro Hanzomon Line
Mitsukoshimae Station
Tokyo Character Street (p.203)
B5 B6
Eitai-dori
Nihonbashi(p.83)
Imperial Palace(p.85)
Shin-Marunouchi Building
Tokyo Mizube Cruising Line "Kawasemi"
B9 B12
Marunouchi Trust Tower Main
Nihombashi Station
Tokyo Station Marunouchi Station Builbing(p.83)
DAIMARU Tokyo
Yaesu Naka-dori
Tokyo Nihombashi Tower
Marunouchi Central Exit
Yaesu North Exit
Yaesu Central Exit
Yaesu-Kitaguchi-dori
TAKASHIMAYA Nihombashi Store
Toei Mita Line
Marunouchi Building
Marunouchi South Exit
JR Tokyo Station
First Avenue Tokyo Station(p.203)
Tokyo Central Post Office
Yaesu South Exit
Matsumoto kiyoshi (B1F)
Chuo-dori
Showa-dori
Toei Asakusa Line
Sky Bus Tokyo(p.187)
JP Tower KITTE
Tokyo Metro Ginza Line
Yaesu-dori
Mitsubishi Ichigokan Museum,Tokyo(p.174)
Tokyo Okashi Land(p.203)
Tokyo Building TOKIA
Sotobori-dori
Kyobashi Edogrand
Tokyo Chuo City Tourist Information Center
Yanagi-dori
Tokyo Expressway
JR Yokosuka Line
Hibiya Station
Kyobashi Station
Tokyo International Forum
Tokyo Metro Marunouchi Line
Hato Bus (MARUNOUCHI-MINAMIGUCHI Bus Stop) (p.187)
Takaracho Station
Ginza Station
N
0 100 200m

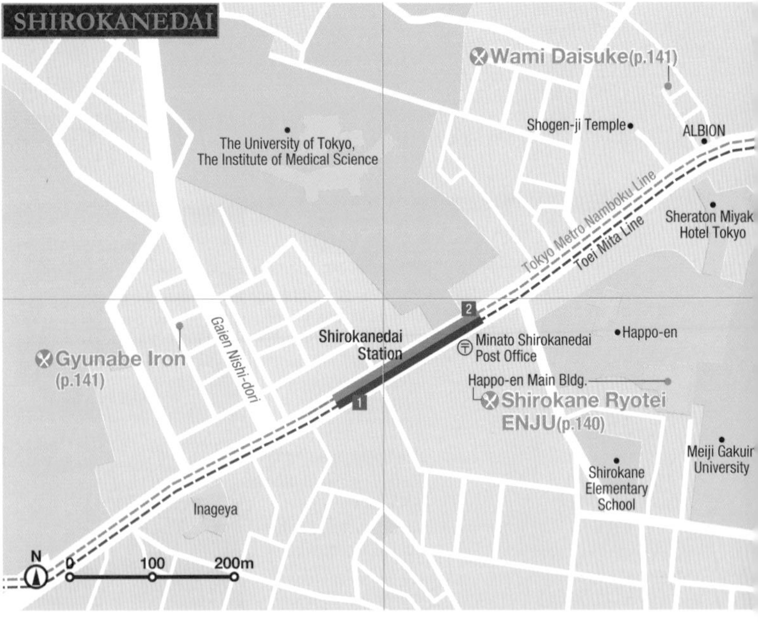

SHIROKANEDAI

Wami Daisuke(p.141)
Shogen-ji Temple
ALBION
The University of Tokyo, The Institute of Medical Science
Tokyo Metro Namboku Line
Toei Mita Line
Sheraton Miyako Hotel Tokyo
2
Happo-en
Gaien Nishi-dori
Shirokanedai Station
Minato Shirokanedai Post Office
Gyunabe Iron (p.141)
Happo-en Main Bldg.
Shirokane Ryotei ENJU(p.140)
1
Meiji Gakuin University
Shirokane Elementary School
Inageya
N
0 100 200m

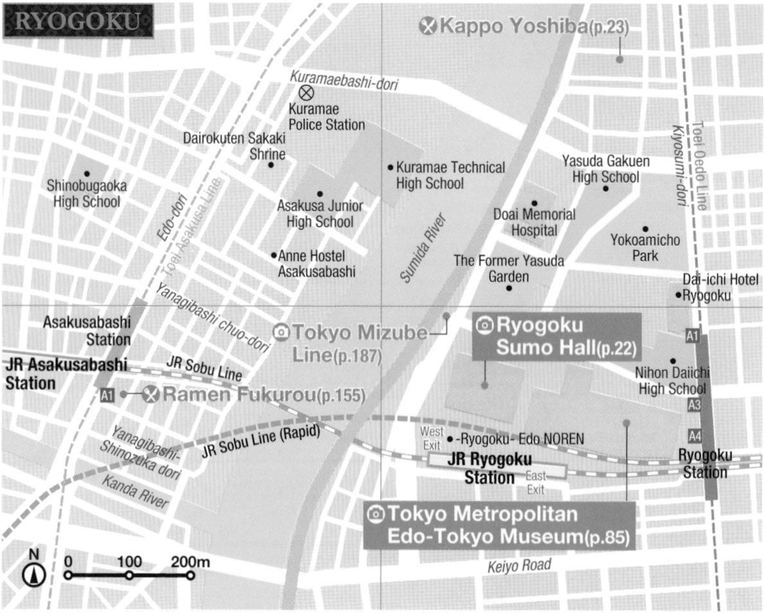

C

D

RYOGOKU

Kappo Yoshiba(p.23)

Kuramaebashi-dori

Kuramae Police Station

Dairokuten Sakaki Shrine

Shinobugaoka High School

Kuramae Technical High School

Yasuda Gakuen High School

Toei Oedo Line

Kiyosumi-dori

Asakusa Junior High School

Edo-dori

Toei Asakusa Line

Doai Memorial Hospital

Sumida River

Yokoamicho Park

Anne Hostel Asakusabashi

The Former Yasuda Garden

Dai-ichi Hotel Ryogoku

Yanagibashi chuo-dori

Asakusabashi Station

Tokyo Mizube Line(p.187)

Ryogoku Sumo Hall(p.22)

JR Asakusabashi Station

JR Sobu Line

A1

Ramen Fukurou(p.155)

Nihon Daiichi High School

A3

A4

Yanagibashi-Shinozuka dori

JR Sobu Line (Rapid)

West Exit

-Ryogoku- Edo NOREN

JR Ryogoku Station

East Exit

Ryogoku Station

Kanda River

Tokyo Metropolitan Edo-Tokyo Museum(p.85)

N

0 100 200m

Keiyo Road

1

2

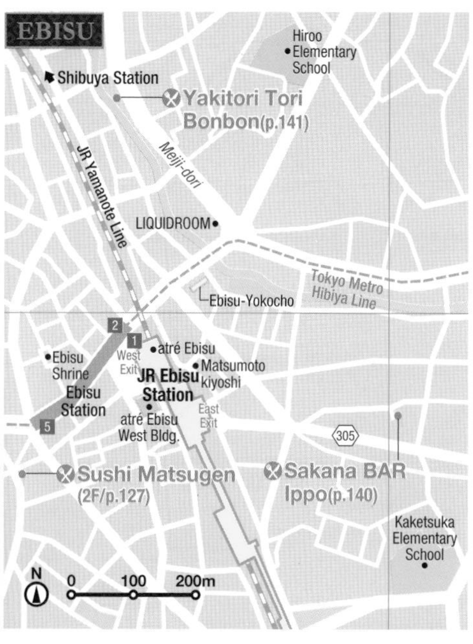

3

4

Railway Map

*Some stations are omitted

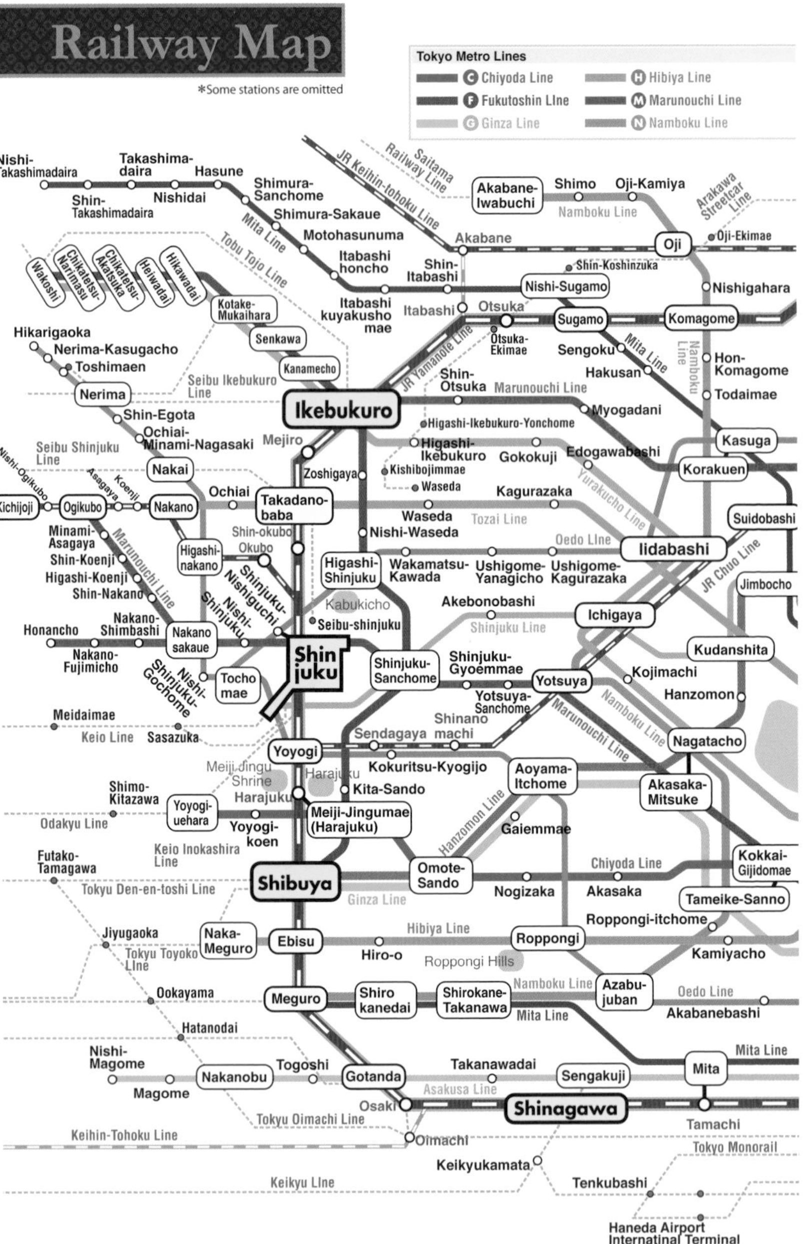

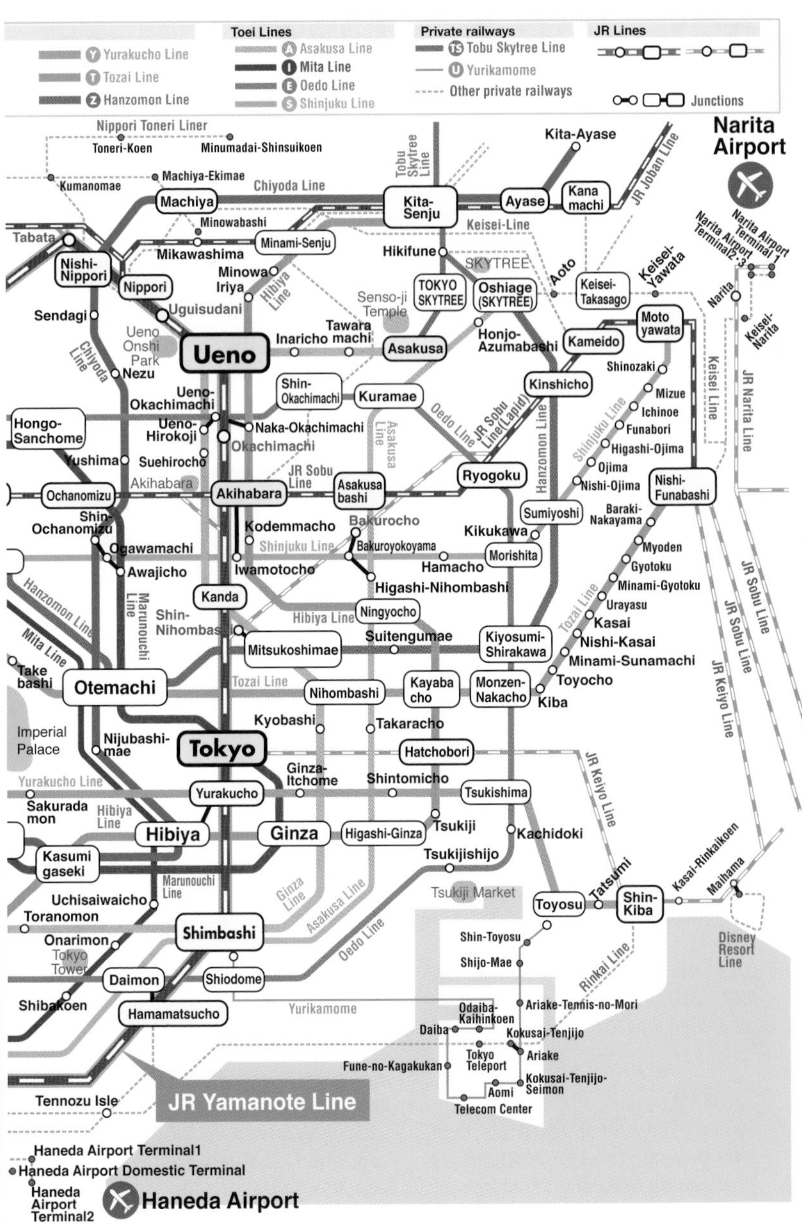

Toei Lines
Private railways
JR Lines
Yurakucho Line
Tozai Line
Hanzomon Line
Asakusa Line
Mita Line
Oedo Line
Shinjuku Line
Tobu Skytree Line
Yurikamome
Other private railways
Junctions
Nippori Toneri Liner
Toneri-Koen
Minumadai-Shinsuikoen
Machiya-Ekimae
Kumanomae
Chiyoda Line
Machiya
Minowabashi
Kita-Senju
Ayase
Kana machi
Kita-Ayase
JR Joban Line
Narita Airport
Narita Airport Terminal 1
Narita Airport Terminal2·3
Narita
Keisei-Narita
Tabata
Nishi-Nippori
Nippori
Mikawashima
Minami-Senju
Minowa
Iriya
Hikifune
Keisei-Line
SKYTREE
TOKYO SKYTREE
Oshiage (SKYTREE)
Aoto
Keisei-Takasago
Keisei-Yawata
Sendagi
Uguisudani
Ueno Onshi Park
Ueno
Senso-ji Temple
Tawara machi
Inaricho
Asakusa
Honjo-Azumabashi
Kameido
Moto yawata
Nezu
Ueno-Okachimachi
Shin-Okachimachi
Kuramae
Kinshicho
Shinozaki
Mizue
Ichinoe
Funabori
Higashi-Ojima
Ojima
Nishi-Ojima
Keisei Line
JR Narita Line
Hongo-Sanchome
Ueno-Hirokoji
Naka-Okachimachi
Okachimachi
Suehirocho
Yushima
Oedo Line
JR Sobu Line(Lapid)
Hanzomon Line
Shinjuku Line
Ryogoku
Akihabara
Ochanomizu
JR Sobu Line
Asakusa Line
Asakusa bashi
Nishi-Funabashi
Sumiyoshi
Baraki-Nakayama
Shin-Ochanomizu
Kodemmacho
Bakurocho
Kikukawa
Ogawamachi
Bakuroyokoyama
Myoden
Awajicho
Iwamotocho
Hamacho
Morishita
Gyotoku
Minami-Gyotoku
Higashi-Nihombashi
Urayasu
Hanzomon Line
Mita Line
Marunouchi Line
Kanda
Hibiya Line
Ningyocho
Tozai Line
Kasai
Nishi-Kasai
Minami-Sunamachi
Shin-Nihombashi
Mitsukoshimae
Suitengumae
Kiyosumi-Shirakawa
Take bashi
Otemachi
Tozai Line
Nihombashi
Kayaba cho
Monzen-Nakacho
Toyocho
Kiba
JR Keiyo Line
Kyobashi
Takaracho
Imperial Palace
Nijubashi-mae
Tokyo
Hatchobori
Yurakucho Line
Ginza-Itchome
Shintomicho
Yurakucho
Tsukishima
Sakurada mon
Hibiya Line
Hibiya
Ginza
Higashi-Ginza
Tsukiji
Kachidoki
Kasai-Rinkaikoen
Maihama
Kasumi gaseki
Tsukijishijo
Marunouchi Line
Ginza Line
Asakusa Line
Tsukiji Market
Uchisaiwaicho
Toyosu
Tatsumi
Shin-Kiba
Toranomon
Shimbashi
Oedo Line
Disney Resort Line
Onarimon
Tokyo Tower
Shin-Toyosu
Shijo-Mae
Rinkai Line
Daimon
Shiodome
Shibakoen
Hamamatsucho
Yurikamome
Odaiba-Kaihinkoen
Ariake-Tennis-no-Mori
Daiba
Kokusai-Tenjijo
Tokyo Teleport
Ariake
Fune-no-Kagakukan
Kokusai-Tenjijo-Seimon
Aomi
Telecom Center
Tennozu Isle
JR Yamanote Line
Haneda Airport Terminal1
Haneda Airport Domestic Terminal
Haneda Airport Terminal2
Haneda Airport

Tokyo is that kind of place

First of all, let's learn about basic information regarding Tokyo. Get to know the means of transportation and different item prices, and use that info to plan your journey!

Tokyo is the capital of Japan. Tokyo is largely divided into East and West areas, the East side is referred to as Tokyo special wards (23 wards), and the West as Tama area (26 cities, 3 towns, 1 village). Furthermore, on the South side, islands such as the Ogasawara Islands and Izu Islands are also included (2 towns, 7 villages). Almost is concentrated in the 23 wards, population, economy, culture, etc.

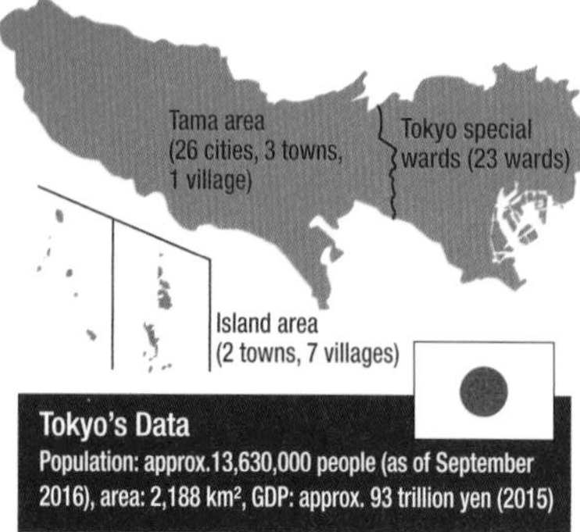

Tokyo's Data

Population: approx.13,630,000 people (as of September 2016), area: 2,188 km², GDP: approx. 93 trillion yen (2015)

Prices

1 bottle of mineral water (500ml) is around 100 yen, a pack of cigarettes is around 450 yen, taxi starting fare is 410 yen, train base fare is 140 yen (JR Line). "McDonald's" Big Mac is 380 yen.

Visa

If the period of stay in Japan is up to 90 days, and, no activities with remuneration are performed, some countries (currently 67 countries) are also visa exempt. For further information, let's check the Ministry of Foreign Affairs HP.
URL:http://www.mofa.go.jp/j_info/visit/visa/index.html

Tip

Basically there is not tip custom. However, there are cases for which service charges and other additional fees are paid in hotels and luxury Restaurants.

Rate & Currency

1$ = approx.113 yen (as of January 2017). Currency used is the yen (YEN). There are four types of paper bill: 1,000 yen, 2,000 yen, 5,000 yen, and 10,000 yen bills. Six types of coin: 1 yen, 5 yen, 10 yen, 50 yen, 100 yen, and 500 yen coins.

Language

The official language is Japanese. Japanese is written using three types characters: hiragana, katakana, and kanji.

Means of transportation

Train (JR), and subway are the main means of transportation. Apart from that, taxi is also convenient. There are also many taxis, so it's easy to catch one. Although it depends on traffic conditions for taxis, public transports are almost running on time.

Best season

There are four seasons, and the change of season is relatively clear. Spring is from March to May, summer from June to August, autumn from September to November, and winter from December to February. Summer is hot, and rainy. In particular, in June cloudy and rainy days are persisting due to the "rainy season". In winter, days are often dry and sunny. The best season in Tokyo is when the weather stabilizes in April and May, and in September and October.

Tokyo's average temperature and average rainfall

	January	February	March	April	May	June	July	August	September	October	November	December
temperature (℃)	5.2	5.7	8.7	13.9	18.2	21.4	25	26.4	22.8	17.5	12.1	7.6
rainfall (mm)	52.3	56.1	117.5	124.5	137.8	167.7	153.5	168.2	209.9	197.8	92.5	51

*It is based on the normal value obtained from the Japan Meteorological Agency

Public holidays

January 1 New Year's Day
A day to celebrate the beginning of the year

Second Monday of January Coming-of-Age Day
A day to celebrate and encourage people who reached the age of maturity (20 years old)

Feburary 11 Foundation Day
A day to remember the founding of the nation

March 20 or 21 Vernal Equinox Day
A day celebrating the coming of spring and honoring nature

April 29 Showa Day
A day to reflect on the turbulent Showa period
*A day to commemorate the birthday of Emperor Showa

May 3 Constitution Memorial Day
A day to commemorate the day Japanese Constitution came into effect

May 4 Greenery Day
A day to commune with nature

May 5 Children's Day
A day to wish for the happiness of children

Third Monday of July Ocean Day
A day to show gratitude to the sea

August 11 Mountain Day
A day to show gratitude to the mountain

Third Monday of September Respect for the Aged Day
A day to honor elderly people

September 22 or 23 Autumnal Equinox Day
A day to honor ancestors

Second Monday of October Sports Day
A day to cultivate a healthy mind and body
*Associated with the day when the Tokyo Olympic Games were opened

November 3 Culture Day
A day to praise culture
*A day to commemorate the promulgation of Japan's constitution

November 23 Labour Thanksgiving Day
A day to honor labor

December 23 The Emperor's Birthday
A day to celebrate the birth of the Emperor

*Many shops have different business hours on public holidays, so let's be careful

Safety

Safety is relatively good. Tokyo earned 1st place in the "Safe Countries and Cities Ranking" published in the British weekly magazine "The Economist". However, a minimum of attention is required, like trying to avoid walking in deserted streets at night alone, etc.

Ordinances of the Capital

In addition to Japanese law, Tokyo has its own ordinances. In particular regarding smoking, the "Ordinance on Street Smoking Ban" defines strict conditions on smoking while walking and on the streets so let's be careful.

Keyword 1

Lick your lips with Japanese gastronomy

Tokyo Gourmet → P.14

Keyword 2

The spirit of Japanese tradition is alive

Shrines and Temples → P.18

©Senso-ji Temple

What you really want to experience in Tokyo since you came all the way here!

The 8 for enjoying

Keyword 5

Masterpieces created with the commitment of craftsmen

Treasures made in Japan → P.24

Keyword 6

Representing the Japanese aesthetic

Wagashi → P.28

Keyword 3
It has a 400-year history
Kabuki → P.20

©Shochiku Co., Ltd.

Picture provided by the Nihon Sumo Kyokai

Keyword 4
An overwhelmingly intense national sport
Grand "Sumo" → P.22

Keywords Tokyo

An introduction of keywords for enjoying Tokyo, such as its food, traditional culture, pop culture, and more. Feel the unique charms of Tokyo and make unforgettable memories!

Keyword 7
Attracting attention from all around the world!
POP Culture → P.30

Keyword 8
Can you feel Neo-Tokyo!?
Tokyo's Night view → P.32

Tokyo Gourmet

Japanese food is famous all over the world. Here, we introduce some diverse Japanese cuisine you can easily try in Tokyo.

Check!

The true pleasure of eating sushi is at the counter seats. At Sushi Matsugen, sushi is carefully made one by one right in front of the customers

Many of the most popular Japanese dishes were established during the Edo era. Dishes that use vegetables cultivated in the surrounding of Edo and Edo-mae ingredients (fish and shellfish caught in Tokyo Bay) represent the local cuisine of Tokyo. Japanese cuisine focuses on sense of season by bringing out the flavor of materials and seasonal ingredients (the time of the biggest harvest, when the produce is at its most delicious). In particular, it is important to know what seafood is in season for sushi and Kaisendon.

Kaiseki cuisine, a course meal in which dishes served one by one, also uses the theme of "seasons".

In addition, example of seasonal dishes include unaju and unadon that are cooked using eels. Eel is often eaten during summer, but in fact eel is naturally in season from autumn to winter. It turned into a classic summer dish after it was advertised to sell during summer and became a huge hit at the end of the Edo period.

Tokyo Gourmet 1

Sushi スシ / Kaisendon (Seafood Rice Bowl) 海鮮丼

Sushi, in which vinegar-flavored rice is lightly pressed and combined with seafood sashimi or cooked ingredients, is also called "Edo-mae sushi".

[→**P.93** Maguro Donya Miuramisakiko Megumi
→**P.127** Ginza Kyubey
→**P.127** Sushi Matsugen]

A rice bowl dish in which white rice or vinegar-flavored rice is topped with seafood sashimi. The kind of seafood used varies depending on the restaurant.

[→**P.133** Minatoya Ueno Store No.2]

Tokyo Gourmet 2

Kaiseki Cuisine 会席料理

Course meal for banquets and dinners. You can have as many as 8 to 10 dishes, including soup, sashimi, grilled and simmered dishes.

[→**P.44** Koshitsukaiseki KITAOHJI Shinjukusaryo
→**P.138** Inshotei]

Tokyo Gourmet 3

Eel ウナギ

A dish featuring rice put into a lacquered box or a bowl, topped with broiled eel and kabayaki sauce.

[→**P.77** Unagi Maekawa]

Soba ソバ

Noodles processed using buckwheat flour made of buckwheat grains. Enjoy a variety of ways to eat soba. It is important to know that buckwheat allergies exist.

[→**P.111** GONBEE]

Tokyo Gourmet 5

Nabe (hot pot) cuisine ナベ

Put the main ingredients (chicken, seafood, vegetables, etc.) into the pot, distribute at the table, and eat after dipping in liquid seasoning.

[→**P.23** Kappo Yoshiba
→**P.76** Asakusa Imahan
→**P.77** Komakata Dojo Asakusa Main Shop]

There are various ways to eat soba. For mori-soba, zaru-soba, and other kinds of soba, you put tsuyu sauce in a small bowl, then take a bite-size portion of noodles with chopsticks and dip it into the sauce. There are many variations, including kake-soba with hot sauce and soba topped with various ingredients. You can order your noodles warm or cold.

There are also plenty of dishes that use a hot pot, (nabe-ryouri) such as yose-nabe, chanko-nabe, motsu-nabe, and more. In this hot-pot cuisine, the leftover soup is then consumed with white rice, udon, or ramen. In Japan, this is refered to as shime, or “finishing dish”, and it is sometimes included in the course. Hot pot cuisine is also subdivided into o-den, sukiyaki, and shabu-shabu.

Tempura is different from other deep-fried foods, and the method for coating and frying tempura is difficult. The tempura created in specialty shops by chefs who’ve accumulated years of learning is a masterpiece. Tempura is eaten with special tsuyu sauce or salt. We recommend the ten-don, which features white rice topped with tempura served in a bowl, as well as tempura-soba.

Tokyo Gourmet 6

Tempura and Ten-don 天ぷら・天丼

A dish in which seafood and vegetables are coated with a batter of egg and flour, then fried in vegetable oil.

[→**P.58** Tempura Kondo
→**P.77** Masaru
→**P.125** Japanese Cuisine Yamazato]

Tokyo Gourmet 7

Ramen ラーメン

A dish featuring noodles put into a hot soup and topped with ingredients (barbecued pork, bamboo shoots, vegetables, etc.). You can eat it at an affordable price.

→P.45 Fu-unji
→P.155 Ramen Fukurou

Tokyo Gourmet 8

Wagyu 和牛

The are four breeds of Wagyu cattle: the Akaushi (Japanese Brown), the Kuroushi (Japanese Black), the Japanese Polled, and the Japanese Shorthorn. Wagyu is characterized by the tenderness of the meat.

→P.111 Aoyama Manpuku
→P.139 Gyukatsu AONA Okachimachi Main Restaurant
→P.141 Gyunabe Iron

Tokyo Gourmet 9

Sake 日本酒

An alcohol using rice, water and malted rice as main ingredients, brewed with a Japan-specific process. Breweries are called kuramoto.

[→P.112 Juban Ukyo]

Nowadays Japanese ramen noodles are so famous that you can find ramen restaurant all around the world. It is originally Chinese noodles arranged to suit Japanese tastes. The basic ramen flavors are soy-sauce, salt, and miso. There are also differences in the dashi soup, such as chicken, seafood, or pork bone. There are countless varieties of ramen, since you can also find differences in terms of thickness of the soup as well as the ingredients used depending on the region.

The Wagyu, a luxury brand of cattle, is famous as well. Kobe beef, Matsuzaka beef, Omi beef, and Yonezawa beef are highly popular. Steak is the way to it that allows you to taste the most of the beef umami. Although it can be prepared rare, medium rare, medium, and well-done, we recommend you try it medium-rare with the rare meat inside still warm.

Many kinds of Japanese sake are available, and there's a specific way to drink each brand. The temperature of the sake and taste of the accompanying snacks are also important. There are brewery tours and workshops available in English. Kikizake events, tastings in which you can enjoy small samples of various brands of sake, are held all throughout Japan.

Keyword 2

Shrines and Temples

Even though shrines and temples may look the same at first sight, they each have their own kind of religious services. You must be careful, since the ways of worship and manners are different.

There are a torii indicating the entrance to the shrine and guardian lion-dogs (imaginary animals).

Temples are Buddhist religious institutions. Worshippers can look at the Buddhas and offer their prayers. There are also temples with colossal Buddha statues and bells.

In Japan, the Shinto faith and Buddhist faith (Buddhism in Japan) have been mixed and reconstructed into a religious phenomenon called "Shinbutsu-shugo" (syncretism of gods and buddhas) as one unique belief. For example, oftentimes you can find a Shinto altar to worship gods and a Buddhist altar, which is a place of Buddhist worship, standing together in Japanese houses. Regarding shrines and temples as well, they both worship faith the same way.

Originally, both faiths originated separately. Shinto is the faith of the native tribes since ancient times, a polytheism paying respect to mountains and seas, rivers and nature, as well as natural phenomena, and also venerates gods appearing in mythology. Each of the enshrined gods located throughout the country are also respectively different.

Buddhism was introduced in Japan in the 6th century, and it had a major impact on the people. Since the Nara period (710-794 *various theories exist), the relationship between gods and Buddhas grew closer gradually, and after that the use of Jinguji (Buddhist temple within a Shinto shrine, based on the philosophy of gods and Buddhas syncretism) was widespread. However, because they are different faiths, prayers and manners are also different depending on the place of worship. Although both have an offertory box in which you put a money offering, you will not find the large bell that the shrine has in a temple. At the time of worship in a temple, you must not clap your hands in prayer, like in the shrine. It is important to know how to worship properly in each place in order to avoid a faux pas.

After worshipping, many people draw omikuji, or fortunes, write their wishes on ema (wooden plaques), or buy good luck charms.

Omikuji are small pieces of paper you draw at shrines and temples in order to have your fortune told. It is custom to attach those pieces of paper to the branches of trees in the precincts. English omikuji are also available depending on the location.

A charm that helps give protection, considered to contain a blessing from the gods. Various types of protection are available, such as for marriage, traffic safety, health, safe birth, studies, etc.

How to worship in shrines

In all shrines located around Japan, there are proper ways and procedures for worshipping. These ways are different from those used in temples, so be careful.

When you pass through the torii, bow once before entering the precincts.

*Photos show Meiji Jingu Shrine (worshipping manners, and the presence or absence of omikuji may vary depending on the shrine and region)

→

Take water at Temizuya (place for ritual cleansing) using a ladle, and cleanse both your hands, your mouth, and the ladle handle. It is forbidden to put your mouth directly in contact with the ladle.

→

Bow lightly and ring the bell. Put a money offering in the offertory box, bow twice in a row, clap your hands twice immediately after, and bow once again in the end.

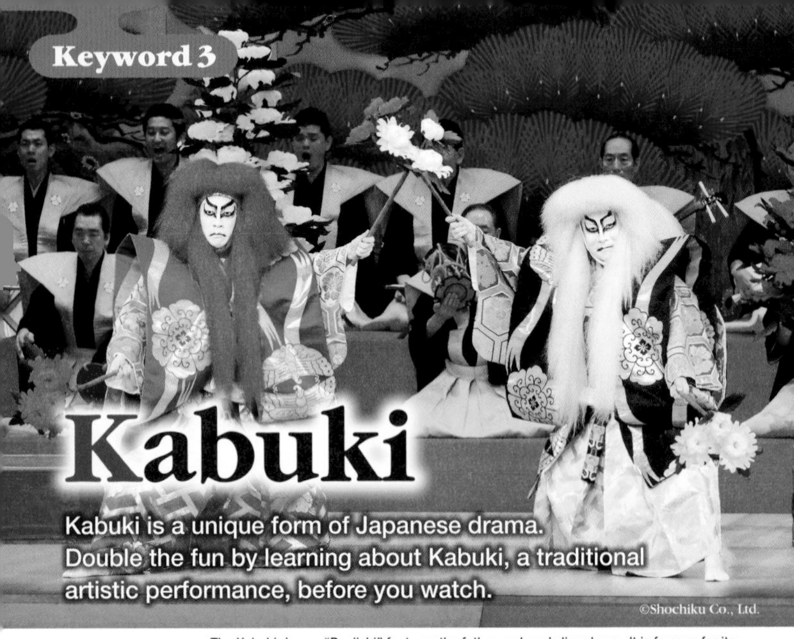

Keyword 3
Kabuki
Kabuki is a unique form of Japanese drama.
Double the fun by learning about Kabuki, a traditional artistic performance, before you watch.
©Shochiku Co., Ltd.

The Kabuki dance, "Renjishi" features the father and son's lion dance. It is famous for its choreography specifically the turning of head with great strength while holding his long hair

It is said that Kabuki was created by Izumo-no-Okuni in Kyoto around 1600. Because female actors were banned on grounds that their performances were disturbing public morals, it changed into an all-male form of entertainment called "yaro-kabuki".

The characteristic of kabuki is its stylized beauty. This includes the makeup technique called kumadori, which lets viewers understand different character portrayals by using different colors depending on the role. Red is for virtue and heroes. Blue is for evil and enemies. Brown is used for demons, ghosts, etc. You can also understand the identity and role according to the wig (hairstyle) and costume. Costumes come equipped with a variety of contraptions, so costumes can be changed in the blink of an eye right in the middle of a dance.

In the repertory, the aragoto, or rough style of Edo is represented by the Kabuki Juhachiban (Eighteen Best Kabuki Plays) including "Sukeroku Yukari no Edo Zakura" (Sukeroku: Flower of Edo), "Kanjincho" (The Subscription List), etc. The wagoto, or soft style, flourished mainly in Osaka. There are historical plays featuring the stories of samurai, as well as domestic plays about the lives of ordinary people. There are also dances and other types of plays.

Music is indispensable for kabuki performances. The story is told by a tayu (reciter) with a futozao (thick neck) shamisen called gidayu. The long epic song nagauta is indispensable to the dance and performed by an ensemble of about 30 people providing a musical accompaniment with hosozao (thin neck) shamisen, instruments (flute, taiko drum, tsuzumi hand drum, etc.), and vocals. Sound effects are created in a room called kuromisu hidden behind a black bamboo curtain hung on the left side of the stage (shimote).

Description of the Kabuki-za stage

Seri
セリ

A trapdoor-like lifting device for actors and sets placed on the stage. The arrangement and number differ depending on the theater.

Chobo-yuka
チョボ床

A small room located on the upper section (2nd floor) of the kamite. This is the place where the gidayu melody is performed.

Suppon
スッポン

A trapdoor located near the hanamichi stage. Used to make the actors playing spirits and ghosts appear and disappear.

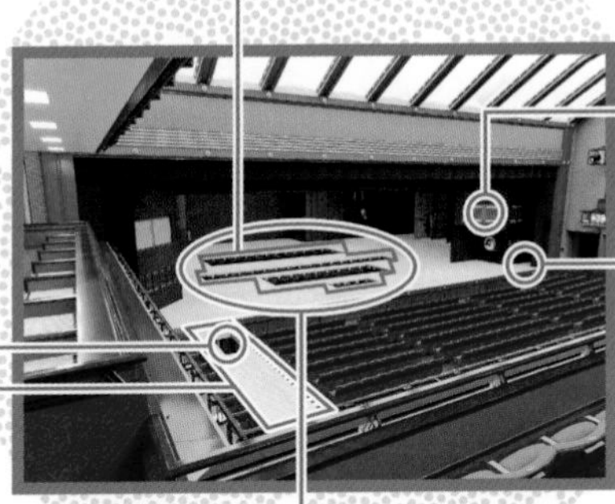

Kamite / Shimote
上手／下手

The stage-right is called kamite, and stage-left called shimote. (When viewed from audience side).

Hanamichi
花道

Passage-like stage section that runs through the audience. The hanamichi allows a sense of presence by having the actors pass close to the audience.

Mawari-butai
廻り舞台

Located at the center stage, this creates scene changes by rotating while carrying the actors and set.

Kurogo
黒衣

In kabuki, black is a color that the audience pretends not to see. Appearing on stage dressed all in black, these stagehands move the props and equipment used by the performers on and off stage.

Kabuki-za 歌舞伎座

Opened in 1889. After being rebuilt several times, this theater, which shows kabuki performances exclusively, was re-opened in 2013. Its external appearance is a vestige of the early period.

Address: Ginza, Chuo-ku 4-12-15 **TEL:**03-3545-6800 **Opening hours/ Closed:** Depending on public holiday and month **Fee:** from 4,000 yen **Access:** directly connected to Tokyo Metro Higashi-Ginza Station Exit 3

HP MAP P.53 C-3

Topics: Recommended for kabuki beginners

Hitomakumiseki 一幕見席

Seats on the 4th floor, from where people can watch just one act of the play. Tickets are sold only on the day of the performance at a special ticket counter located on the 1st floor. From 1,000 yen.

Subtitle guide 字幕ガイド

Gives a description of the scene and script in English. Can be rented at a special counter.

Kabukiza Gallery 歌舞伎座ギャラリー

An interactive gallery that helps you get familiar with kabuki. Located on the 5th floor of the building (Kabuki-za Tower) behind Kabuki-za.

TEL:03-3545-6886 **Fee:**600 yen

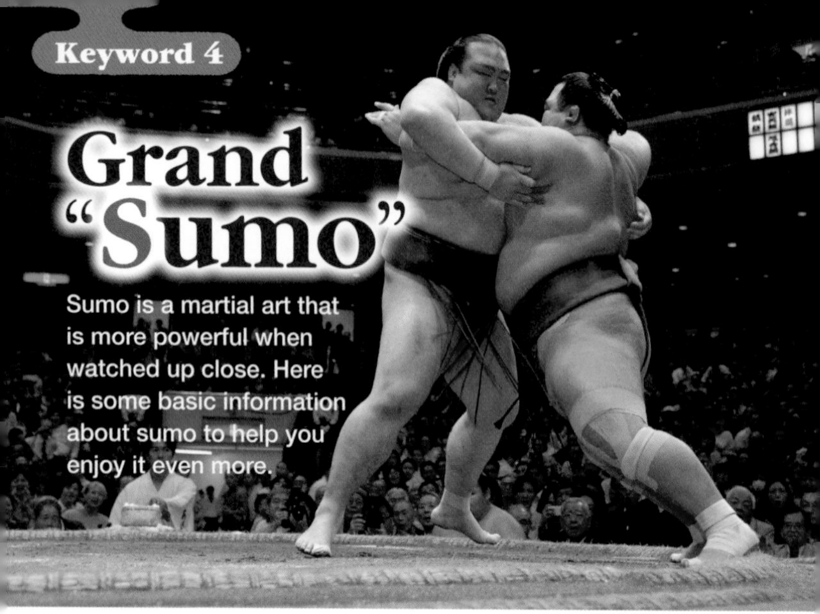

Keyword 4

Grand "Sumo"

Sumo is a martial art that is more powerful when watched up close. Here is some basic information about sumo to help you enjoy it even more.

Pictures provided by the Nihon Sumo Kyokai

Sumo, the national sport of Japan, is a form of Japanese ancient ritual or festival in which sumo wrestlers fight in a wrestling ring. It is also a martial art. Men blessed with strong health and power unleash all their strength before an altar in an act performed to show gratitude and respect to the gods. That is why great importance is attached to the etiquette and formalities, one of them being that sumo wrestlers do not wear anything more than a loincloth called mawashi.

Under the rules of sumo, 2 wrestlers holding each other by the mawashi compete in a circular ring, and defeat is declared for the one who is forced out of the ring first, any part of his body except the soles of his feet touch the ground, or if a foul is committed.

The origins of sumo date back to around from 3rd to 7th century, but it was during the 17th century that sumo wrestling was organized as a public performance. Nowadays, professional performances are called Grand Sumo, with official tournaments held six times a year (in odd months), each of them running for 15 days in a row. Wrestlers always belong to a sumo stable (institution for training sumo wrestlers, with all groups led by a stable master) where they live together. Depending on the sumo stable, there are tours that let the public view morning practice available, making them popular among tourists.

両国国技館

Ryogoku Sumo Hall

Address:1-3-28 Yokoami, Sumida-ku **TEL:**03-3623-5111 **Opening hours:**10:00 - 16:30 (8:00 - 18:00 during the Grand Sumo tournament) **Closed:** On Saturdays, Sundays and public holidays (open everyday during the Grand Sumo tournament) **Fee:**From 2,200 yen **Access:**3 min. walk from JR Ryogoku Station West Exit

HP

MAP P.7 D-2

*Entry to the Sumo Museum is free of charge except during tournaments

Gyoji (Sumo referee) 行司

The referee responsible for determining the sumo winner. The war-fan they hold in their hand is used to indicate the winner's side. Gyoji have names passed down from generation to generation. Famous gyoji are Kimura Shonosuke and Shikimori Inosuke.

Dohyo (Wrestling ring) 土俵

Made of mounted clay, this is where sumo wrestling matches are held. A circle 4.55m in diameter is placed on the center of a mounted platform of clay that sides measure 6.7m. It is a sacred place.

Mage (Top-knot) まげ

Although the "Mage" was a male hairstyle during the Edo period, the wrestler's hairstyle is particularly large and called "Oichou" (ginkgo-leaf top-knot). Its name comes from the fact that the tip is shaped like a ginkgo leaf.

Mawashi (Loincloth) まわし

The mawashi covers the waist of a sumo competitor, supporting the area around the waist and belly, thus protecting the body, and it is used to put forth even more strength.

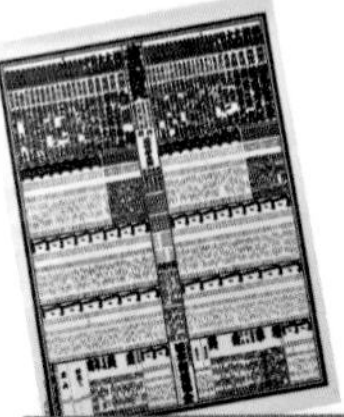

Banzuke-hyo (Sumo Ranking) 番付表

The Grand Sumo wrestlers ranking chart. There are 10 classes in total, and the strongest one is "Yokozuna". The characters size gets gradually bigger for higher-rank sumo wrestlers.

Shiko (Leg stomps) しこ

Sumo's basic movement, warm-up exercise, and training method. The left and right legs are placed in a wide stance, and one leg is raised high in the air.

Rikishi (Wrestler) 力士

Wrestlers belong to a sumo stable, have a professional stage name, and take part in Grand Sumo. Strictly speaking, people practicing at university sumo clubs and amateur sumo participants are not rikishi.

Chanko Nabe (hot pot) specialty restaurant using a former sumo stable

You can taste this Restaurant's own original chanko nabe. We recommend the "Chanko Yoshiba Nabe" with its famous minced swordfish. The restaurant uses a building of the sumo stable established by the 43rd Yokozuna Yoshibayama.

Kappo Yoshiba 割烹吉葉

Address:2-14-5 Yokoami, Sumida-ku **TEL:**03-3623-4480 **Opening hours:**11:30 - 14:00 (last order 13:30), 17:00 - 22:00 (last order 21:10) **Closed:**On Sundays and public holidays **Price:**Lunch from 880 yen, Dinner from 6,500 yen **Access:**9 min. walk from Toei Subway Ryogoku Station Exit A1 MAP P.7 D-1

In the restaurant there is a real wrestling ring, and events are held featuring Sumo-Jinku (sumo-themed songs), Tsugaru-jamisen

Keyword 5

Treasures made in Japan

Give Japanese products a try!

Japanese techniques are not only used in consumer electronics, but can be found in crafts made by skilled artisans.

Traditional crafts are everyday goods made using traditional techniques cultivated for many years amid the climate and history of Japan. In Japan, you can find traditional craft items designated by the country in each prefecture. Their number comes to about 1,200 items.

The main ones are: textiles, dyed articles, ceramics, lacquerware, woodwork, bamboowork, metalwork, Buddhist altars, Buddhist altar fittings, washi (Japanese paper), stationery (writing brush, ink, ink stone, abacus), masonry products, dolls, craft tools, and craft materials.

These traditional crafts have a handmade rustic flavor, familiarity, and superior functionality. Compared to mass-produced products, they provide richness and charm to one's life. Some of these arts and crafts have been designated as important cultural properties and important tangible folk cultural assets by Law for the Protection of Cultural Properties.

Edo-Kiriko (Edo-style faceted glass)
江戸切子

Skilled techniques are required in the delicate craftsmanship used for Edo-kiriko. There are also various patterns available, from traditional to modern.
[→**P.75** Sumida Edo-Kiriko kan]

Tenugui (hand towel) 手ぬぐい

The patterns have names, including ones containing jokes. This store is filled with products that cannot be bought anywhere else.

[→P.73 Some-e Tenugui Fujiya]

Nail clippers, Tweezers, grip Gcissors, Cutting scissors ツメ切り、毛抜き、握り鋏、裁ち鋏

Nail clippers, tweezers, and other items are useful as souvenirs. ❶

Knives 包丁

Offers a wide variety of types and sizes of Japanese kitchen knives, Western kitchen knives, etc. The superb cutting sharpness is obtained by the techniques of skilled craftsmen. ❶

Cosmetics コスメ

Offering only products with special commitment to materials, including hand creams made of natural ingredients that can even be used before cooking and eating, Japanese-paper towels, etc. ❷

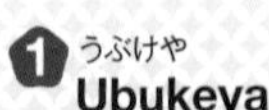

❶ うぶけや Ubukeya

Knife store passed down for 8 generations since 1783

This shop takes cutting tools made by craftsmen and turns them into products at the shop. The three major items are the knives, scissors, and tweezers. It is also possible to repair the products you purchased here.

Address:3-9-2 Ningyocho, Nihonbashi, Chuo-ku **TEL:**03-3661-4851 **Opening hours:**9:00-18:00, 9:00-17:00 on Saturdays **Closed:**On Sundays and public holidays **Access:**2 min. walk from Tokyo Metro Ningyocho Station Exit A5

MAP P.80

❷ まかないこすめ 東急プラザ銀座店 Makanai Cosme Tokyu Plaza Ginza Shop

A natural cosmetics brand born of a gold leaf shop

Selling additive-free and gentle-to-the-skin cosmetics using natural plant components. In the shop, there is also space to try out popular products, such as the "konnyaku Sponge" and more.

Address: Tokyu Plaza Ginza 6F, 5-2-1 Ginza, Chuo-ku **TEL:**03-6274-6130 **Opening hours:**11:00-21:00 **Closed:**Irregular holidays **Access:**Immediate access from Tokyo Metro Ginza Station Exit C2

MAP P.52 B-2

Traditional crafts are of high quality, but their price is often high as well. Also, since elaborate handmade techniques can not be learned during a short apprenticeship, the number of people who can make these crafts has been decreasing year after year. For this reason, the number of people who have no opportunity to learn about the virtues of traditional crafts is growing.

Consequently, in recent years traditional industries have been cooperating with different businesses through creating a movement that aims to develop new products and markets. This includes, for example, collaborations between well-known brands and traditional crafts.

Craft products have excellent design that goes well also with modern life, letting you feel the craftsmanship as well. Countries around the world are also interested in this refined design. Traditional Tokyo crafts were also created from a mix between tradition and contemporary design, such as Edo Mokuhanga (woodblock prints) featuring famous artists represented in ukiyo-e style, as well as Edo Kiriko lighting fixtures and T-shirts using design components of Tama Ori (woven fabric), etc.

These items seek something that goes beyond the criteria of traditional item while paying respect to the traditions of Japanese craft.

Momotaro Jeans
桃太郎ジーンズ

Jeans are instantly recognizable by the two white lines and the Momotaro mark leather patch. They also provide denim shirts. ❸

❸ 桃太郎ジーンズ青山店 Momotaro Jeans Aoyama Shop

Jeans made with a special commitment to the handmade process

A brand of jeans originally from Kojima, Okayama Prefecture. The products are made with an unwavering commitment to design and quality, and have many fans in Japan and abroad. Jeans you buy at the shop can be hemmed on the spot.

Address: Ao 2F, 3-11-7 Kita-Aoyama, Minato-ku
TEL:03-6427-9721 **Opening hours:**11:00-20:00
Closed: None **Access:**1 min. walk from Tokyo Metro Omote-Sando Station Exit B2

MAP P.102 B-3

❹ オニツカタイガー表参道 Onitsuka Tiger Omotesando

Offering a rich variety of shoes made in Japan

Flagship store of the sports fashion brand Onitsuka Tiger. This is the largest Onitsuka Tiger store in the world. In this store, you can find a wide assortment of high-quality products made in Japan.

Address:4-24-14 Jingumae, Shibuya-ku
TEL:03-3405-6671 **Opening hours:**11:00-20:00
Closed: Irregular holidays
Access:5 min. walk from Tokyo Metro Meiji-Jingumae (Harajuku) Station Exit 5

MAP P.102 B-2

Sneakers スニーカー

The distinctive features of Onitsuka Tiger are a slim silhouette and lines on the side. They combine design and comfort. ❹

Kantoui (Japanese-style poncho) 貫頭衣

They are comfortable, since they are made with Ise cotton towel fabric. They use traditional Japanese colors. ❻

Canvas bag 帆布バッグ

Bags are reputed to be light and easy-to-use. You can choose from 11 different colors, and also have a name embroidered on it. ❺

Jikatabi shoes 地下足袋

The pop style jikatabi shoes are all made in Japan. They are also extremely comfortable. ❻

❺ 犬印鞄製作所 浅草２丁目店 Inujirushi Kaban Seisakujo Asakusa 2 Chome Shop

A shop founded in 1953 specializing in canvas bags

A shop that specializes in bags using canvas, a thick and robust fabric. Products are made by hand at the shop, which uses only fabrics and metal fittings that have been made in Japan. It is possible to visit the workshop, built as an annex.

Address: Fujita Bldg. 2F, 2-1-16 Asakusa, Taito-ku **TEL:**03-5806-0650 **Opening hours:**9:30-18:30, 9:30-18:00 on Sundays and public holidays **Closed:**None **Access:**3 min. walk from Tokyo Metro Asakusa Station Exit 6

 MAP P.66 B-1

❻ SOU・SOU KYOTO 青山店 Sou・Sou Kyoto Aoyama Shop

A brand generating "evolved Japanese clothing"

With its flagship store located in Kyoto, this shop is lined with jikatabi shoes and kimonos, small items and accessories, as well as children's clothing, all made using original textiles. At the Aoyama shop, you can also find a tea room built as an annex.

Address:A La Croce 1F, 5-4-24 Minami-Aoyama, Minato-ku **TEL:**03-3407-7877 **Opening hours:**11:00-20:00. Tea Room: 13:00-18:00 **Closed:**None **Access:**8 min. walk from Tokyo Metro Omote-Sando Station Exit B1

MAP P.103 C-3

Keyword 6

Wagashi

Japanese confectionaries were originally developed as refreshments for tea ceremonies. Therefore, importance is of course given to their taste, as well as to the beauty of their appearance.

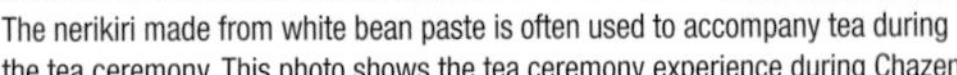

The nerikiri made from white bean paste is often used to accompany tea during the tea ceremony. This photo shows the tea ceremony experience during Chazen

Wagashi is Japanese traditional confectionery. The main types include mochigashi, yokan, manju, monaka, rakugan, and senbei. A wide variety of sweets are made depending on the season, region, ingredients, and craftsmanship. The main ingredients used in the major confectioneries are carefully selected rice and wheat, red beans, soy, arrowroot powder, and sugar. The creation of An (red bean paste) is particularly important. The sweetness and taste of red bean paste are slightly different depending on the Wagashi artisan preparing it.

The history of the Wagashi is long. They have existed since ancient times, with the creation of the prototype in the 7th century. In particular, the tea ceremony, which started to get popular around 1191, had a huge impact on Wagashi. Japanese sweets are made assuming that they will be enjoyed with matcha or with the daily cup of green tea.

Wagashi are used as souvenirs, but also as gifts for events held all throughout the year and on occasions for celebration or condolence. In addition, Wagashi have strong ties with the four seasons. High-grade fresh Wagashi represent seasonal sense not only through their taste, but also through color and shape, making them visually beautiful as well. Although Japanese confectionery makers study for many years to learn the basics of red bean paste-making, they are also required to have an artistic sense at the same time.

Yokan (sweet bean jelly) 羊羹

Red bean paste solidified with agar. There are many different types, including some with chestnuts, and others using matcha, sweet potato, and other ingredients.

Sakuramochi 桜餅

Red bean paste wrapped in a pink-colored dough made of mochi (sticky rice cake), and rolled in a pickled cherry blossom leaf. There is the Kanto-style Chomeiji mochi (left) and the Kansai-style Domyoji mochi (right).

Manju 饅頭

Steamed confectionery consisting of red bean paste wrapped in a dough made of flour and other ingredients. It is said to have been introduced from China.

Mamegashi (bean confectioneries) 豆菓子

Beans (mainly peanuts) are broiled and combined with a variety of seasonings. The mamegashi of Higashiya are available in various flavors, such as black sesame, bamboo coal, kelp, and others. [→**P.61** HIGASHIYA GINZA]

Dorayaki どら焼き

Red bean paste sandwiched between a dough made from wheat, eggs, and other ingredients. It is thought to have existed since the Edo period, but the dough was only in one side at that time. [→**P.79** Kamejuu]

Dango 団子

Round, bite-sized Joshinko (Top-grade rice flour made from non-glutinous rice) balls put onto a bamboo skewer and covered with shoyu-based sauce (mitarashi), sesame, or red bean paste.

Experience an authentic Japanese tea ceremony

Experience an authentic Japanese tea ceremony, from the grinding of the green tea to manners, in a tea room made by master carpenters. In addition to showing a video about tea ceremony, masters with over 30 years experiencein tea ceremony will teach you all you need to know, so feel free to take part in this experience.

Chazen 茶禅

Address: Ginza Ishikawa Bldg. 5F, 4-12-17 Ginza, Chuo-ku **TEL:**03-6264-0690 **Opening hours:**10:00-20:00 **Closed:**None **Fee:**3500 yen (45 min.) **Access:**1 min. walk from Tokyo Metro Higashi-Ginza Station Exit 3

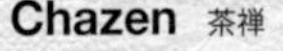 MAP P.53 C-3

Keyword 7

POP Culture

Experiencing Japanese pop culture for yourself is the best way to enjoy it. Enjoy "Cool Japan" in districts like Akihabara, Ikebukuro, Harajuku, and more!

Japan's pop culture has gained worldwide support, especially from younger generations, with manga, anime, movies, games, light novels (Entertaining, easy-to-read novels aimed at young people), J-pop, etc. Manga and anime have been translated into many languages and have helped spread Japanese culture, known as "Cool Japan". Recently in Tokyo, the unique culture created by OTAKU who love this pop culture and the KAWAII culture represented by Harajuku fashion have undergone further development into a hands-on movement.

This includes animal cafés where you can pet cute creatures. Maid cafés as well as butler cafés, spots where you can transform into Lolita fashion, nail salons that will paint your favorite anime characters on your nails. Go-karts for which you can actually drive on public roads dressed as characters. In pop culture epicenters such as Akihabara, Ikebukuro and Harajuku, you can enjoy an unforgettable experience!

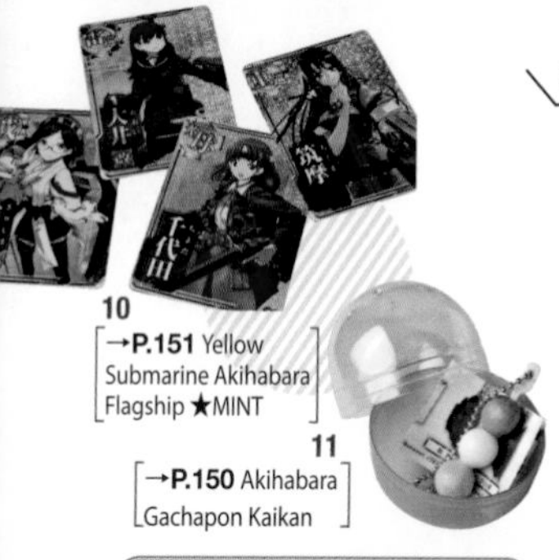

10

→P.151 Yellow Submarine Akihabara Flagship ★MINT

11

→P.150 Akihabara Gachapon Kaikan

OTAKU Culture

12

→P.146 Akiba Kart

13

→P.151 Nail Salon VenusRico

1. Whether it is fancy (NILE PERCH Harajuku Main shop)
2. casual (SPINNS Harajuku Takeshita Street Shop),
3. cute (lilLilly TOKYO)
4. Lolita Ⓒ, rock Ⓐ or other, Harajuku is the place where your own favorite fashion style is accepted
5. Many eccentric fashion styles are born in Harajuku as well Ⓑ
6,7. Animal cafés with cats, owls, rabbits, and other animals are also popular
8. You can find many cute character goods as well Ⓓ
9. "Takeshita Street" is a popular street in Harajuku where young people gather
10,11. In Akihabara, there is a large number of exciting products for the fans
12. Drive around town in a go-kart!
13. You'll be surprised at their quality of reproduction!

Experience in these places!

Ⓐ LISTEN FLAVOR Harajuku Shop

Offering all the Harajuku "kawaii" fashion items

A lineup of unique and original products that combine fancy and dark. Collaboration products featuring anime and game characters are also available.

Address:1-7-5 Jingumae, Shibuya-ku **TEL:**03-3408-6311 **Opening hours:** 11:00-20:00 **Closed:**None **Access:**5 min. walk from JR Harajuku Station Takeshita Exit

MAP P.102 A-1

Ⓑ KAWAII MONSTER CAFE HARAJUKU

A new type of restaurant that cannot be found anywhere else

Not only the interior, but also the staff as well as dishes are colorful, making a huge impact! Dance shows and other performances are held as well.

Address:YM Square Bldg. 4F, 4-31-10 Jingumae, Shibuya-ku **TEL:**03-5413-6142 **Opening hours:**11:30-16:30 (last admission 15:30, 90 minute system), 18:00-22:30 (last order 22:00), 11:00-20:00 (last order 19:30) on Sundays and public holidays **Closed:**None **Price:**Lunch from 1,500 yen, Dinner from 3,000 yen. 500 yen charge **Access:**3 min. walk from Tokyo Metro Meiji-Jingumae (Harajuku) Station Exit 5

MAP P.102 B-2

*2-hour seat system when crowded

Ⓒ Maison de Julietta

Transform yourself into a Lolita in Harajuku

A specialized shop where you can experience full-fledged Lolita fashion. Choose your favorite Lolita dress, and get your hair, makeup, and pictures done by professionals.

Address: Laforet Harajuku B1.5F, 1-11-6 Jingumae, Shibuya-ku **TEL:**03-6434-5464 **Opening hours:**11:00-21:00 (last admission 19:00) **Closed:**None **Price:**From 9,980 yen **Access:**1 min. walk from Tokyo Metro Meiji-Jingumae (Harajuku) Station Exit 4

MAP P.102 A-2

Ⓓ KIDDY LAND Harajuku store

A large selection of character goods

Goods shop offering trendy items and goods featuring characters popular in Japan and abroad. Events where people wear character costumes are also held on weekends.

Address:6-1-9 Jingumae, Shibuya-ku **TEL:**03-3409-3431 **Opening hours:**11:00-21:00, 10:30-21:00 on Saturdays, Sundays and public holidays **Closed:**Irregular holidays **Access:**4 min. walk from Tokyo Metro Meiji-Jingumae (Harajuku) Station Exit 4

MAP P.102 B-2

Tokyo's Night view

Look down from above, or up from the ground. There are many ways to enjoy Tokyo's night view. Enjoy it by changing your point of view.

With a population of about 13 million people, Tokyo transforms into a sea of lights when night falls. Of all the lights produced by glittering buildings and downtown areas such as Shinjuku and Roppongi, Tokyo Tower and TOKYO SKYTREE are the most remarkable. See this night view from elevated places such as observation decks to really get the feeling that "This is Tokyo". Also, illuminations projected on each building are filled with the unique Japanese aesthetic sense.

Since ancient times, Japanese people have felt elegance in soft shades created by lights, such as the faint light of the moon passing through shōji (paper doors) and small candles burning in the dark. Feel this unique Japanese elegance in lights that make use of different shades, such as at TOKYO SKYTREE, Kabukicho, and others. In addition, these days you can also enjoy illuminations created to celebrate daily or seasonal events such as Christmas, etc.

1. Spend your time in elegance as you listen to a live performance from a jazz band 2. Reputed also for its original cocktails, such as the "L.I.T", inspired by the movie

NEW YORK BAR ニューヨーク バー

A bar with an outstanding view that also appeared in a movie

Located on the 52nd floor, this bar has a sparkling view of the Tokyo night. Offers the best selection of California wines in Tokyo. It also appeared in the Hollywood movie "Lost in Translation".

Address: Park Hyatt Tokyo 52F, 3-7-1-2 Nishi-Shinjuku, Shinjuku-ku **TEL:**03-5323-3458 **Opening hours:**17:00-24:00 (last order), 17:00-25:00 (last order) from Thursday to Saturday **Closed:**None **Price:**Drinks from 2,000 yen **Access:**18 min. walk from JR Shinjuku Station South Exit

HP MAP P.38 A-3

*Cover charge: 2,400 yen from 20:00 (from 19:00 on Sunday)

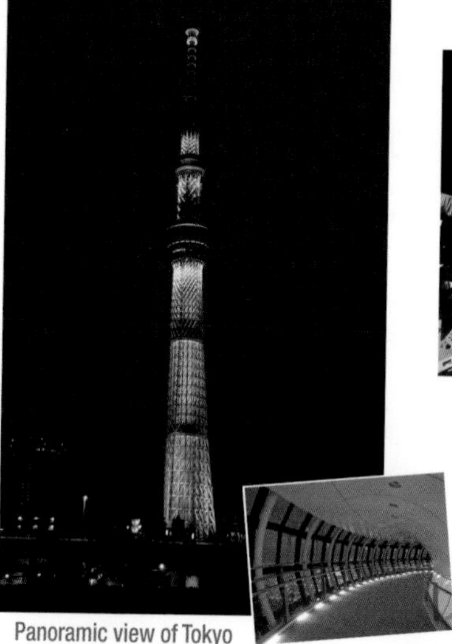

©TOKYO TOWER

Enjoy a spectacular view from the foot of the tower!

The foot of the Tokyo Tower

The interlacing truss structure is rising up beautifully. Although it is generally orange, different colored lights can also be seen on Saturdays and on special days.

[→P.122 Tokyo Tower]

Panoramic view of Tokyo from the observatory deck of the world's tallest self-supporting tower!

TOKYO SKYTREE observation deck

©TOKYO-SKYTREE

With the "Tembo Deck" at 350m and the "Tembo Galleria" at 450m, you can enjoy the view of the Tokyo nightscape from different heights. Lit up from sunset to midnight.

[→P.70 TOKYO SKYTREE]

Illuminations

The illumination of Kabuki-za. Colors differ depending on the time of year, representing the change of seasons ©Shochiku Co., Ltd.

The illumination of Odaiba's Rainbow Bridge is usually white. It also sometimes features rainbow colors during events

©Bureau of Port and Harbor, Tokyo Metropolitan Government

Small lanterns lining the alleys

Drinking district

When night falls in the drinking districts, the pub signs and lanterns light up. The sight of lighted small shops lined up is something you can find only in Japan.

[→P.46 Golden Gai]

An outstanding presence in the neon light district

Kabukicho's signboard

A signboard located in Shinjuku Kabukicho 1-chome. It is the next photo spot after Kabukicho Ichibangai Gate.

[→P.48 Kabukicho]

These are their features!

Seven features to express Japanese people

Take a look at these keywords to help you figure out the character traits of Japanese people and how to interact with them. However, be aware that these traits do not apply to every Japanese person.

Feature1 Clean

Japanese people love cleanliness to the point that you may be surprised to see that there is no trash in the streets and that the toilets are clean. They believe that public places should not be made dirty.

Feature2 Punctual

Railway companies are almost always punctual, so much so that if the train is even one minute late, they will apologize over the speakers. They believe that honoring commitments leads to trust.

Feature3 Hospitable

Japanese people naturally give more importance to others, and have the culture of honoring others. This is shown in proactive hospitality, such as providing guests with wet towels at the start of a meal, etc.

Feature4 Shy

You might have the impression that Japanese people run away when you try to talk to them, and also that Japanese people do not express their own opinions. Many people are shy and not willing to appear in front of others.

Feature5 Hardworking

Japanese are serious and hardworking people, but are said to be stubborn. Recently, a growing number of people think they can work even harder if they make more time for their interests and family.

Feature6 Courteous

Japanese learn to do proper greetings from an early age, and to respect others. Protecting the established rules and establishing order is considered a good thing.

Feature7 Always apologizing?

Japanese people say sumimasen (sorry) in all kinds of situations. Sumimasen has various uses besides as an apology, such as gratitude, solicitation, calling out to someone, and expressing humility.

The hot areas of Tokyo

Each district of Tokyo is unique. Among its many districts, we'll introduce 9 must-see sightseeing areas, along with an overview of each place that includes ways to have fun and recommended spots.
Have a fulfilling journey in Tokyo!

AREA 1

新宿

SHINJUKU

Shinjuku Station South Exit where many people come and go. “Busta Shinjuku” and the commercial facility “NEWoMan” are located on the opposite side

What kind of town?

Shinjuku is the biggest terminal station in Tokyo, used by about more than 3.5 million passengers per day. It boasts the largest number of passengers not only in Japan, but also in the world. The station is largely divided between west side and east side.

On the west side, you can find the business district where skyscrapers, including the Tokyo Metropolitan Government Building, are lined up.

The east side is a commercial area where there are long-established department stores and other shops. There is also “Kabukicho”, the largest entertainment district in Asia, which offers plenty of restaurants and the nostalgic bar street “Shinjuku Golden Gai”, making it a district that never runs out of things to do from morning to night.

In April 2016, Shinjuku Expressway Bus Terminal “Busta Shinjuku” was opened, and has become a center for accessing regional areas.

1. The west side business district
2. Large-scale shopping facilities such as “Isetan Shinjuku store” and “Shinjuku Marui” line Shinjuku-dori

1. Shinjuku is a city visited by many foreign tourists
2. The stairs in front of "Shinjuku Flags" that lead to the East South Exit of the station. You can also go to the east side of the station using these stairs
3. The "Robot Restaurant", where robots perform a spectacular show every night
4. Shinjuku is recommended for shopping as it offers all kind of goods

How to enjoy

There are three main ways to enjoy Shinjuku. The first above all is shopping. There are the long-established department store "Isetan Shinjuku store" and the popular roadside stores which dot the surroundings. Since there are rows of several buildings in various sizes, it is interesting to explore the area on foot.

The second way to enjoy is to look at Tokyo cityscape from skyscrapers of the business district. There are observation decks that can be used free of charge at the Tokyo Metropolitan Government Building No.1. In buildings that have restaurants on their upper floors, you can enjoy dining as you view the cityscape.

The third is to feel the four seasons of Japan in an urban oasis. In Shinjuku Gyoen, which is located on the southeast side, a variety of plants are grown a vast space.

©Shinjuku Gyoen National Garden

1.The gate of "Kabukicho Ichibangai", the symbol of Kabukicho
2. The Japanese garden in the "Shinjuku Gyoen". Wisterias bloom in the early summer

Must-visit tourist spots

Sightseeing

- Tokyo Metropolitan Government Building Observation Decks →P.40
- Shinjuku Gyoen →P.41
- Seiji Togo Memorial Sompo Japan Nipponkoa Museum of Art →P.41

Gourmet

- Koshitsukaiseki KITAOHJI Shinjukusaryo →P.44
- Fu-unji →P.45
- Shinjuku Golden Gai →P.46

Shopping

- Tokyu Hands Shinjuku Store →P.42
- Isetan Shinjuku Store →P.43
- Shinjuku Takashimaya →P.43

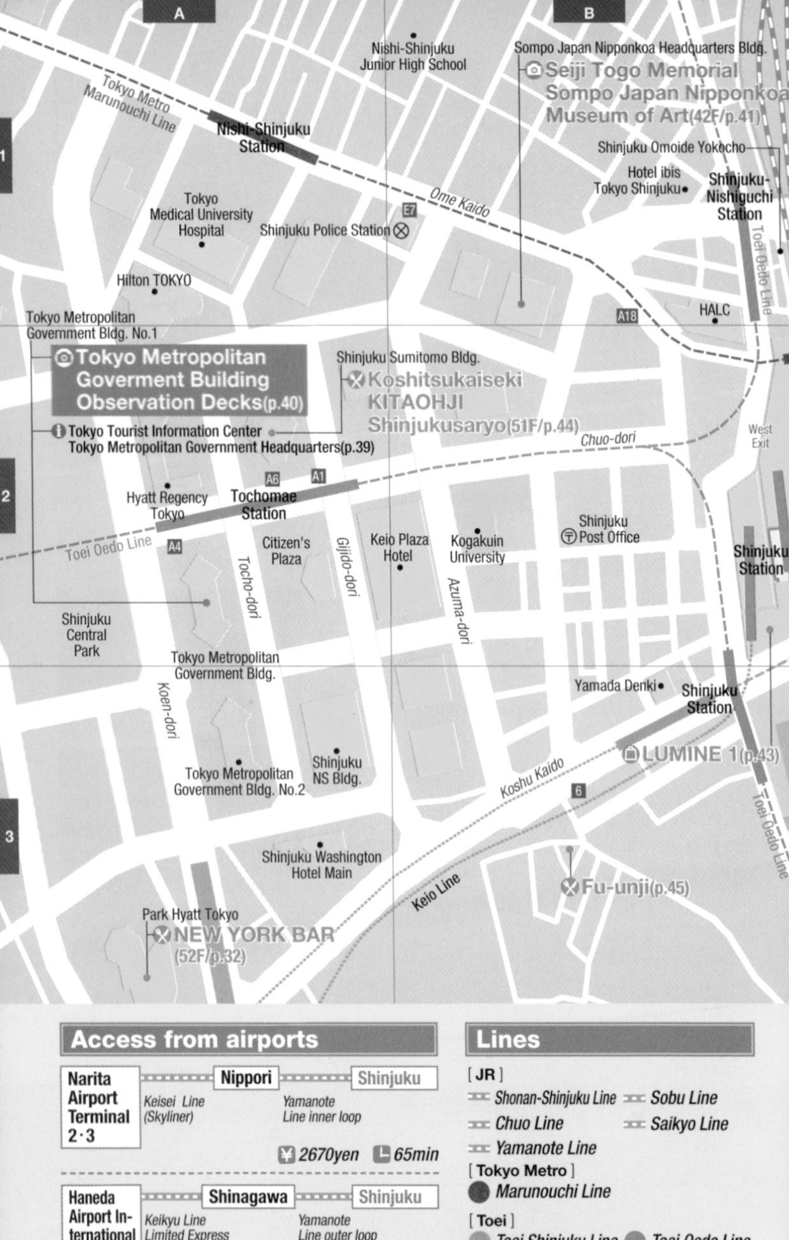

Access from airports

Narita Airport Terminal 2·3 — Keisei Line (Skyliner) — **Nippori** — Yamanote Line inner loop — **Shinjuku**

2670yen 65min

Haneda Airport International Terminal — Keikyu Line Limited Express and more — **Shinagawa** — Yamanote Line outer loop — **Shinjuku**

610yen 45min

Lines

[**JR**]

- *Shonan-Shinjuku Line*
- *Sobu Line*
- *Chuo Line*
- *Saikyo Line*
- *Yamanote Line*

[**Tokyo Metro**]

- *Marunouchi Line*

[**Toei**]

- *Toei Shinjuku Line*
- *Toei Oedo Line*

[**Private railway**]

- *Odakyu Odawara Line*
- *Keio Line*

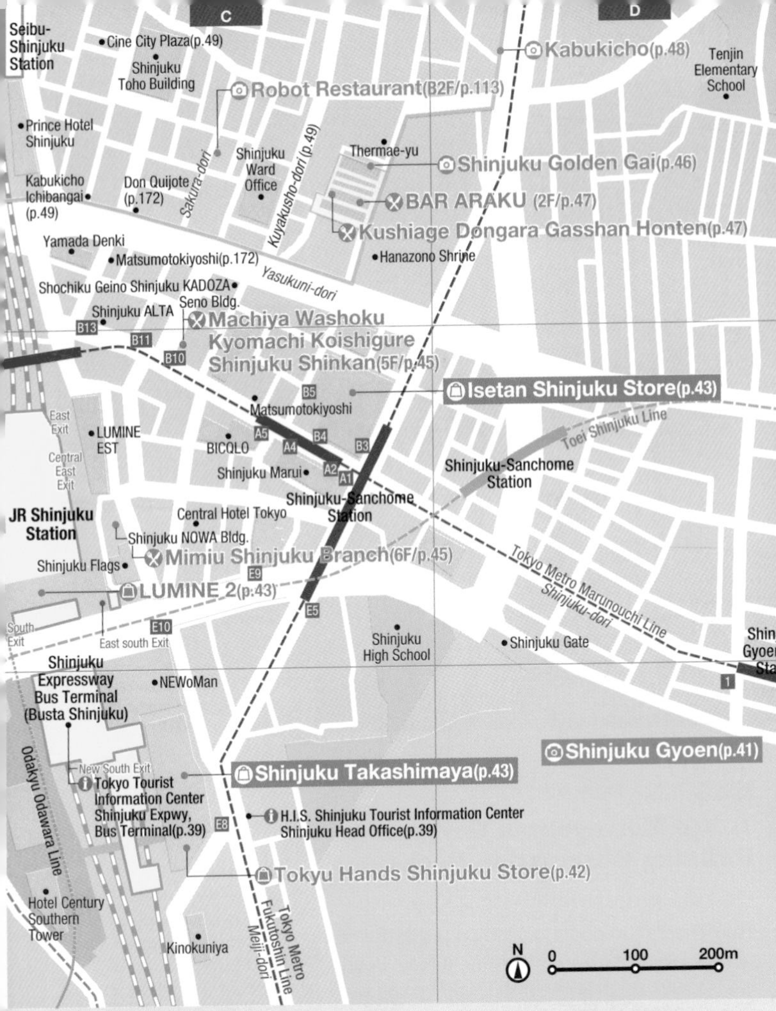

C D

Seibu-Shinjuku Station
Cine City Plaza(p.49)
Shinjuku Toho Building
Robot Restaurant(B2F/p.113)
Kabukicho(p.48)
Tenjin Elementary School
Prince Hotel Shinjuku
Sakura-dori
Shinjuku Ward Office
Kuyakusho-dori (p.49)
Thermae-yu
Shinjuku Golden Gai(p.46)
Kabukicho Ichibangai (p.49)
Don Quijote (p.172)
BAR ARAKU (2F/p.47)
Kushiage Dongara Gasshan Honten(p.47)
Yamada Denki
Matsumotokiyoshi(p.172)
Hanazono Shrine
Yasukuni-dori
Shochiku Geino Shinjuku KADOZA
Seno Bldg.
Shinjuku ALTA
Machiya Washoku Kyomachi Koishigure Shinjuku Shinkan(5F/p.45)
B13 B11 B10 B5
Isetan Shinjuku Store(p.43)
Matsumotokiyoshi
East Exit
LUMINE EST
BICQLO
A5 A4 B4 B3
Toei Shinjuku Line
Central East Exit
Shinjuku Marui
A2 A1
Shinjuku-Sanchome Station
Shinjuku-Sanchome Station
JR Shinjuku Station
Central Hotel Tokyo
Shinjuku NOWA Bldg.
Mimiu Shinjuku Branch(6F/p.45)
Tokyo Metro Marunouchi Line
Shinjuku-dori
Shinjuku Flags
E9
LUMINE 2(p.43)
E5
South Exit
E10
East south Exit
Shinjuku High School
Shinjuku Gate
Shinjuku-Gyoemmae Station
1
Shinjuku Expressway Bus Terminal (Busta Shinjuku)
NEWoMan
Shinjuku Gyoen(p.41)
Odakyu Odawara Line
New South Exit
Tokyo Tourist Information Center Shinjuku Expwy, Bus Terminal(p.39)
Shinjuku Takashimaya(p.43)
H.I.S. Shinjuku Tourist Information Center Shinjuku Head Office(p.39)
E8
Tokyu Hands Shinjuku Store(p.42)
Hotel Century Southern Tower
Kinokuniya
Meiji-dori
Tokyo Metro Fukutoshin Line
N
0 100 200m

2

3

Tourist information centers

H.I.S. Shinjuku Tourist Information Center Shinjuku Head Office

H.I.S新宿ツーリストインフォメーションセンター 新宿本社

Offer services such as booking for tours and cultural experiences, Tokyo Metro Pass, Wi-Fi rental, luggage storage, Yukata sales and rental, etc.

Address: South Gate Shinjuku Bldg. 1F, 5-33-8 Sendagaya, Shibuya-ku **TEL:** 080-4869-0514 **Opening hours:** 11:00-19:00, 11:00-18:30 on Saturdays, 11:00-18:00 on Sundays and public holidays **Closed:** None **Access:** 3 min. walk from JR Shinjuku Station New South Exit

HP MAP P.39 C-3

◆ Other tourist information centers

Tokyo Tourist Information Center Tokyo Metropolitan Government Headquarters

東京観光情報センター 都庁本部 MAP P.38 A-2

Tokyo Tourist Information Center Shinjuku Expwy, Bus Terminal

東京観光情報センター新宿高速バスターミナル MAP P.39 C-3

©TCVB

1. The building was designed by Kenzo Tange, an architect who worked both in Japan and abroad
2. The "Tokyo Café 202" located in the South Observation Deck. You can enjoy dishes related to Tokyo
3. The night view is also beautiful. Go up to the observation decks from the 1st floor observatory elevator

Observation Deck 東京都庁展望室

Tokyo Metropolitan Government Building Observation Decks

Shinjuku's symbolic high-rise building

The observation decks located on the 45th floor of Tokyo Metropolitan Government Main Building No.1 are open to the public and can be used free of charge, so they are recommended. There are also souvenir shops, cafés and restaurants.

Address:2-8-1 Nishi-Shinjuku, Shinjuku-ku **TEL:** 03-5320-7890 ※Weekdays: 10:00-17:00 **Opening hours:**North Observation Deck: 9:30-23:00, South Observation Deck: 9:30-17:30 ※Open until 23:00 when North Observation Deck is closed. Admission ends 30 minutes before closing time **Closed:**North Observation Deck: 2nd and 4th Monday of each month, South Observation Deck: 1st and 3rd Tuesday of each month. Tokyo Metropolitan Government Building Inspection Date **Access:** Directly connected with Toei Subway Tochomae Station A4 Exit

HP MAP P.38 A-2

For Tourists

You can see a superb view of the buildings in Shinjuku, Tokyo Tower, Meiji Shrine, etc. You can see Mount Fuji from the North Observation Deck if weather conditions are good.

Garden 新宿御苑

Shinjuku Gyoen

A beautiful garden called "the urban oasis"

A garden with more than a 100-year history. Originally built as garden of the imperial family, it has been opened to the public after the war. In this garden, you can see a variety of garden styles including English Landscape Garden, French Formal Garden, Japanese Traditional Garden.

Address: 11 Naito-machi, Shinjuku-ku
TEL: 03-3350-0151
Opening hours: 9:00-16:00
Closed: Mondays **Fee:** 200 yen
Access: 5 min. walk from Tokyo Metro Shinjuku-Gyoemmae Station Exit 1
HP
MAP P.39 D-3

*Bringing alcohol into the garden and drinking it there is prohibited. Using toys, sports equipment and the like is also prohibited in the garden

1. "Tamamo Pond" in the Japanese garden in the summertime. Sometimes waterfowl gather around the pond 2. You'll want to visit the "Lawn Area" during cherry-blossom season

For Tourists

Although you can enjoy this beautiful garden throughout the year, various varieties of cherry-blossoms bloom from the end of March until around the end of April. You can see the "Chrysanthemum Exhibition" from November 1 to 15 (no holiday), and autumn leaves from early November until early December.

1. Van Gogh's "Sunflowers". A work painted in 1888
2. The scene of the exhibition room. Decorated with Seiji Togo's works

For Tourists

Because it is located on 42nd floor, you can overlook the scenery of downtown Tokyo from the building's east corridor. It is possible to see TOKYO SKYTREE and Tokyo Tower both at the same time.

Art Museum 東郷青児記念 損保ジャパン日本興亜美術館

Seiji Togo Memorial Sompo Japan Nipponkoa Museum of Art

The museum where you can find "Sunflowers".

A collection of works from Japanese and foreign artists, including the western-style Japanese painter Seiji Togo. Holds exhibitions spanning a wide range of arts, such as western painting and modern art. You can see "Sunflowers", which is the only Van Gogh in Japan.

Address: Sompo Japan Nipponkoa Headquarters Bldg. 42F, 1-26-1 Nishi-Shinjuku, Shinjuku-ku **TEL:**03-5777-8600 (Hello Dial Service) **Opening hours:**10:00-18:00 (entry by 30 minutes before the closing time)
Closed: Mondays (open if public holiday), and during exhibit changes
Fee: Different depending on exhibitions **Access:** 9 min. walk from JR Shinjuku Station West Exit
HP MAP P.38 B-1

1. Many products perfect for souvenirs are on the 7th floor
2. On the second floor, you can find Tokyu Hands original products such as suitcases, umbrellas, etc.
3. There are also demonstration sales
4. There are also members of staff who can speak foreign languages Check for the mark on their chest!
5,6. 8th floor, a stationery area rich in variety

DIY Store 東急ハンズ 新宿店

Tokyu Hands Shinjuku Store

Many convenient everyday commodities together in one place!

A seven-floor large-scale home center offering about more than 150,000 products. Boasts a wide assortment of goods such as travel goods, kitchenware, stationery, etc. The store is located in Shinjuku Takashimaya Times Square.

Address: Times Square Bldg.2-8F, 5-24-2 Sendagaya, Shibuya-ku
TEL:03-5361-3111
Opening hours:10:00-21:00
Closed: Irregular holidays
Access:2 min. walk from JR Shinjuku Station New South Exit
MAP P.39 C-3

For Tourists

Foreign tourists can get a 5% OFF coupon by showing their passport. Members of staff fluent in foreign languages are on hand at the Information Counter on the 2nd floor.

Department Store 伊勢丹新宿店

Isetan Shinjuku Store

A popular department store selling first-class goods

A department store representing Shinjuku with a history of more than 80 years since its foundation. It consists of the Main Building and Men's Wing, offering a lineup of products for refined tastes. The food floor, which is the largest in the metropolitan area, is also a must-see.

Address:3-14-1 Shinjuku, Shinjuku-ku **TEL:**03-3352-1111 **Opening hours:** 10:30-20:00. 7th floor restaurants: 11:00-22:00 **Closed:** Irregular holidays **Access:**Immediate access from Tokyo Metro Shinjuku-Sanchome Station Exit B3 to B5

HP MAP P.39 C-2

The 3rd floor of the Main Building is the "International Designers" floor, which features fashion items from the world

For Tourists

There is a garden with lush greenery on the roof. Since there are chairs and tables, it can be used as a spot to relax or have lunch.

Department Store 新宿タカシマヤ

Shinjuku Takashimaya

A highly convenient department store near the station

A department store located on the south side of Shinjuku Station. Contains a variety of shops offering foodstuffs, clothing and accessories, and restaurants as well. Provides plenty of services for foreigners such as facility information and deliveries available in foreign languages, interpreters, etc.

Address:5-24-2 Sendagaya, Shibuya-ku **TEL:**03-5361-1111 **Opening hours:**10:00-20:00, 10:00-20:30 on Fridays and Saturdays **Closed:**None **Access:**2 min. walk from JR Shinjuku Station New South Exit

HP MAP P.39 C-3

Cosmetics and high-brand shops lined up on the 1st floor

For Tourists

You can get a 5% OFF coupon by showing your passport. Currency exchange machines are available on the 2nd floor.

Fashion Building ルミネ新宿

LUMINE Shinjuku

Offering a great line-up of elegant products

A shopping facility popular among Japanese working women. Features a variety of shops conscious of the latest trends, including fashion, accessories, cosmetics, restaurants, etc.

Address:1-1-5 Nishi-Shinjuku, Shinjuku-ku **TEL:**03-3348-5211 **Opening hours:**Shops: 11:00-22:00. Restaurants and bookstore: 11:00-23:00 (different for some shops) **Closed:**Irregular holidays **Access:** Immediate access from JR Shinjuku Station South Exit

HP MAP P.38 B-2/P.39 C-2

The two facilities LUMINE 1 and LUMINE 2 are located around Shinjuku Station South Exit

For Tourists

Offers plenty of services, such as floor information in English and Chinese, simultaneous interpretation support by phone, etc.

1. "Sushi Kaiseki" available only in Shinjuku. You can eat popular Japanese dishes such as sushi, tempura, sukiyaki and others all together 2. Window side guest room offers a nice view. Recommended also during night time for the beautiful night view 3. Female member of staff entertaining in a kimono

Kaiseki Cuisine 個室会席 北大路 新宿茶寮

Koshitsukaiseki KITAOHJI Shinjukusaryo

Kaiseki dishes enjoyed in a Japanese atmosphere

Experience the taste of Japanese cuisine using seasonal ingredients. The restaurant features the traditional tea house-style called "Sukiya-zukuri", letting you enjoy your meal in a Japanese atmosphere. Offering course meal only.

Address: Shinjuku Sumitomo Bldg. 51F , 2-6-1 Nishi-Shinjuku, Shinjuku-ku **TEL:**03-5909-7227 **Opening hours:**11:30-14:00 (last order 13:00), 17:00-22:30 (last order 21:00). Saturdays: 11:30-15:00 (last order 13:00), 17:00-21:00 (last order 19:00) **Closed:**Sundays and public holidays **Price:**Lunch from 2,000 yen, dinner from 7,000 yen **Access:**12 min. walk from JR Shinjuku Station West Exit

MAP P.38 A-2

For Tourists

All seating is in private rooms with tatami floors and require that shoes be removed. You will not feel pain in your legs when sitting on the tatami, for the table is over a hole in the floor.

Izakaya 町屋和食 京町恋しぐれ 新宿 新館

Machiya Washoku Kyomachi Koishigure Shinjuku Shinkan

Fully enjoy the taste and atmosphere of Kyoto in Tokyo

A Japanese food izakaya based on the image of a Machiya (traditional merchant's house) in Kyoto. You can enjoy the taste of Kyoto-style cuisine and Japanese sake produced in Kyoto. The interior and the river flowing in the Izakaya are also worth seeing.

Address: Seno Bldg. 5F, 3-18-4 Shinjuku, Shinjuku-ku **TEL:**03-3226-2855 **Opening hours:**17:00-24:00 (last order 23:00) **Closed:**None **Price:**From 3,500 yen **Access:**4 min. walk from JR Shinjuku Station East Exit

P.39 C-2

The signature dish is the "Seiro Mushi" made of meat and vegetables

For Tourists

You can also sometimes take a commemorative picture with the staff dressed as Maiko (not regular)

"Tokusei Tsukemen". Ingredients feature chashu (sliced roast pork), miso-flavored egg, laver, etc. You can upgrade to a large portion of noodles for free

Ramen 風雲児

Fu-unji

A ramen shop where people are always queuing

You have to try the "Tokusei Tsukemen". The soup made with dashi from anchovy and bonito is thick but still refreshing. The interior of the shop is decorated in Matsuri-style, and the entrance is a reproduction of a shrine curtain.

Address: Hokuto Dai-ichi Bldg. 1F, 2-14-3 Yoyogi, Shibuya-ku **TEL:**03-6413-8480 **Opening hours:**11:00-15:00, 17:00-21:00 **Closed:**Sundays and public holidays **Price:**From 950 yen **Access:**8 min. walk from JR Shinjuku Station South Exit

MAP P.38 B-3

For Tourists

You can see the hot water draining performance at the open kitchen in the shop. You will not get bored even when waiting.

*Even when there is a queue, you will be able to eat if you queue before the end of business hours.

Udon 美々卯 新宿店

Mimiu Shinjuku Branch

A long-established udon restaurant that originated in Osaka

This restaurant, which has continued for about 200 years, opened in 1925 under its current name. Its specialty is the "Udonsuki" which is made using a cooking method passed down since the restaurant's foundation, and it is popular with many people.

Address: Shinjuku NOWA Bldg. 6F, 3-37-12 Shinjuku, Shinjuku-ku **TEL:**03-5379-7241 **Opening hours:** 11:30-15:00 (last order 14:30), 17:00-22:30 (last order 21:30), 11:30-23:00 (last order 22:00) on Fridays and Saturdays, 11:30-22:00 (last order 21:00) on Sundays and public holidays **Closed:**Corresponds with NOWA Bldg. **Price:**Lunch from 2,000 yen, Dinner from 6,000 yen **Access:**3 min. walk from JR Shinjuku Station East Exit

MAP P.39 C-2

The "Udonsuki", full of toppings in a dashi of frigate mackerel, is Mimiu's signature dish

For Tourists

The menu is also rich in variety, offering Yuba (tofu skin), chicken and others, and the menu with items using typical Kansai ingredients and cooking methods is popular as well.

What is Shinjuku Golden Gai?

On the East side of Shinjuku, next to the Hanazono Shrine, there is bar street which is famous all over Japan called "Shinjuku Golden Gai". The Golden Gai started in 1945 as a post-war black market and evolved to its current form. In this area with its retro atmosphere, there are rows of tenement-style buildings and more than 280 shops doing business. It is special in that it is home to many unique shops specializing in hobbies such as music, movies, manga, literature, etc.

In 1975, Kenji Nakagami received the Akutagawa Prize and Ryuzo Saki the Naoki Prize, and since both of them were regular customers of the Golden Gai, the fact that they received two major literary prizes from Japanese literary circles at the same time made this bar area known as a place where intellectuals gather.

Even nowadays this area draws a lot of attention, known as a bar street where artists, authors, and people in entertainment gather. Most of the shops are small scale and offer around 10 seats. Bar-hopping around the shops is one way to have fun, and beginners should ask for recommended places from shopkeepers and regular customers as well. The true charm of this area is in trying to talk with the people around you.

1. The "BAR ARAKU" crowded with foreign tourists. In recent years, many foreign tourists also come here
2. BAR ARAKU's bartender
3. Golden Gai sign. Although it is in Japanese, a map of the whole area is available at the G1 entrance
4. An alley that makes you feel like you have traveled back in time. There are also shops on the 2nd floor of the building

MAP P.39 C-1

Fried Skewers Izakaya 串揚げ どんがらがっしゃん本店

Kushiage Dongara Gasshan Honten

Relish freshly fried crispy kushiage

You can eat about 40 types of kushiage including meat, fish, vegetables, etc. It is among the places easy to enter even for beginners in the Golden Gai, as it has space for 22 seats. Kushiage skewers from 80 yen, drinks from 400 yen.

Address: Golden Gai G2 1F, 1-1-9 Kabukicho, Shinjuku-ku **TEL:**03-3207-3718 **Opening hours:**17:00 to following day 5:00 (last order 4:00), 17:00 to following day 2:00 on Sundays and public holidays (last order 1:00) **Closed:**Irregular holidays **Price:**From 1,000 yen **Access:**10 min. walk from JR Shinjuku East Exit

MAP P.39 C-1

1. The unique signs in the shop are written by the employees 2.The handmade "Shoyu Koji Karaage" marinated in malted rice is tender and juicy 3. The "Horoyoi Set" is a good bargain with skewers and drink set for 1,000 yen. Orders from 17:00 to 19:00, 24:00 to following day 5:00

For Tourists

Order for kushiage goes smooth when you fill in the English order sheet on the table with the number of skewers you want. Double-dipping the kushiage in the sauce is forbidden, so be careful.

*Kushiage is the term for bite-size cut ingredients put on skewers, coated with batter and deep-fried in oil

1. Cocktails using Japanese alcohol such as Japanese sake, matcha liquor, and others are popular 2. Bills from many countries cover the walls and ceiling of the shop

For Tourists

Bills with messages covering the inside of the shop have been left by visiting foreign tourists. Why not leaving one in memory of your visit to the shop?

*Bringing drinks in the shop is not allowed but food is OK

Bar BAR ARAKU

BAR ARAKU

A lively bar bustling with discourse between customers

A shop started by its Australian owner who loves the Golden Gai. The name of the shop means "to enjoy Asia". 80% of the customers are foreigners and there is no extra charge, making it a place easy for foreigners living in Japan to visit.

Address: Golden Gai G2 2F, 1-1-9 Kabukicho, Shinjuku-ku **TEL:**03-5272-1651 **Opening hours:**20:00-following day 4:00 (last order 3:30) **Closed:**None **Price:**From 650 yen **Access:**10 min. walk from JR Shinjuku Station East Exit

MAP P.39 C-1

The safest entertainment district in the world!?

Kabukicho

In Shinjuku there are many different districts, each has its own features. Kabukicho is one of the districts you absolutely cannot miss if you go sightseeing in Japan.

Kabukicho is also referred to as "Asia's largest entertainment district"

What kind of district is it?

Located in Tokyo's Shinjuku Ward, Kabukicho is an entertainment district lined with restaurants, amusement facilities and movie theaters. It is a home to many manga cafes, izakayas, and adult entertainment establishments as well, and with its neon signs brightly lighting up the night, it is also referred to as "the town that never sleeps". It offers a strange and unique atmosphere where the legal and illegal are mixed together.

The history of Kabukicho

The site where Kabukicho is currently located used to be a residential area that got razed to the ground following the bombing of Tokyo in 1945. After Second World War, it was named "Kabukicho" as its reconstruction project planned to build a kabuki theater.

In the mid-1950s, in addition to all kinds of restaurants, a movie theater, a bowling alley, saunas, and amusement facilities, as well as adult entertainment establishments started getting more and more prominent. Since 2001, laws have been enforced more strictly by the police , and crime has gone down considerably. In 2004, a large-scale crackdown called the "Kabukicho Purification Operation" was also implemented and in 2005, the revision of a city ordinance (commonly known as street touts banning ordinance) was enforced. In 2015, the Shinjuku Toho Building opened on the site of the old Shinjuku Koma Theater. It has been attracting attention as the new symbol of Shinjuku with its Godzilla head decoration and other attractions.

The Shinjuku Koma Theater opened in 1956

A view of the bustling Kabukicho Ichibangai at the end of the year (1972)

Pictures provided by the Shinjuku Historical Museum

Kabukicho nowadays

Referred to as, "the town that never sleeps" and also, "the nightless city", Kabukicho often appears in novels, comics, movies, dramas and games depicting Tokyo's underworld. This is why it has an unsafe and scary image. However, it is a district for young people where travelers can walk around with peace of mind. Since there are popular cat cafés, manga cafes and also stylish cafés in Kabukicho, it is also a place you can visit with comfort. Lively during daytime, Kabukicho has a different side at night, showing even more splendor. Kabukicho is very wide with its 1-chome and 2-chome districts.

Although there are suspicious people trying to get you into their shops that you should be careful about, you will realize that it is a very fun entertaining district once you actually go there.

Kabukicho is not only about restaurants. You can also enjoy shopping during daytime

At night, Kabukicho turns into a nightless castle covered with innumerable mysterious neon lights

PICK UP

The main area of Kabukicho

The surprisingly vast Kabukicho. Enjoy nighttime amusement to the fullest by knowing the main streets and spots!

Ichibangai

Kabukicho's main street, packed with a variety of restaurants.
The entrance gate is famous as a good place to take pictures.

→MAP P.39 C-1

Cine City Plaza

The plaza in front of Shinjuku Toho Building. You can find many amusement facilities including a bowling alley and a movie theater, and sometimes events are held here as well.

→MAP P.39 C-1

Kuyakusho-dori

Kuyakusho, meaning "ward office", as its name indicates, it is situated in front of the Shinjuku Ward Office, with the Shinjuku Golden Gai area on the east side.
Lit-up with illuminations in winter.

→MAP P.39 C-1

銀座

GINZA

Symbol of Ginza, the "Wako" clock tower located at the Ginza 4-chome intersection

What kind of town?

Ginza is a world-class commercial district, ranked with NY 5th Avenue and the Champs Elysées in Paris. It is known as a sophisticated district for grown-ups district where "first-class" gathers. In the central area, there is the Ginza 4-chome intersection of Chuo-dori and Harumi-dori, with long-established department stores representing Ginza such as "Wako" and "Ginza Mitsukoshi" on its corner. Along the Chuo-dori, apart from other department stores and luxury brands, you can find many long-established gourmet restaurants and famous shops. In addition, new commercial facilities have been opening up one after the other recently, drawing attention as a place that not only offers long-established shops but also as a place to find the latest trends. It is a district where you can enjoy the new and the old at the same time.

1. "GINZA PLACE" opened in September 2016(right) 2. Many people from Japan and overseas visit the "Tokyu Plaza Ginza", which has as its theme Japanese "tradition and innovation"

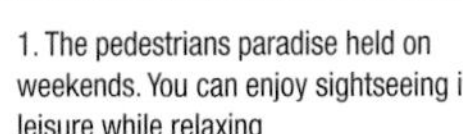

1. The pedestrians paradise held on weekends. You can enjoy sightseeing in leisure while relaxing
2. The parfait of "Ginza Sembikiya". It is also a real pleasure to enjoy the taste of long-established shop
3. At the "Kobikicho Hiroba" located in the underground of Kabuki-za, you can enjoy products and food associated with Kabuki
4. The willows swaying elegantly in the air are symbolic of Ginza

How to enjoy

There are two main ways to enjoy Ginza. First, shopping and dining at the long-established restaurants and luxury brand stores. There are many old shops (established more than 100 years ago) in Ginza, gourmet restaurants that have been popular for many years, and you can also find articles made with a brillant craftsmanship. Since Ginza offers world-renowned high-class brands as well, you can also do "brand-cruising".

The other way to enjoy is to experience both Japanese tradition and trends. Seeing Kabuki performance is definitely a unique experience. If you want to feel modern Tokyo, go to the large shopping facilities that have recently opened one after the other such as "Tokyu Plaza Ginza", "GINZA PLACE", and "EXIT MELSA". They have all the latest Japanese fashion items and gourmet.

1. "Kabuki-za". The Japanese-style garden on the rooftop is also a must-see!
2. Luxury brands together in the "Harumi-dori" and "Ginza Marronnier-dori"

Must-visit tourist spots

Gourmet

- Ginza Bairin →P.58
- Tempura Kondo →P.58
- Rengatei →P.59
- Tofuro Yumemachi Kouji Ginza 1chome Shop →P.59
- Ginza Budonoki →P.60
- Ginza Sembikiya Ginza Main Store Fruit Parlor →P.61

Shopping

- Tokyu Plaza Ginza →P.55
- Tokyo Kyukyodo Ginza Main Shop →P.56
- Ginza Itoya →P.57

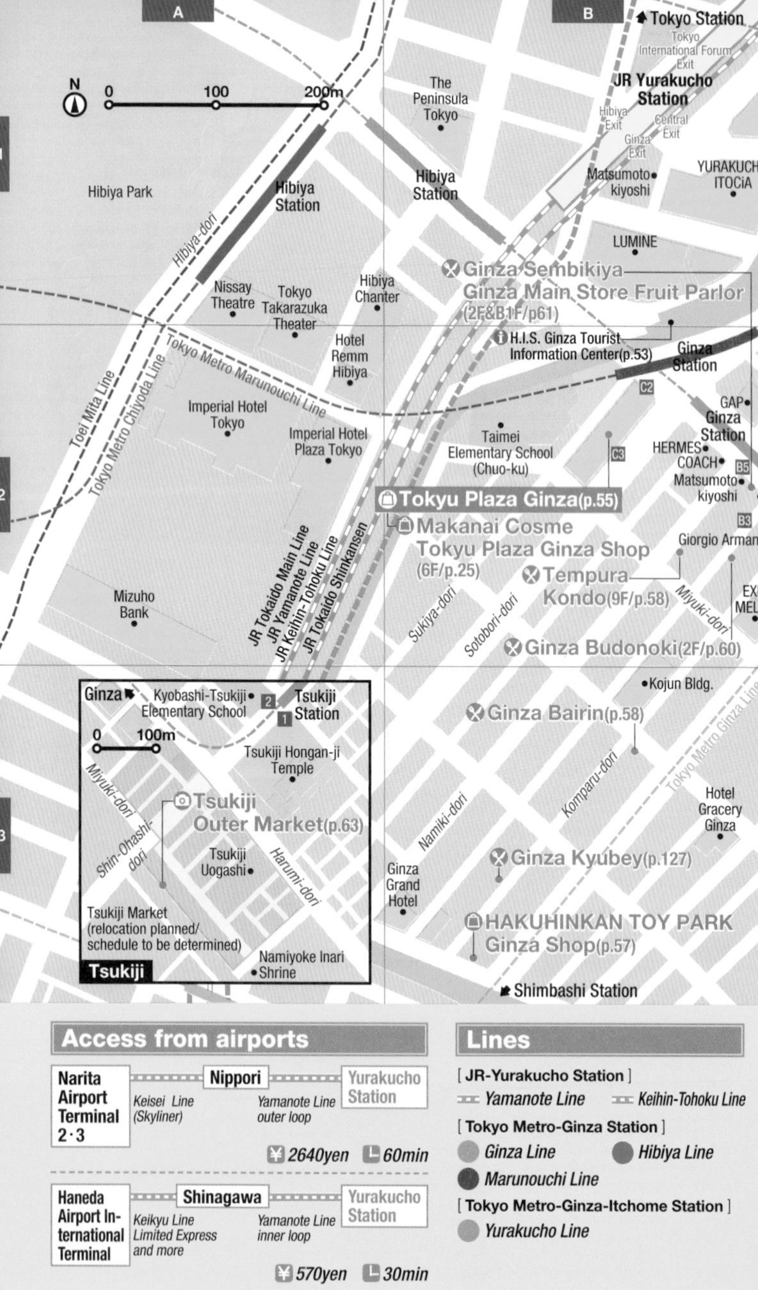

Access from airports

Narita Airport Terminal 2·3 — *Keisei Line (Skyliner)* — **Nippori** — *Yamanote Line outer loop* — **Yurakucho Station**

2640yen 60min

Haneda Airport International Terminal — *Keikyu Line Limited Express and more* — **Shinagawa** — *Yamanote Line inner loop* — **Yurakucho Station**

570yen 30min

Lines

[**JR-Yurakucho Station**]

Yamanote Line *Keihin-Tohoku Line*

[**Tokyo Metro-Ginza Station**]

Ginza Line *Hibiya Line*

Marunouchi Line

[**Tokyo Metro-Ginza-Itchome Station**]

Yurakucho Line

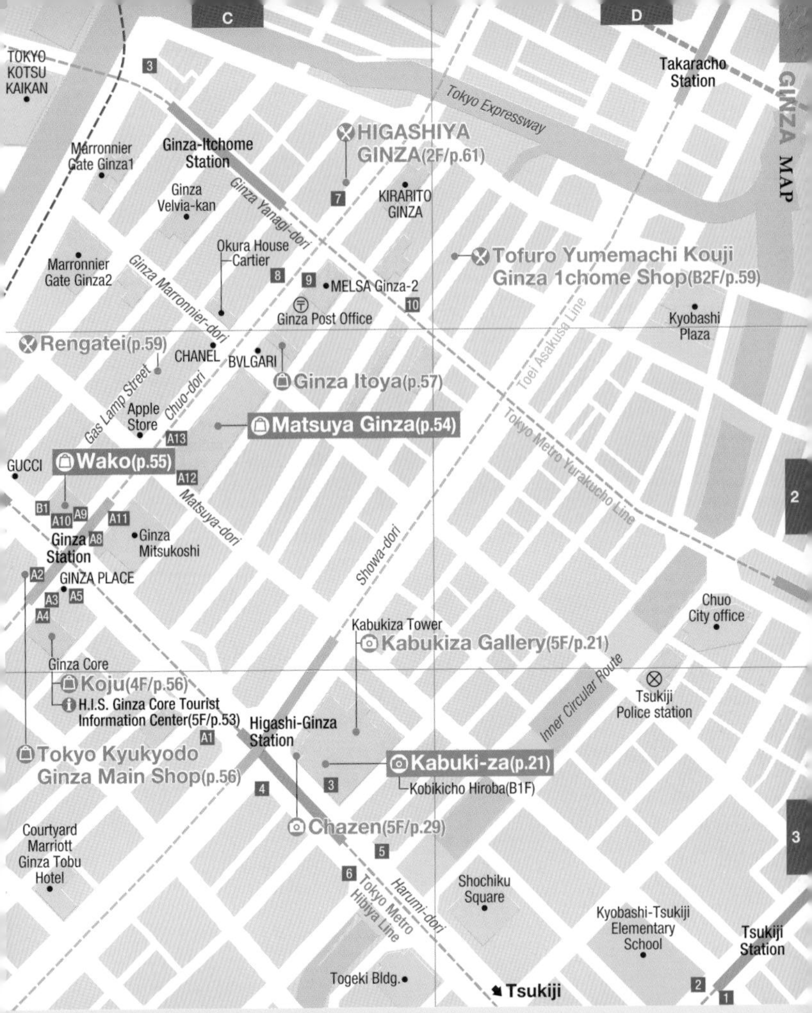

C D

TOKYO KOTSU KAIKAN
Takaracho Station
Tokyo Expressway
HIGASHIYA GINZA(2F/p.61)
Marronnier Gate Ginza1
Ginza-Itchome Station
Ginza Velvia-kan
Ginza Yanagi-dori
KIRARITO GINZA
Okura House Cartier
Marronnier Gate Ginza2
Ginza Marronnier-dori
MELSA Ginza-2
Ginza Post Office
Tofuro Yumemachi Kouji Ginza 1chome Shop(B2F/p.59)
Kyobashi Plaza
Toei Asakusa Line
Rengatei(p.59)
CHANEL
BVLGARI
Ginza Itoya(p.57)
Gas Lamp Street
Chuo-dori
Apple Store
Matsuya Ginza(p.54)
Tokyo Metro Yurakucho Line
GUCCI
Wako(p.55)
Matsuya-dori
Ginza Station
Ginza Mitsukoshi
Showa-dori
GINZA PLACE
Chuo City office
Kabukiza Tower
Kabukiza Gallery(5F/p.21)
Ginza Core
Koju(4F/p.56)
H.I.S. Ginza Core Tourist Information Center(5F/p.53)
Inner Circular Route
Tsukiji Police station
Higashi-Ginza Station
Tokyo Kyukyodo Ginza Main Shop(p.56)
Kabuki-za(p.21)
Kobikicho Hiroba(B1F)
Courtyard Marriott Ginza Tobu Hotel
Chazen(5F/p.29)
Shochiku Square
Harumi-dori
Tokyo Metro Hibiya Line
Kyobashi-Tsukiji Elementary School
Tsukiji Station
Togeki Bldg.
Tsukiji

Tourist information centers

H.I.S. Ginza Core Tourist Information Center

H.I.S. 銀座コア ツーリストインフォメーションセンター

Offer services such as booking for tours and cultural experiences, Tokyo Metro Pass, Wi-Fi rental, luggage storage, Yukata sales and rental, etc.

Address: Ginza Core 5F, 5-8-20 Ginza, Chuo-ku **TEL:** 080-3215-7539
Opning hours: 11:00-19:00
Closed: Corresponding with Ginza Core Bldg. **Access:** Immediate access from Tokyo Metro Ginza Station Exit A3

MAP P.53 C-2

◆ Other tourist information centers

H.I.S. Ginza Tourist Information Center

H.I.S. 銀座ツーリストインフォメーションセンター

MAP P.52 B-1

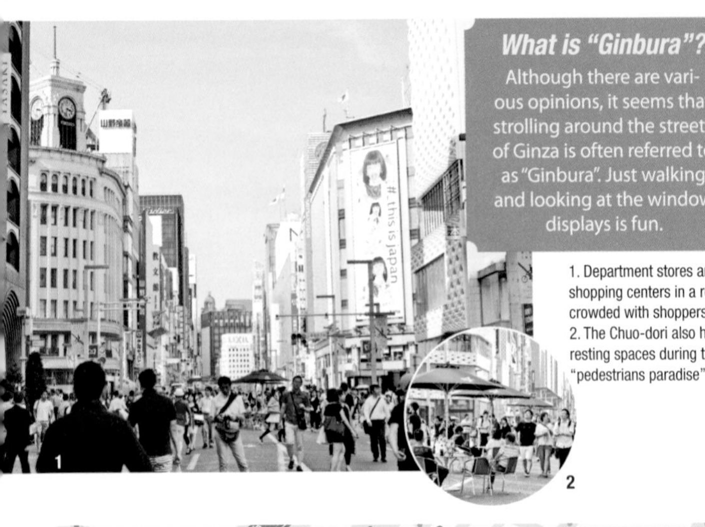

What is "Ginbura"?

Although there are various opinions, it seems that strolling around the streets of Ginza is often referred to as "Ginbura". Just walking and looking at the window displays is fun.

1. Department stores and shopping centers in a row, crowded with shoppers
2. The Chuo-dori also has resting spaces during the "pedestrians paradise"

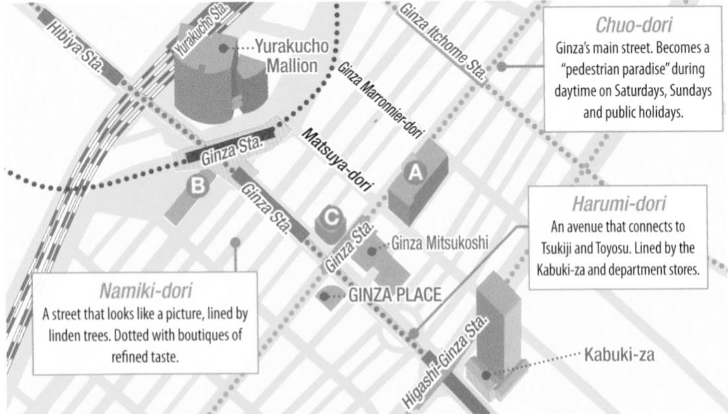

Chuo-dori
Ginza's main street. Becomes a "pedestrian paradise" during daytime on Saturdays, Sundays and public holidays.

Harumi-dori
An avenue that connects to Tsukiji and Toyosu. Lined by the Kabuki-za and department stores.

Namiki-dori
A street that looks like a picture, lined by linden trees. Dotted with boutiques of refined taste.

A Department Store 松屋銀座 Matsuya Ginza

A department store representing Ginza

A long-established department store in Ginza. It's Handing fashion and household goods, also it have many famous Japanese confectionery shops and a bar which you can enjoy many kinds of sake from Japan. All this shops are the representative place of Japanese food culture.

Address:3-6-1 Ginza, Chuo-ku **TEL:**03-3567-1211
Opening hours:10:00-20:00 **Closed:**Irregular holidays
Access: Directly connected with Tokyo Metro Ginza Station Exit A12
HP MAP P.53 C-2

1. The "Hands Expo" combines "shopping, eating and experiencing"
2. The "LOTTE DUTY FREE GINZA" is located on 8th and 9th floor
3. The 6th floor event space "Kiriko Lounge"

Commercial Facility 東急プラザ銀座

Tokyu Plaza Ginza

New shops opening one after another

A shopping center established in March 2016. It is composed of two underground floors and eleven above ground floors and offers a rich lineup, from long-established Japanese brands to overseas brands.

Address:5-2-1 Ginza, Chuo-ku **TEL:**03-3571-0109 (11:00-21:00) **Opening hours:**11:00-21:00. Restaurants and food: 11:00-23:00 *Some shops may differ **Closed:**Irregular holidays twice a year **Access:**1 min. walk from Tokyo Metro Ginza Station Exit C2 and C3

MAP P.52 B-2

Specialty Store 和光

Wako

The clock tower is the city's landmark

Offers high-quality articles from Japan and abroad, such as watches, jewellery, clothing, and others. It has an established reputation particularly for its vast selection of watches, with the largest number of items from domestic brands and Seiko in Japan.

Address:4-5-11 Ginza, Chuo-ku **TEL:**03-3562-2111 **Opening hours:**10:30-19:00 **Closed:**None **Access:**Immediate access from Tokyo Metro Ginza Station Exit A9 and A10

MAP P.53 C-2

Column

Delicatessen section in department store basement

↑ Lunch boxes from all the shops are sold at "Momokozen" corner during lunch time

↓ At "Ebisu Daikoku", you can buy Japanese side dishes which sold by weight

↑ The patisserie of the "Hotel Seiyo Ginza", which used to located in Ginza. Top-selling products are "Ginza Macaron" and "Seiyo Mont Blanc"

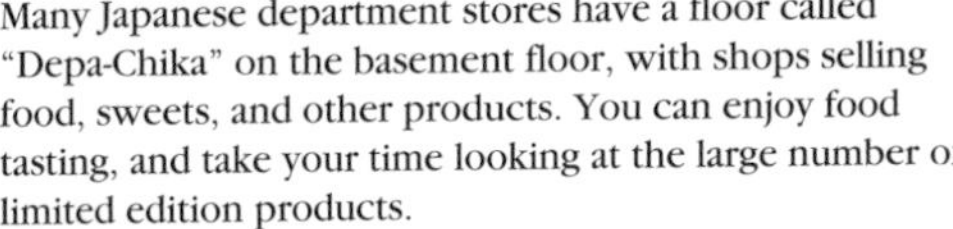

Many Japanese department stores have a floor called "Depa-Chika" on the basement floor, with shops selling food, sweets, and other products. You can enjoy food tasting, and take your time looking at the large number of limited edition products.

*All pictures are the property of "Matsuya Ginza"

Incense 香十

Koju

An incense shop with more than 440 years of tradition

A shop specializing in incense that was also loved by historical figures such as Hideyoshi Toyotomi, Ieyasu Tokugawa, and others. This shop, which has passed down incense culture from ancient times, offers blended and manufactured instruments for incense burning.

Address: Ginza Core 4F, 5-8-20 Ginza, Chuo-ku **TEL:**03-3574-6135
Opening hours:11:00-20:00
Closed: Corresponding with Ginza Core
Access:1 min. walk from Tokyo Metro Ginza Station Exit A3

MAP P.53 C-2

1. "Tokusen Hana-no-Hana". "Kosuiko" incense, blended at the end of the 19th century, passed down to today
2. "Shippo Kouzara" and "Aritayaki Koutatezuru". The crane motif is recommended for celebrations

For Tourists

Offering incense as a gift to ancestors during memorial services has been a custom in Japan since ancient times. Don't hesitate to try this incense, which calms the mind.

1. Just looking at the colorful Yuzen paper is a pleasant experience. Offering also plenty of Japanese-style accessories using Yuzen paper
2. Apart from postcards, stationery and Chiyogami, the calligraphy items are also very popular

For Tourists

Subtle Japanese paper patterns and durability can only be achieved through traditional techniques of craftsmen. Duty-free shopping available for purchases over 10,000 yen without tax (passport required).

Japanese Arts and Crafts 東京鳩居堂 銀座本店

Tokyo Kyukyodo
Ginza Main Shop

Take home the culture of Japanese paper and incense

A famous shop originating in Kyoto with a history of more than 350 years. Offers products combining tradition and practicability, centered around incense and Japanese paper. One appeal of this shop is that you can check the texture, thickness and other aspects before you buy.

Address:5-7-4 Ginza, Chuo-ku **TEL:**03-3571-4429 **Opening hours:**10:00-19:00, 11:00-19:00 on Sundays and public holidays
Closed: Irregular holidays **Access:**Immediate access from Tokyo Metro Ginza Station Exit A2

MAP P.53 C-2

Miscellaneous Goods 銀座・伊東屋

Ginza Itoya

Offering a rich variety of stationery items

This stationery shop has been popular since its establishment was renewed in 2015. On every floor, there is a display of stationery items needed for each kind of situation. There are also a café and juice stand.

Address:2-7-15 Ginza, Chuo-ku
TEL:03-3561-8311
Opening hours:10:00-20:00, 10:00-19:00 on Sundays and public holidays. 12th floor café: 10:00-22:00 (last order 21:00)
Closed: None **Access:**2 min. walk from Tokyo Metro Ginza Station Exit A13

MAP P.53 C-2

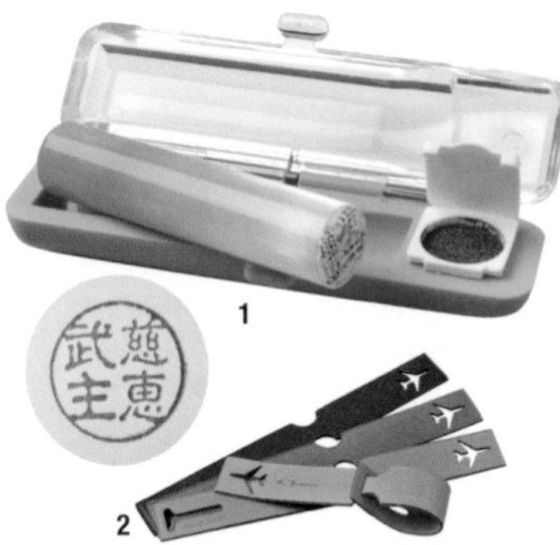

1. A hanko stamp that converts European alphabets into kanji. The picture shows the kanji for "James"
2. Travel baggage tag. It is possible to put a name on leather goods

For Tourists

The concept is "hands-on". You can have a variety of experiences, such as a desk where you can write and post a letter, make an original notebook, etc.

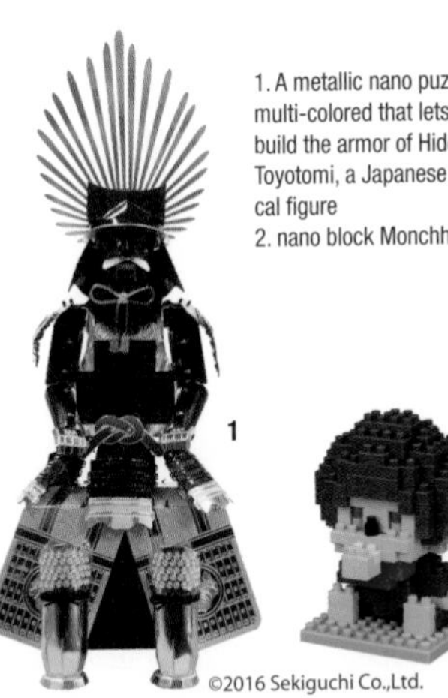

1. A metallic nano puzzle multi-colored that lets you build the armor of Hideyoshi Toyotomi, a Japanese historical figure
2. nano block Monchhichi

©2016 Sekiguchi Co.,Ltd.

For Tourists

The shop has been created to be easy to understand with multi-language signs as well as many product monitors and samples.

Toys 博品館TOY PARK銀座本店

HAKUHINKAN TOY PARK Ginza Shop

A toy treasure house Japan can be proud of

A shop specializing in toys, offering approximately 200,000 products. You will find the items you are looking for, with toys, character goods, and even typical Japanese goods that let you feel Japanese culture.

Address:8-8-11 Ginza, Chuo-ku
TEL:03-3571-8008
Opening hours:11:00-20:00 **Closed:**None
Access:6 min. walk from JR Shimbashi Station Ginza Exit

MAP P.52 B-3

*Some items may be sold out

Tonkatsu 銀座 梅林

Ginza Bairin

A shop specializing in Tonkatsu where queues are inevitable

This tonkatsu, made from high-quality meat, for which particular attention was paid to the texture, and fresh bread crumbs with low sugar that efficiently drains off the oil, is refreshing and has many fans. The shop also sells its special sauce.

Address: Shibuya Bldg. 1F, 7-8-1 Ginza, Chuo-ku **TEL:**03-3571-0350 **Opening hours:**11:30-21:00(last order 20:45) **Closed:**None **Price:**From 2,000 yen **Access:**5 min. walk from Tokyo Metro Ginza Station Exit A2

MAP P.52 B-3

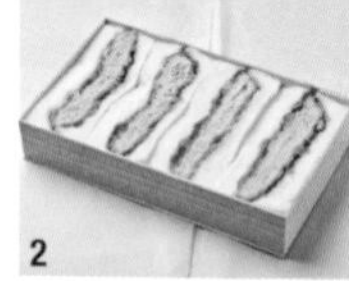

1. "Rōsukatsu (pork loin) Set Meal". Eat this with the Chūno (medium-thick) sauce with stewed onions and pork 2. The "Hirekatsu (pork fillet) Sandwich" is also recommended for take-away. Delicious even when cold

For Tourists

A historic shop that opened in 1927 as the first tonkatsu specialty store in Ginza. Since reservations are not required, try to avoid visiting it during peak hours.

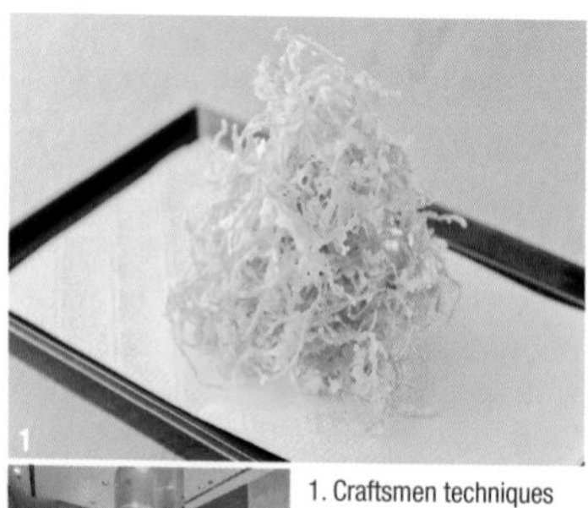

1. Craftsmen techniques are also used to fry shredded carrots from all angles 2. Dishes come in turns. It feels like the perfect live performance as tempura are fried over the counter

For Tourists

Enjoy the taste of the quintessence of Edo-mae Tempura. Dishes using not only the classic ingredients but also more creative ones are marvelous.

Tempura てんぷら近藤

Tempura Kondo

It goes without saying that this is Tempura at the highest level

A well-established restaurant visited by celebrities from all around the world. This tempura, which uses seasonal vegetables, is gorgeous, as the thin batter-coating highlights the ingredients colors and shapes, making it look like a work of art. Since it is a popular restaurant, early reservation is required.

Address: Sakaguchi Bldg. 9F, 5-5-13 Ginza, Chuo-ku **TEL:**03-5568-0923 **Opening hours:**12:00-15:00 (last order 13:30), 17:00-22:30 (last order 20:30) **Closed:**Sundays and Mondays on public holidays **Price:**Lunch from 7,000 yen, Dinner from 12,000 yen **Access:**3 min. walk from Tokyo Metro Ginza Station Exit B5

MAP P.52 B-2

Western Food 煉瓦亭

Rengatei

Enjoy Japan's original Western-style menu

Established in 1895. Known as the first restaurant to serve omu-rice (rice omelet) and cutlets which are now iconic dishes for Western-style menus. Burned bricks remaining from the Ginza Renga-gai district which existed during Meiji era were used for the walls in the restaurant, creating a retro atmosphere.

Address:3-5-16 Ginza, Chuo-ku **TEL:**03-3561-3882 **Opening hours:**11:15-15:00 (last order 14:15), 16:40-21:00 (last order 20:30), 11:15-15:00 (last order 14:15), 16:40-20:45 (last order 20:00) on Saturdays and public holidays **Closed:**Sundays **Price:**Lunch from 2,000 yen, Dinner from 3,000 yen **Access:**2 min. walk from Tokyo Metro Ginza Station Exit A9

MAP P.53 C-2

1. "The Original Pork Cutlet" using Sagami pork in the background of the picture, and the "The Original Omu-rice" in the foreground
2. Table seats from B1F to 2F, and tatami seats on 3F

For Tourists

"Pork Cutlets", in which thickly sliced pork is coated with bread crumbs and deep-fried, and the "Omu-rice", which combines eggs and rice into one dish, originated here.

1. The "Otakara-mori", which uses plenty of seasonal ingredients. A rich selection of Japanese sake is also available 2. The elegant lights in the restaurant seem to burn like candles, it is just as if you went back to the Edo period

For Tourists

The entire space, with its entrance decorated in bamboo and its riverside tatami rooms, is used to make you feel the atmosphere of Japan.

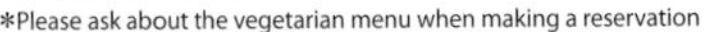

*Please ask about the vegetarian menu when making a reservation

Izakaya 土風炉 夢町小路 銀座1丁目店

Tofuro Yumemachi Kouji Ginza 1chome Shop

Travelling back in time to the Edo period?!

Offers a rich variety of Japanese dishes, including sashimi, soba, tempura, and other preparations using ingredients from all over Japan. The interior of the store is also fascinating, inspired by an Edo era town, and features a vermillon bridge.

Address: Ginza First Bldg. B2F, 1-10-6 Ginza, Chuo-ku **TEL:**03-3563-3033 **Opening hours:**11:30-14:30 (last order 14:00), 17:00-23:30 (last order 22:55), 11:30~23:30 (last order 22:55) on Saturdays, Sundays and public holidays **Closed:**None **Price:**Lunch from 900 yen, Dinner from 3,500 yen **Access:**Directly connected with Tokyo Metro Ginza-Itchome Station Exit 10

MAP P.53 D-1

1. The "Crepe Suzette" with the aromas of orange and cognac. Large pieces of nuts put in the homemade macadamia nut sorbet
2. Many of the ornaments and furniture in the store are custom-made
3. The powerful flambé service has been performed since the time of opening

Dessert 銀座ぶどうの木

Ginza Budonoki

A specialty shop where you can taste exquisite desserts

A shop founded in 1979 specializing in desserts served on plate. You can taste freshly-made desserts, as the pastry chefs start to make them right after you order. The menu offers 10 to 12 types of desserts at all times, and there is also a limited time menu using seasonal fruits.

Address:THE STONE Bldg. 2F, 5-6-15 Ginza, Chuo-ku
TEL:03-5537-3140 **Opening hours:**11:00-20:00 (last order 19:15), 11:00-19:00 (last order 18:15) on Sundays and public holidays **Closed:**None **Price:**From 1620 yen
Access:1 min. walk from Tokyo Metro Ginza Station Exit B3
MAP P.52 B-2

For Tourists

Most of the tableware is composed of original pieces drawn by an exclusive painting master. The staff appear to be choosing the tableware in accordance with the customers' taste in clothing.

Fruit Parlor 銀座千疋屋 銀座本店フルーツパーラー

Ginza Sembikiya Ginza Main Store Fruit Parlor

The fresh fruits are exquisite

In 1913, the first fruit parlor to open in the world. You can eat desserts that use seasonal fruits from all regions in Japan. The most popular is the "Ginza Parfait", which also looks gorgeous.

Address:5-5-1 Ginza, Chuo-ku **TEL:**03-3572-0101 **Opening hours:**2F:11:00-20:00 (last order19:30), 11:00-19:00 (last order 18:30) on Sundays and public holidays. B1F:11:00-17:30 (last order 17:00), 11:00-18:00 (last order 17:30) on Saturdays, Sundays and public holidays **Closed:**None **Price:**From 1,000 yen **Access:**1 min. walk from Tokyo Metro Ginza Station Exit B5

MAP P.52 B-2

*Under renovation. Scheduled to open in early March 2017

1. The "Fruits Ponche" (right) and "Ginza Parfait" (left) with ice and sorbet
2. You can look over the Harumi-dori from the store. There are pictures of seasonal fruits on the wall

For Tourists

In 1923, it offered the "Fruits Ponche" for the first time in Japan. The original syrup, which uses red wine and western liquor, is also delicious.

1. The cute modern packages, which you won't believe contain Japanese confectioneries, are also charming
2. The Japanese afternoon tea "Samajiki", through which you can enjoy "inari zushi" and a rich variety of Japanese confectioneries

For Tourists

The tea ordered at the teahouse is carefully brewed at the space in the center of the shop. You will also want to watch the gentle way the tea is brewed.

Japanese Confectionery HIGASHIYA GINZA

HIGASHIYA GINZA

Tasting the traditional Japanese confectioneries and teas

Offers traditional Japanese confectioneries that go with modern-day living. You can enjoy Japanese confectioneries such as Monaka (wafer cake filled with bean jam) prepared in sticks that make them easy to eat, as well as "Hitokuchigashi"(one-bite wagashi) along with sake and more.

Address: Pola Ginza Bldg. 2F, 1-7-7 Ginza, Chuo-ku **TEL:**03-3538-3240 **Opening hours:**Shop: 11:00-19:00. Tea salon: 11:00-22:00 (last order 21:00), 11:00-19:00 (last order 18:00) on Sundays and public holidays **Closed:**Mondays *Tuesday if Monday is a public holidays **Price:**Lunch from 3,780 yen, Dinner from 5,400 yen **Access:**1 min. walk from Tokyo Metro Ginza-Itchome Station Exit 7

MAP P.53 C-1

Eat delicious seafood

Learn about Tsukiji Market!

Tsukiji is synonymous with the Japanese market. It not only brings together fish from all around the world, but has now also become a famous tourist destination. Learn information about Tsukiji you can put to use when dining and shopping.

Tsukiji Outer Market brings together a variety of shops

Photos povided by Tokyo Metropolitan Central Wholesale Market

The origins of Tsukiji Market

Tsukiji Market is a market located in Tokyo Chuo-ku that deals in seafood products, fruits, and vegetables. It handles the world's largest volume of seafood products. Its official name is Tokyo Metropolitan Central Wholesale Market - Tsukiji Market. The history of Tsukiji Market is surprisingly short.

The market that had been in Nihombashi since the Edo period (1603-1868) and other fish and vegetable markets, were destroyed by fire following the Great Kanto Earthquake of 1923. This is why it was moved to the current location. It has now become famous all around the world as the fish market of Japan. The reasons behind this include the excellent quality of its fresh products as well as the fact that the food of the surrounding restaurants are now featured in all kinds of media.

In addition, Tsukiji includes Tsukiji Market as well as Tsukiji Outer Market Shopping Street (known as Jogai Market).This is an area where many visitors enjoy dining and shopping in their pursuit of seafood. Jogai Market is as friendly as an ordinary shopping street, and is special in that it is easily accessible for tourists.

Tsukiji Market in the 1930's

The famous tuna auction is held at the Tsukiji Market. It is planning to be held at the Toyosu Market after the market has moved

An area of about 23 ha. Goods handled include marine seafood, fruits and vegetables, eggs, and various processed products in 2005

The future of Tsukiji

Tsukiji Market was supposed to be relocated to Toyosu, but in August 2016 it was announced that the relocation had been postponed. The relocation destination of Toyosu is vast and offers smooth distribution of goods. A course for visitors has been prepared, as they plan to accept tourists as well.

Since it was decided that Tsukiji Outer Market (Jogai Market) Shopping Street will remain as is, business activities have continued as usual so far. For tourists who want to enjoy Jogai Market, Tsukiji's place as a vibrant tourist destination remains unchanged. They hold events as well, among them the popular "Tsukiji Pub Crawl" held each year in early November where you can hop from place to place all night. This event uses a ticket system.

Tsukiji Uogashi opened Tsukiji Outer Market in November 2016. Besides seafood, fruits, and vegetables shops, it also offers a food court.

Photo provided by Chuo Ward

Market 築地場外市場

Tsukiji Outer Market

Its official name is "Tsukiji Outer Market Shopping Street". It houses around 400 shops over an area of 400m by 120m, stretching over Tsukiji 4-chome and 6-chome in Chuo-ku, Tokyo.

Address:4~6 Tsukiji, Chuo-ku

TEL:03-3541-9444 (Council Bureau for the promotion of Tsukiji gastronomic district)

Access:1 min. walk from Toei Subway Tsukijishijo Station Exit A1

URL:http://www.tsukiji.or.jp/english/index.html

MAP P.52 A-3

PICK UP

Go to the new market!

It's around a 30-minute train ride away from Tsukiji Outer Market in Tsukiji to Toyosu, where Toyosu Market is located. Experience this new much-discussed facility!

Toyosu Market 豊洲市場

Toyosu Market is the new Tokyo Metropolitan Central Wholesale Market, a closed facility that can properly manage temperature. They have plans to build a passage and deck especially for visitors, as well as allow visits from tourists.

Address: Part of 6th and 7th district, 6-5 Toyosu, Koto-ku

Access: Around 4 min. walk from Yurikamome Shijo-Mae Station

URL:http://www.shijou.metro.tokyo.jp/english

MAP P.5 C-2

Toyosu Market. Opening unscheduled as of 2017 January

AREA 3

浅草・押上

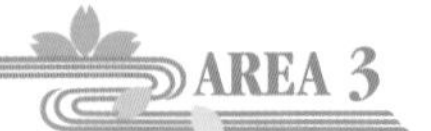

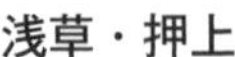

ASAKUSA/OSHIAGE

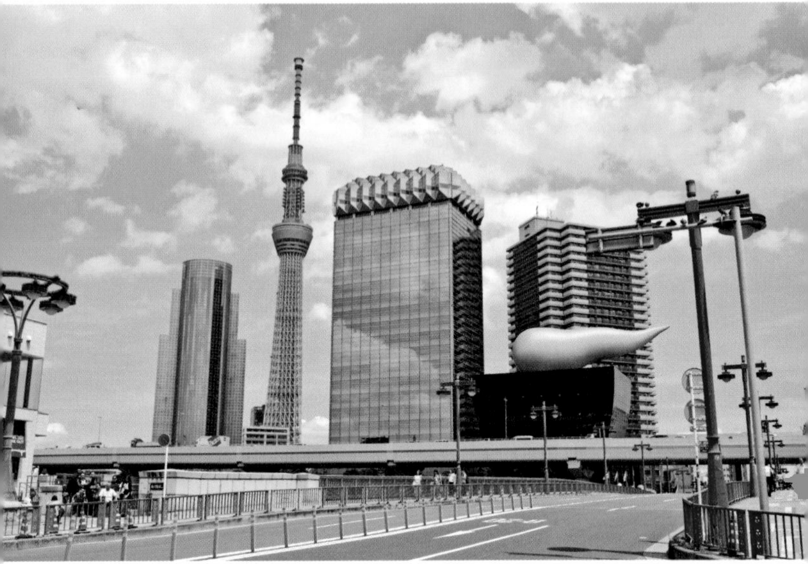

The red Azumabashi (Bridge) that continues to Oshiage is a historic bridge built in 1774 (Edo period)

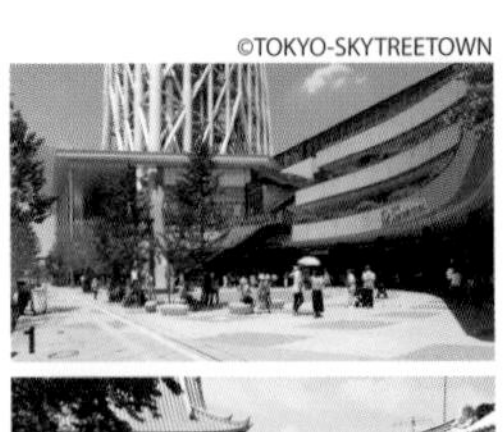

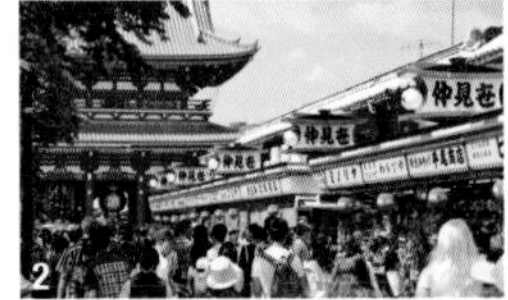

1. East Yard on the 1st floor of Solamachi Square. A place of recreation and relaxation for visitors
2. The lively Nakamise-dori, bustling with people whenever you visit

What kind of town?

Asakusa, which has flourished since the Edo period, is an area where you can experience traditional Japanese culture. It forms a temple town covering the West side of the Sumida River centered on Senso-ji Temple, a standard tourist destination. The surroundings are dotted with Japanese confectionery shops and Japanese restaurants, as well as halls where you can enjoy popular entertainment such as Rakugo (traditional comic storytelling) and more.

Situated on the East side of Sumida River,

Oshiage has suddenly become a popular tourist destination thanks to the opening of TOKYO SKYTREE. You can enjoy sightseeing all day long with the world's tallest tower and entertainment facilities, and other shopping spots.

1. The pond in front of Yogodo within the grounds of the Senso-ji Temple 2. Asakusa Engei Hall, with banners featuring star performers flapping in the wind 3. The Asakusa bar district, Hoppy-dori, is always humming with activity 4. At the Edo Shumi Kogangu Nakamise Sukeroku, you can find many toys requiring delicate craftsmanship

How to enjoy

In Asakusa, a visit to Senso-ji Temple is a must. This temple has many sightseeing spots, including of course the Main Hall, the two gates, a five-storied pagoda, and more. After visiting Senso-ji temple, we recommend the famous gourmet specialties on Nakamise-dori, lined with small food stalls, or a walk around Denbouin-dori, a shopping street that recreates an Edo-era district. Since there are water bus stops along the Sumida River, you can also take a tour of Tokyo on the water.

At TOKYO SKYTREE TOWN in Oshiage, go first to the observation deck of TOKYO SKYTREE. Enjoy an unbroken view of the metropolitan area from the sky. TOKYO Solamachi located at its base is a treasure trove of gourmet food and souvenirs. Get a guide map, and walk around without missing anything.

1. The water bus goes from Asakusa to Odaiba
2. You can get a rickshaw after talking to the driver

Must-visit tourist spots

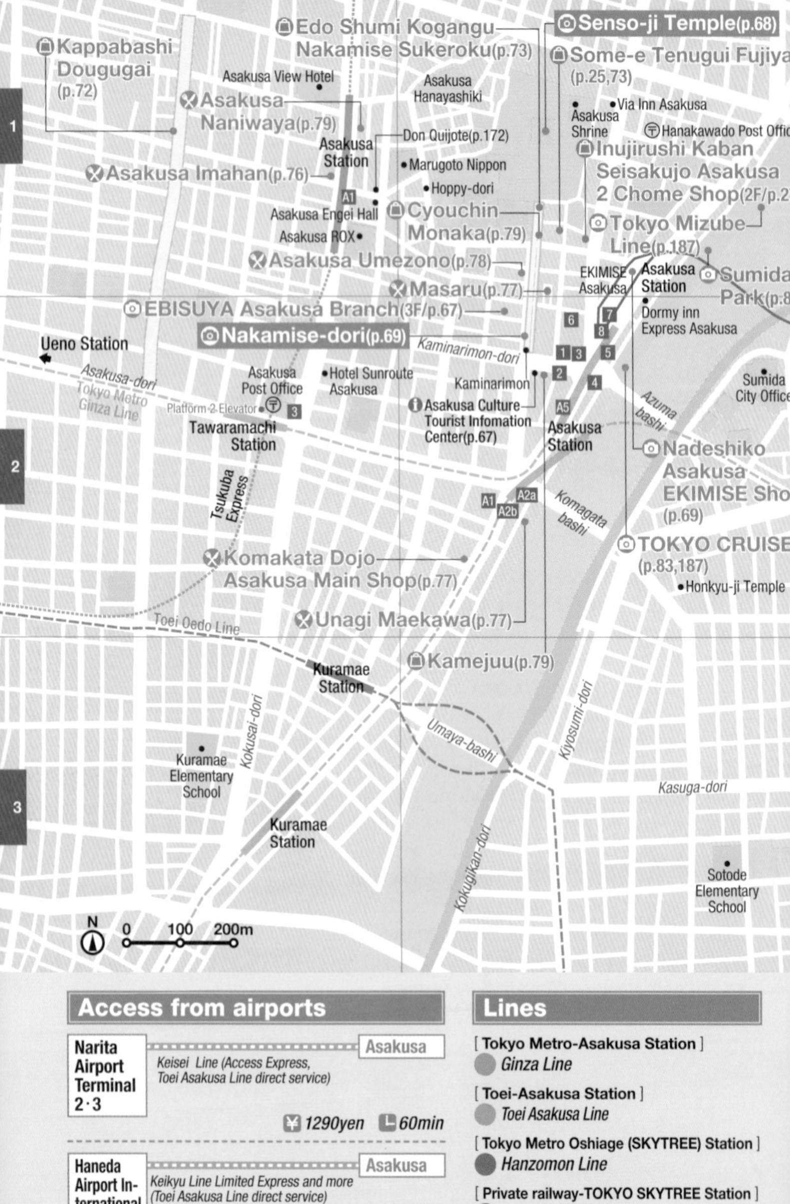
A
B
1
2
3
Edo Shumi Kogangu Nakamise Sukeroku(p.73)
Senso-ji Temple(p.68)
Kappabashi Dougugai (p.72)
Asakusa View Hotel
Asakusa Hanayashiki
Some-e Tenugui Fujiya (p.25,73)
Asakusa Naniwaya(p.79)
Asakusa Shrine
Via Inn Asakusa
Hanakawado Post Office
Asakusa Station
Don Quijote(p.172)
Inujirushi Kaban Seisakujo Asakusa 2 Chome Shop(2F/p.27
Asakusa Imahan(p.76)
Marugoto Nippon
Hoppy-dori
A1
Asakusa Engei Hall
Cyouchin Monaka(p.79)
Tokyo Mizube Line(p.187)
Asakusa ROX
Asakusa Umezono(p.78)
EKIMISE Asakusa
Asakusa Station
Sumida Park(p.83
Masaru(p.77)
EBISUYA Asakusa Branch(3F/p.67)
Dormy inn Express Asakusa
Nakamise-dori(p.69)
Ueno Station
Kaminarimon-dori
Asakusa-dori
Tokyo Metro Ginza Line
Asakusa Post Office
Hotel Sunroute Asakusa
Kaminarimon
Sumida City Office
Platform 2 Elevator
Asakusa Culture Tourist Infomation Center(p.67)
Azuma bashi
Tawaramachi Station
Asakusa Station
Nadeshiko Asakusa EKIMISE Shop (p.69)
Tsukuba Express
A2a
A2b
A5
Komagata bashi
TOKYO CRUISE (p.83,187)
Komakata Dojo Asakusa Main Shop(p.77)
Honkyu-ji Temple
Unagi Maekawa(p.77)
Toei Oedo Line
Kamejuu(p.79)
Kuramae Station
Kokusai-dori
Kiyosumi-dori
Umaya-bashi
Kuramae Elementary School
Kasuga-dori
Kuramae Station
Kokugikan-dori
Sotode Elementary School
N
0
100
200m
Access from airports
Narita Airport Terminal 2·3
Asakusa
Keisei Line (Access Express, Toei Asakusa Line direct service)
1290yen
60min
Haneda Airport International Terminal
Asakusa
Keikyu Line Limited Express and more (Toei Asakusa Line direct service)
620yen
35min
Lines
[Tokyo Metro-Asakusa Station]
Ginza Line
[Toei-Asakusa Station]
Toei Asakusa Line
[Tokyo Metro Oshiage (SKYTREE) Station]
Hanzomon Line
[Private railway-TOKYO SKYTREE Station]
Tobu SKYTREE Line

C D

えびす屋 浅草店

EBISUYA Asakusa Branch

Going around Asakusa on a rickshaw is recommended as well. Rickshaw drivers have a rich knowledge of the area and can explain the tourist attractions. You can get a rickshaw at Kaminarimon-dori, etc.

Address: East Bldg. 3F, 1-20-4 Asakusa, Taito-ku **TEL:**03-3847-4443
Opening hours:9:30 to sunset *differs depending on season **Closed:**None
Fee: From 4,000 yen per area for 2 persons **Access:**1 min. walk from Tokyo Metro Asakusa Station Exit 3
MAP P.66 B-2

Sumida River
Mimeguri Shrine
Bokutei-dori
Kototoi bashi
Koume Elementary School
Mito Kaido
Ushijima Shrine
Tobu SKYTREE Line
TOKYO SKYTREE Station
Sumida Aquarium
Seiou-ji Temple
nsho-ji Temple
Toei Asakusa Line
Narihirabashi
Honjo-Azumabashi Station
Oshiage (SKYTREE) Station
B3 A2 B2 B1
TOKYO SKYTREE TOWN(p.70)
TOKYO Solamachi(p.71)
Industrial Tourism Plaza Sumida Machidokoro(p.67)
Yokokawa Elementary School
Honjo Junior High school
Tabacco and Salt Museum
Narihira Elementary School
Tokyo Metro Hanzomon Line
Honjo Police Station
TOKYO SKYTREE(p.33,70)
Tembo Galleria(p.71)
Tembo Deck(p.71)
Kasuga-dori
Mitsume-dori
Yanagishima Elementary School
Sumida Edo Kiriko Kan(p.24,75)
Honjo Post Office
Kinshi Junior High school
Kuramaebashi-dori
Kinshicho Station
OLINAS MALL
OLINAS CORE
2
3

Tourist information centers

Asakusa Culture Tourist Information Center

台東区立浅草文化観光センター

The staff is very kind, and they give information in English : Chinese and Korean. Internet also available for free.

Address:2-18-9 Kaminarimon, Taito-ku
TEL:03-3842-5566 **Opening hours:** 9:00 -20:00. Tearoom: 10:00 -20:00 (last order 19:30). Observatory terrace: 9:00 -22:00
Closed: None **Access:**1 min. walk from Tokyo Metro Asakusa Station Exit 2
MAP P.66 B-2

◆ Other tourist information centers

Industrial Tourism Plaza Sumida Machidokoro

産業観光プラザ すみだ まち処 MAP P.67 D-2

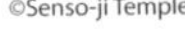

©Senso-ji Temple

1. The entrance of Senso-ji Temple, known as Kaminarimon. On the left and right sides of the lantern you can find statues of Fujin (the god of wind) and Raijin (the god of thunder) in front, and a statue of Ryujin at the back.
2. The incense burner (jōkoro) in front the main hall. Used to waft smoke over the body in order to purify it before visiting the Main Hall
3. The Hōzōmon and five-storied pagoda in front of the main hall. Lit up from sunset until 11:00 p.m.
4. On the bottom of the lantern, you can find the carving of a dragon that symbolizes protection from fire

Temple 浅草寺

Senso-ji Temple

A venerable temple that symbolizes Asakusa

Tokyo's oldest temple, with a history of about 1,400 years. The deity Kannon is enshrined in the Main Hall. Even before reaching the Main Hall, the attractions are never-ending, including the famous Kaminarimon and Nakamise-dori, the Hōzōmon, etc. After visiting the temple, take a walk around the Yogodo, which worships the Buddha, and Asakusa Shrine, situated on the east side of the Main Hall.

Address:2-3-1 Asakusa, Taito-ku **TEL:**03-3842-0181 **Opening hours:**6:00-17:00 (6:30-17:00 between October and March) **Closed:**None **Access:**5 min. walk from Tokyo Metro Asakusa Station Exit 6

HP MAP P.66 B-1

*The five-storied pagoda is under repair until the end of September 2017

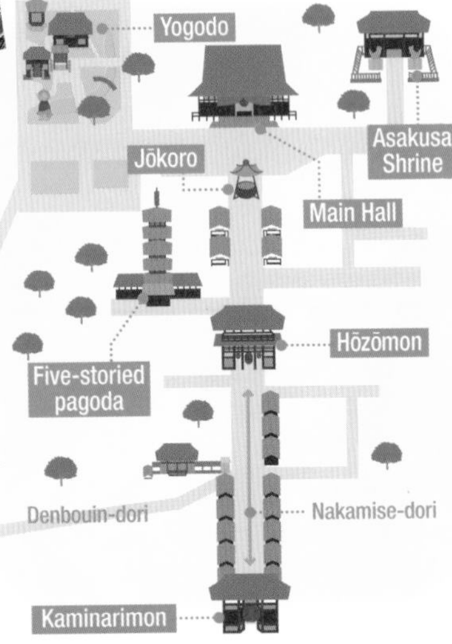

Commercial District 仲見世通り

Nakamise-dori

A bustling shopping district with the longest history in Japan

The road approaching the shrine connects Kaminarimon to the Senso-ji Temple Main Hall. This road has a long history, and it is said to have been built during early Edo period. About 90 shops selling confectionery and crafts are lined up along this 250 meter long street.

TEL:03-3844-3350 (Nakamise Hall)

Opening hours/Closed: Some shops may differ

MAP P.66 B-2

*In order to keep the streets clean, please eat in front or inside the shop where the food was purchased

1. Continuing in a straight line up to the Main Hall, Nakamise-dori is visited by worshipers not only from Japan but from all over the world 2. There are many Nakamise-dori gourmet specialties, such as the Age-manju (fried buns), Kaminari-okoshi (crispy puffed rice sweet), Kibi-dango (sweet dumplings), etc. 3. Sightseeing in a kimono is also a unique feature of tourism in Asakusa

Rows of typical Japanese products, including lucky charms and others

Each of the masks has a different meaning, such as bringing good luck or protecting against evil spirits

Column

Stroll around the Asakusa area in a kimono

A kimono shop on the 4th floor of Asakusa EKIMISE where brand-new kimonos can be rented. You may also bring the kimonos home after wearing them (accessories must be returned).

●なでしこ浅草EKIMISE店

Nadeshiko Asakusa EKIMISE Shop

Address:EKIMISE 4F, 1-4-1 Hanakawado, Taito-ku **TEL:**03-3842-5210

Opening hours:10:00-20:00 **Closed:**None

Price: Kimono rental from 5400 yen **Access:**Directly connected to Tokyo Metro/Tobu Skytree Line Asakusa Station

HP MAP P.66 B-1

*Reservation is required for kimono rental. Socks are sold separately

What is TOKYO SKYTREE TOWN?

The generic name of the complex including TOKYO SKYTREE and the commercial facility TOKYO Solamachi at the foot of the tower. It is a commercial complex where you can enjoy not only a superb view of Tokyo, but also gourmet food, shopping, and all kinds of entertainment.

1. The official characters of TOKYO SKYTREE, from left to right: Teppenpen, Sorakara-chan, and Sukoburuburu
2,3. The Sumida Aquarium located on the 5th and 6th floors of West Yard is popular with its unique displays, such as a large tank atrium space, etc

Tower 東京スカイツリー

634m

① TOKYO SKYTREE

The world's tallest tower

Boasting a height of 634 meters, TOKYO SKYTREE is the world's tallest self-supporting tower. You can get a bird's eye view of Tokyo from the observatories located in two places. The entrance is on the fourth floor. You may buy an admission ticket at the ticket counter.

Address:1-1-2 Oshiage, Sumida-ku **TEL:**0570-55-0634 (TOKYO SKYTREE Call Center) **Opening hours:**8:00-22:00 (last admission one hour before closing time) **Closed:**None **Fee:**Tembo Deck: 2,060 yen, Tembo Galleria: 1,030 yen *There is also a convenient ticket for foreigners only. **Access:**Immediate access from TOBU SKYTREE Line TOKYO SKYTREE Station, and Tokyo Metro/Toei Subway/Keisei Line Oshiage (SKYTREE) Station **URL:**http://www.tokyo-skytree.jp/en

MAP P.67 C-2

The Food Marche on the 2nd floor offers a variety of foods

Commercial Facility 東京ソラマチ

2 TOKYO Solamachi

A new shitamachi at the foot of TOKYO SKYTREE

Bringing together more than 300 stores, including restaurants, shops, and entertainment facilites, under the concept of a new shitamachi. There are many items that can only be purchased here, such as sweets and other Solamachi-limited miscellaneous.

TEL:0570-55-0102 (TOKYO Solamachi Call Center) **Opening hours:**10:00-21:00. Restaurant floors on 6F, 7F, 30F, 31F: 11:00-23:00 *business hours may differ depending on the shop **Closed:**Irregular holidays

MAP P.67 D-2

Tembo Galleria

450m

An observation deck located at a height of 450 meters. After walking up the slope-shaped corridor, you will reach the highest point called Sorakara Point.

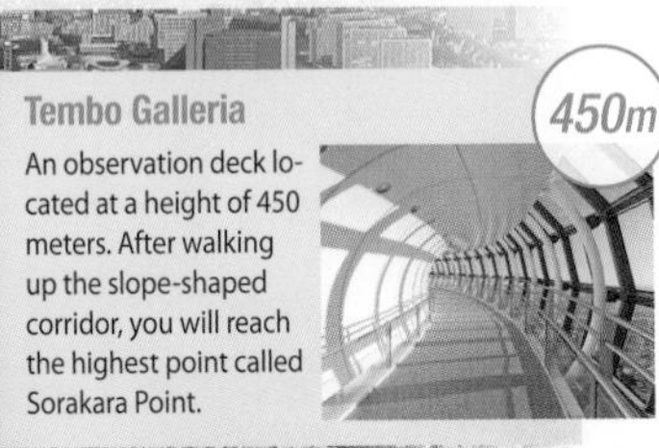

Tembo Deck

350m

Located at a height of 350 meters is an observatory made up of three floors of different height. Restaurants and shops are available on the floors.

Also recommended at night with its lighting

Iki / Miyabi

Representing the spirit, Iki uses the water of Sumida River as a motif. Representing aesthetics, Miyabi has Edo purple as its color scheme, and its main feature is its performance of moving lights.

Column

About the shape of TOKYO SKYTREE

TOKYO SKYTREE extends straight up to the sky. Although it looks conical, its bottom is, in fact, triangular. It was built using traditional curve construction techniques, and is rare in that as it goes upward, its shape changes from planar to circular. Depending from where you view it from, TOKYO SKYTREE never appears to have the same shape, sometimes looking wrapped or swollen. Besides being a communication tower and tourist destination, this building also serves as a giant work of art incorporating traditional Japanese techniques.

The base is triangular and changes into a circular shape starting around a height of 300 meters. On the Group Floor on the 1st floor, the steel frame supporting the tower can be seen, with cross-sections with a maximum size diameter of 2.30 meters, and a thickness of 10 centimeters

Picture provided by: Obayashi-gumi

1. The high-impact jumbo cook model of Niimi Western Tableware Shop is the landmark of Kappabashi Kitchen Town 2. There are also rows of different kinds of tableware 3. The Kappa Kawataro Statue, a symbol of Kappabashi Kitchen Town, is considered to bring prosperity in business through the divine 4. Fake food made in an elaborate way

Kitchen Town かっぱ橋道具街®

Kappabashi DouguGai

The Kitchen Town where even restaurant professionals go

An area with shops that specialize in kitchen supplies with a history of more than 100 years. The street, about 800 meters long, is lined by shops related to food, cookware and tableware, cutlery, fake food, etc. Since it is an area with specialized shops, many of these shops are closed on Sunday.

Address:1~3 Nishi-Asakusa, Taito-ku, 1~4 Matsugaya, Taito-ku **TEL:**03-3844-1225 (Tokyo Kappabashi Shopping Street Promotion Association) **Access:**5 min. walk from Tokyo Metro Tawaramachi Station platform 2 elevator

HP MAP P.66 A-1

For Tourists

At shops belonging to Kappabashi Kitchen Town Union, you can find a map of the area streets. Places where you can get Wi-Fi are also on the map.

Hand Towel 染絵てぬぐい ふじ屋

Some-e Tenugui Fujiya

These bright colors are the work of craftsmen!

A shop that specializes in tenugui (hand towels), boasting more than 70 years of history since its founding. All items in the store have original patterns, carefully dyed by craftsmen. They sell a variety of goods, featuring plants and animals, traditional patterns, lucky charms, etc.

Address:2-2-15 Asakusa Taito-ku
TEL:03-3841-2283
Opening hours:10:00-18:00
Closed: On Thursdays
Access:3 min. walk from Tokyo Metro Asakusa Station Exit 6

MAP P.66 B-1

1. Tenugui is sold for 970 yen a piece. It is available in 4 different sizes: 45 cm, 55 cm. 90 cm, and 110 cm 2. Offers more than 200 different designs at all times

For Tourists

You can also put names on towels for an order of more than 30 pieces. Since it takes more than two weeks, they can be delivered if you are not able to pick them up.

1. Rows of items in the shop. Items are priced starting at 300 yen
2. Their flagship product is the basket wearing dog. In kanji characters, dog is the radical for the character meaning smile. This item contains a wish to see children grow up happily and in good health

For Tourists

There is word play and meaning in each and every toy, so ask the shopkeeper when you choose one.

Toys 江戸趣味小玩具　仲見世 助六

Edo Shumi Kogangu Nakamise Sukeroku

The only place in the world you can find these traditional toys

Founded in 1866. The only shop in Japan that specializes in Edo mame (bean-shaped) toys. Here, toys are referred to as beans toys, and their size is about 1 to 5 cm. In the store, you can find about 3,500 items. Many of these are personified into animals and more.

Address:2-3-1 Asakusa, Taito-ku
TEL:03-3844-0577
Opening hours:10:00-18:00
Closed: None **Access:**5 min. walk from Tokyo Metro Asakusa Station Exit 6

MAP P.66 B-1

*If you want to take pictures of the items, ask first

“The necessity of evolving with the times while still protecting craft and tradition”

The charms of Edo Kiriko

Edo Kiriko is the name given to household goods made of glass cut with traditional Japanese patterns. By overlaying thin colored glass on transparent glass, cut glass (Kiriko) is set with surprisingly fine handwork.

There are about 12 types of traditional Japanese patterns, including chrysanthemum, checkered patterns and more, and the charm of these creations is that their brilliance differs depending on design, as well as the beauty of the patterns and the fine texture that can be obtained only by hand.

In addition to its designation from Tokyo Metropolitan Government, it has also been designated as National Traditional Craft.

Edo Kiriko craftsman

Kozo Kawai

We approached a craftsman who has inherited the craft of Edo Kiriko, a manufacturing method designated as a Traditional Craft Industry by the Tokyo Metropolitan Government.

Profile

Kozo Kawai

Edo Kiriko craftsman in the Sumida Edo Kiriko Kan. He has worked as a craftsman for 25 years and is recognized as Sumida Meister, a skilled artisan who creates high-quality products that support Sumida Ward's industry.

What do you think about while working ?

Actually, if you think all the time only about Edo Kiriko, you cannot create good products. In the process of making, even if you pay attention to faithfully reproducing a design, if you focus too intensively, you won't be able to see what's around it and won't notice distortions of subtle cuts as well as other points. In addition, it is also important to have a firm shift between your work and private life. You will be able to concentrate on work even more if you have a fulfilling private life. I think enjoying your work and continuing it for a long time leads to good workmanship.

How are the Sumida Edo Kiriko Kan products created?

Products made in our atelier are based on an idea given by the director, for which I draw a sketch. Since our work is to make a two-dimensional picture into a three-dimensional object, even if it looks perfect as a picture, it will not necessarily be beautiful once actually cut. After repeated trials, we produce functional products that also have a beautiful appearance.

About how much training do you need to become a full-fledged craftsman?

To produce fine works, it is essential to have a deep understanding of the material itself. In my case, I think that it took me 5 to 10 years to learn a series of production processes comprised of sumitsuke (inking), arazuri (rough grinding), sanbangake (fine cutting), ishikake (stone processed with water and used to make surface cuts smoother), and kenma (polishing). Since you remember it with your body, you don't get any immediate results. There are many things that you must remember, but perhaps constant working on it might be the training itself.

What aspects do you put importance on when it comes to the charms of Edo Kiriko or its creation process?

I think it's different when you consider making a finished product into a commodity or a piece of work. As a craftsman who makes products requested by clients, I think that the charms of Edo Kiriko reside in functional products that can be used in everyday life and not in works that would look like flashy decorative art. When you make Edo Kiriko, you incorporate techniques and patterns handed-down over 180 years of history, and create products wanted by clients living these days.

In the future, how are you going to convey the charms of Edo Kiriko to foreign tourists?

At the Sumida Edo Kiriko Kan, it is possible to see, buy, and experience with a workshop tour, Kiriko lesson, and other activities. I think that the charms of Edo Kiriko can be conveyed to foreign tourists by having them experience it.

The "History of Edo Kiriko"

told by the Director of Sumida Edo Kiriko Kan

Edo Kiriko started when in the 1830s (late Edo period) a vidro (glass) wholesaler set fine carved cuts on glass products brought from overseas. At that time, patterns were set on transparent glass. Later, thin colored glasses were cut to cover clear glass bowls. By overlaying colored glass, Edo Kiriko evolved into a more spectacular and beautiful product. Traditional patterns existing since the Edo period, such as chrysanthemum, checkered, hemp, and other patterns, were cut into the glass.

In recent years, we are making Edo Kiriko modern by adding contemporary arrangements to traditional patterns. Since ancient times, Edo Kiriko craftsmen have expressed familiar and beautiful things, such as seasons and nature, and have polished their techniques in order to make such creations possible. You should definitely try these finely cut glass products that reflect Japanese sensibility.

Director of Sumida Edo Kiriko Kan
Mr. Tatsuo Hirota

Sumida Edo Kiriko Kan すみだ江戸切子館

Experience the shining craftsmanship of Edo Kiriko

Edo Kiriko workshop and store founded more than 100 years ago. Offers original products featuring contemporary arrangements set with traditional patterns. It is possible to experience glass-cutting through workshop tours and other activities.

Address: 2-10-9 Taihei, Sumida-ku
TEL:03-3623-4148 **Opening hours:**10:00-18:00
Closed: On Sundays and public holidays
Fee:4,320 yen (Workshop tour. It is possible to bring your work home on the same day)
Access:8 min. walk from JR Kinshicho Station North Exit

MAP P.67 D-3

Take the Edo Kiriko challenge!

At the Sumida Edo Kiriko Kan, you can experience Kiriko using a polishing machine. Draw your favorite pattern and work on cutting. Junior high school students and older can make paperweights, and high school students and older can make a glass.

1.Listen to a description given by skilled craftsmen on how to use the machines and practice cutting. Hold the receptacle firmly as you move back and forth. The blade used won't cut your hand even if you touch it

2.After practicing, draw a pattern that you'd be able to handle on your own.

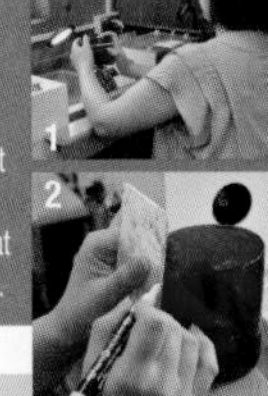

1. The Sukiyaki Lunch Meal is available at a reasonable price (Photo shows the serving for 2 persons)
2. There are private rooms on the 2nd floor. The 1st and 3rd floors also have a large hall and table seats
3. Staff dressed in kimono wait on customers

Sukiyaki / Shabu-Shabu 浅草今半

Asakusa Imahan

The most famous sukiyaki and shabu-shabu restaurant

A long-established restaurant for sukiyaki and shabu-shabu founded in 1895. For its beef, this shop uses only the meat of female cattle whose quality is considered as high as Japanese Black beef. The sukiyaki with its savory secret sauce is exquisite and has many fans in Japan and abroad.

Address:3-1-12 Nishi-Asakusa, Taito-ku
TEL:03-3841-1114
Opening hours:11:30-21:30 (last order 20:30)
Closed: None **Price:**Lunch from 4,000 yen, Dinner from 10,000 yen **Access:**8 min. walk from Tokyo Metro Tawaramachi Station Exit 3

MAP P.66 A-1

*Smoking space is available. The 2nd floor can be used only at night and during lunchtime on Saturdays and Sundays

For Tourists

The Nambu ironware pot, which has the characters, Imahan, inscribed on it, and Kyoto's Chojifu are custom-made products. They pay particular attention to even the finest details.

Tendon まさる

Masaru

Relish exquisite tempura (picky about using natural products)

A tempura rice bowl specialty shop nestled in a back alley. This Edo-style tempura that uses fresh seafood is so popular that people line up even before the store opens. Since the shop closes when it runs out of ingredients, you should come here early.

The Oiri Edomae Tendon— topped with prawns, conger eel, big-eyed flathead, silage, etc.

Address:1-32-2 Asakusa Taito-ku **TEL:**03-3841-8356 **Opening hours:**11:00-15:00 (last order 14:45) **Closed:** Wednesdays and Sundays **Price:**From 3,700 yen **Access:**2 min. walk from Tokyo Metro Asakusa Station Exit 6

MAP P.66 B-1

*Playing games on smartphones is not allowed *It is required to order at least one item per person

For Tourists

The restaurant is also picky about other ingredients, such as all seafood and the sesame oil and dried bonito, using only the products that satisfy the owner.

Dojo Nabe 駒形 どぜう 浅草本店

Komakata Dojo Asakusa Main Shop

A restaurant that specializes in dojo dishes since 1801

The dojo (loach) nabe is made with cooking methods that have remained unchanged since the restaurant was founded, offering a taste that cannot be appreciated anywhere else.

Eat this dojo nabe, uniquely prepared with sauce and leeks

For Tourists

Since everything from head to tail can be eaten in the dojo nabe, you can have it all, nutrients included.

Address:1-7-12 Komagata, Taito-ku **TEL:**03-3842-4001 **Opening hours:**11:00-21:30 (last order 21:00) **Closed:**None **Price:**Lunch from 2,600 yen, Dinner from 4,000 yen **Access:**2 min. walk from Toei Subway Asakusa Station Exit A1

MAP P.66 B-2

Eel 鰻 駒形 前川

Unagi Maekawa

A restaurant that specializes in eel dishes founded 200 years ago

A long-established restaurant offering eel dishes located along the Sumida River. Reputed, of course, for its Kabayaki (fish preparation) using a sauce that remains unchanged since the time of founding, as well as for grilling without any seasoning, which allows enjoyment of the natural taste of the ingredients.

Una-juu, rice topped with broiled eel. The eel is produced by high-grade aquaculture in Japan, and has a flavor close to the natural one

Address:2-1-29 Komagata, Taito-ku **TEL:**03-3841-6314 **Opening hours:**11:30-21:00 (last order 20:30) **Closed:**None **Price:**Lunch from 3,000 yen, Dinner from 5,000 yen **Access:**1 min. walk from Toei Subway Asakusa Station Exit A2a

MAP P.66 B-2

For Tourists

From the parlor seats on the 2nd to 4th floor, you can see the Sumida River and TOKYO SKYTREE.

1. The "Awa Zenzai" have existed since the time of founding. Warm red bean paste on a freshly pounded yellow millet rice cake. The perilla seeds are served between main dishes 2. "Anmitsu" with sweet bean paste, ice cream, agar and fruit. The balance between the specially made black sugar syrup and the sweet bean paste is exquisite 3. Orders are made in advance. Choose your dish by looking at the food samples placed at the entrance

Japanese Confectionery 浅草 梅園

Asakusa Umezono

A traditional taste that has been loved since ancient times

A Japanese traditional confectionery shop founded in 1854. The name of the shop originates from the fact that there were many plum trees called Ume at the time the teahouse was opened at a branch temple of the Senso-ji Temple called Baion-in. You can enjoy these Japanese confectioneries made with specially prepared ingredients and recipe.

Address:1-31-12 Asakusa, Taito-ku **TEL:**03-3841-7580
Opening hours:10:00-20:00 (last order 19:45)
Closed: Irregular holidays on Wednesdays (twice a month)
Price: From 700 yen **Access:**5 min. walk from Toei Subway Asakusa Station Exit 1

MAP P.66 B-1

For Tourists

Tsubuan (coarse sweet red bean paste) used in a variety of Umezono confectioneries is carefully made everyday at the shop. Taste elegant sweetness.

Taiyaki 浅草浪花家

Asakusa Naniwaya

Exquisite Taiyaki (fish-shaped Pancakes)

A shop managed by a shopkeeper who mastered baking techniques at Naniwaya Sohonten, a long-established taiyaki shop founded in 1909. Each and every taiyaki baked here has thin dough and is generously filled with red bean paste.

Address:2-12-4 Asakusa, Taito-ku **TEL:**03-3842-0988 **Opening hours:**10:00-19:00 **Closed:**Tuesday **Price:**Taiyaki is priced starting at 150 yen. Kakigori (shaved ice dessert) is priced starting at 550 yen **Access:**3 min. walk from Tsukuba Express Asakusa Station Exit A1

MAP P.66 A-1

With the Taiyaki Set, you can have your Taiyaki with a drink. You choose from 7 different drinks, including tea, coffee, and others

For Tourists

Kakigori on which you put homemade syrup, is also one of their signature dishes. You may also have anmitsu, udon, etc.

*Taiyaki is available for takeaway

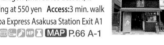

Japanese Confectionery 亀十

Kamejuu

Speciality Dorayaki with inevitable queues

A Japanese confectionery shop located on Kaminarimon-dori that has been open for more than 90 years. Visited everyday by people who come for its famous dorayaki. The dorayaki sell out around the evening so you should come early. Dorayaki (→P.29): 1 piece for 325 yen.

Larger Dorayaki of about 10cm are handmade at the factory located at the back of the shop. It is characterized by its soft dough.The expiration date is 3 days after the production date

For Tourists

Apart from Dorayaki, the Matsukaze with its delicious dough using brown sugar is also reputed.

Address:2-18-11 Kaminarimon, Taito-ku **TEL:**03-3841-2210 **Opening hours:**10:00-19:00 **Closed:**Irregular holidays (about once a month) **Access:**1 min. walk from Tokyo Metro Asakusa Exit 2

MAP P.66 B-2

Monaka 浅草ちょうちんもなか

Cyouchin Monaka

The specialty Ice Monaka is the top food in nakamise-dori

A shop famous for its Ice Monaka (ice cream sandwich wafers), located on Nakamise-dori. The specialty named Lantern Monaka has a design inspired by the Kaminarimon of Senso-ji Temple.The combination of a 100 % glutinous rice skin and ice is perfect.

Address: East 21 Nakamise-dori, 2-3-1 Asakusa, Taito-ku **TEL:**03-3842-5060 **Opening hours:**10:00-17:30 (may vary depending on season) **Closed:**Irregular holidays **Access:**6 min. walk from Tokyo Metro Asakusa Exit 6

MAP P.66 B-1

Cyouchin Monaka is sold for 330 yen a piece. There are a total of 8 types of ice creams available to sandwich between the monaka

For Tourists

Apart from Monaka Ice Cream, they also sell juice and the Anko Monaka as a souvenir.

1. Amazake Yokocho. Its name, meaning "sweet sake alley" comes from the fact that there was a Amazakeya (sweet sake shop) located at the entrance of the alley in the early Meiji period which was popular among the worshipers of Suitengu Shrine 2. On Ningyocho-dori, there are two doll clocks called "Karakuri Yagura".The doll moves automatically every hour on the hour from 11:00 to 19:00 3. Ningyocho-dori. It is not unusual to find stores that have been in business for a few hundred years since the Edo period 4. At Ningyocho Soka-ya you can see how the shopkeeper prepares "Teyaki" 5. Suitengu Shrine, where Benzaiten, one of the Seven Deities of good luck, is worshipped. It is visited by many people praying for safe and easy child birth

Venture a little further! ❶

Ningyocho

Ningyocho is a district where the traditions of the Edo period remain. Its name, literally meaning "Doll Town", comes from the fact that it had many puppet theaters at the time and people involved in those performances lived in the area.

The main street is Ningyocho-dori. This road going from the intersection with Shin-ohashi Street to the intersection with Edo Street is lined with restaurants, stores, and other shops.

You should visit Amazake Yokocho, an alley stretching some 400m from Ningyocho-dori to Meiji-za. On this street, you can find traditional pastry shops, eateries, furniture dealers, and more.

Although the area is small, it is also home to many shrines. There is a course called a "Shichifukujin meguri", a short pilgrimage tour of the Seven Deities of Good Fortune, and it is said that if you go around and offer prayers to all seven of the gods, that "seven calamities will vanish, and seven good fortunes will come".

Spots to visit

1 日本橋 ゆうま Nihonbashi Yuma

"Kinchaku-iri Otedama", made in Japan

Book covers with patterns of "Okame-Hyottoko" (right), and "Maneki-Neko" (left) are said to bring good fortune

Rows of traditional toys and miscellaneous goods

Selling Japanese goods and toys with original designs. Products with traditional patterns called "Jidai Komon" are particularly popular. The shopkeeper is the model for a character in "SHINZANMONO", a novel written by Keigo Higashino. This shop also appeared in dramas.

Address:2-32-5 Ningyocho, Nihonbashi, Chuo-ku **TEL:**03-3808-1779
Opening hours:10:30-18:30 **Closed:**Irregular holidays **Access:**5 min. walk from Tokyo Metro Ningyocho Station Exit A1

2 にんぎょう町 草加屋 Ningyocho Soka-ya

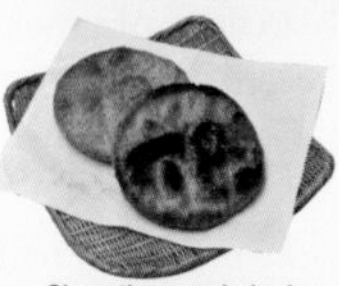

Since they are baked over charcoal, "Teyaki" have savory smell. Two different roasting levels are available

Taste hand-baked crackers that let you experience the taste of rice

A rice cracker shop founded in 1928. We recommend the "Teyaki (hand-baked)" crackers baked one by one at the shop. Depending on the time of your visit, you can taste freshly baked crackers. This shop also appeared in the first episode of "SHINZANMONO", a Japanese TV drama.

Address:2-20-5 Ningyocho, Nihonbashi, Chuo-ku
TEL:03-3666-7378 **Opening hours:**9:00-18:00, 10:00-17:00 on Saturdays and public holidays
Closed: On Sundays **Access:**3 min. walk from Tokyo Metro Ningyocho Station Exit A1

3 自家焙煎ほうじ茶の店 森乃園 Homemade roasted Hojicha Shop Morinoen

Hojicha soft cream

Hojicha specialty shop founded more than 100 years ago

Tea leaves are roasted in the shop every day, and you can taste the hojicha and buy the tea leaves. There is a café on the 2nd floor, and you can taste desserts that use plenty of hojicha.

Address:2-4-9 Ningyocho, Nihonbashi, Chuo-ku
TEL:03-3667-2666 **Opening hours:**9:00-19:00, 11:00-18:00 on Saturdays, Sundays and public holidays. Café: 12:00-18:00 (last order 17:00), 11:00-18:00 (last order 17:30) on Saturdays, Sundays and public holidays
Closed: None **Price:**From 900 yen **Access:**1 min. walk from Tokyo Metro Ningyocho Station Exit A1

*Hojicha is prepared by roasting tea leaves over a strong fire

Let's briefly study the history of Tokyo!

Easy-to-understand "Tokyo History"

Tokyo, the capital of Japan, is a political, economic, commercial and cultural center. Tokyo has been reformed, reconstructed, and developed along with the trends of time. We are now going to study its history, the previous state of Tokyo, and how it has evolved.

Edo period, advancing reforms

The Edo shogunate consolidates the infrastructure of Edo.

In ancient times, Tokyo was called Edo. The era that lasted for about 260 years from 1603, when Ieyasu Tokugawa established the Edo Shogunate after the long Sengoku Jidai (Warring States Period), until its end in 1867, is called the Edo period.

At the time when Ieyasu entered Edo for the first time in 1590, Edo was still a small rural village. Wetlands of swamps and sea were reclaimed after large-scale construction work, consolidating the infrastructure of Edo. The areas of Nihonbashi, Shinbashi and Tsukiji located in the center of the city used to be covered by sea. Several bridges were built, and the Nihonbashi Bridge became the starting point for the five major routes called Gokaido. With these, the town of Edo developed itself as a center for transportation, communication, economy, culture, and trade.

Canals make Edo a City of Water

Ieyasu also made effort to create a castle town. At the same time he placed samurai residences (mansion given by the lord in which samurais lived), he also built a town where craftsmen and merchants taking part in the construction of Edo could live. In addition, waterways for the transportation of large amounts of goods that could not be carried over land were developed. Many waterways leading to canals that changed the flow of the great rivers were built. Thanks to this, domestic consumption goods (rice, sake, oil, paper, cotton, stone, iron, dried bonito) from all across Japan were transported to Edo on ships. In addition, it became possible to transport vegetables, miso, and firewood by riverboats and rafts able to perform small turns. That is how urban development progressed, leading to prosperity.

Developing commerce

At the time Ieyasu Tokugawa had just established the Edo Shogunate, the city was considerably late in terms of trade and industry compared to Osaka and Kyoto since Edo turned rapidly into a big city. The products transported from Kyoto and Osaka were first-class articles. That is why shops from the Kansai region opened in Edo. Particularly famous ones were shops opened from Ise (current-day Mie Prefecture) which sold cotton and paper. In addition, there were also many shops from Omi (current-day Shiga prefecture) which handled products such as kimonos, cotton, raw silk, tatami, and mosquito nets. This is how commerce in Edo was founded by merchants from the Kansai region.

Furthermore, in terms of technical aspects, merchants from the Kansai region transferred production techniques. It increased the productivity of the Kanto region. In the middle of the 18th century, handmade production was performed even in areas around Edo.

PICK UP

History-exploring spots ①

Let's visit spots like places built in the Edo era and others related to it, such as bridges and waterways.

隅田公園

Sumida Park

Popular since Edo period as a place famous for its cherry blossoms

A park located along the Sumida River bank. Believed to have opened after the 8th Tokugawa Shogun Yoshimune Tokugawa planted cherry trees on both sides of the Sumida River during the Edo period.

Address: Hanakawado, Taito-ku
TEL:03-5608-6951 **Access:** 5 min. walk from Tokyo Metro/Toei Subway Asakusa Station Exit 4
MAP P.66 B-1

東京都観光汽船

TOKYO CRUISE

A water bus connecting to popular tourist attractions

Founded in 1898, it operates cruise ships in the Port of Tokyo and on Sumida River. You can enjoy Tokyo sightseeing from the sea, with its skyscrapers, bridges, etc.

Address: (Asakusa Pier) 1-1-1 Hanakawado, Taito-ku **TEL:**0120-977311
Opening hours:10:00-18:00 Days
Closed: None **Fee:**780 yen (Hinode to Asakusa) **Access:** Immediate access from Tokyo Metro Asakusa Station Exit 4
MAP P.66 B-2

日本橋

Nihonbashi

A bridge built in 1603, at the same time as the birth of Edo Shogunate

A bridge that was considered as the starting point of five routes extending to the whole country. It was replaced by the current bridge in 1911. Its sculptures are also a must-see!

Address:1 Nihonbashi, Chuo-ku
Access: Immediate access from Tokyo Metro Mitsukoshimae Station Exit B5
MAP P.6 B-1

東京駅丸の内駅舎

Tokyo Station Marunouchi Station Building

Restored as it was some hundred years ago

A station building also designated as Important Cultural Property of Japan. There is a hotel and a gallery as well.

Address:1-9-1 Marunouchi, Chiyoda-ku
MAP P.6 A-1 →P.203

Continued evolution from Edo period to modern times

Functioning as the capital of Japan

When an expansion of the Edo Castle was constructed, the Edo Shogunate readjusted the districts for townspeople to live, and placed residences of senior statesmen and magistrates as well. As a result, the structure to oversee the administration of Edo and the whole country was almost complete.

After that, Edo was divided into two between a North and a South District, in either of which a district magistrate office was placed. The district magistrate offices not only played the role of a police organization, cracking down on crime, but covered a wide range of duties, including administrative governance, justice, lawmaking, and fire fighting.

Also, in 1635, the "Sankin-kotai" (alternate residence in Edo for major feudal lords) was institutionalized with the purpose of establishing a military service for the Tokugawa Shogunate. This military ritual, organized in order to show the master-servant relationship between the Shogun and the feudal lords, reduced the economic power and military forces of the feudal lords and preserved a peaceful state in which no conflicts occurred.

Developing as a capital of food

When people hear "fish market", they often associate it with Tsukiji; however, the fish market was located in Nihonbashi during the Edo period. (it was transferred to Tsukiji after the great Kanto earthquake of 1923). Starting with Nihonbashi, the number of peddlers selling various kind of foods increased, and offered support to the dining tables of all households.

In the middle of the Edo period, ichizen-meshiya and izakaya became famous as places where people could eat simple dishes and rice in a casual way. Over the late Edo period, together with the popularization of soy sauce, dining out culture selling sushi, soba, tempura, and eel flourished and became established. The number of stalls and shops increased, and the town of Edo became a food capital different from Kyoto and Osaka. It is surprising to see that there were ryori-chaya (restaurants) and side dish rankings (listing shops and dishes like the sumo style ranking chart looked a bit like the Michelin Guide) as well as competitive eating contests.

The development of culture and entertainment

The culture and entertainment of Edo period represent a "common-people culture" developed by Edo townspeople. The noble culture and arts, which had spread only among part of the aristocracy before Edo period, also spread to the common people and developed into a form that was easy to appreciate.

Kabuki and Joruri were developed from Noh and Kyogen. Entertainment was not only viewed, as with sumo, rakugo and ukiyo-e, but also included activities to be experienced and enjoyed, such as chanoyu (common people's version of the tea ceremony), go, shogi, nazokake (riddles), karuta, and kite flying.

The development from Meiji to Showa and to today

The rapidly changing Tokyo, defining eras through reconstruction

The Edo shogunate came to an end, and in September 1868, Edo was renamed Tokyo. Tokyo then began operating full-scale as the center of government and the capital of Japan. In 1872, the first railway in Japan opened. Modernization continued, but in 1923 the Great Kanto Earthquake occurred, affecting approximately 1.9 million people. However, two years later, the Yamanote Circle Line began operations. With Japan's first subway opened in 1927, and the Tokyo Airfield (current-day Tokyo International Airport) completed in 1931, reconstruction was achieved with tremendous speed. Even during the Second World War (1939-1945), Tokyo was burned to the ground through bombing, reconstruction became the objective after the end of the war.

Tokyo Tower was built, the Tokaido Shinkansen line was opened, and in 1964 the Olympic Games were held. At that time, since it had already achieved industrial development, Japan entered into a period of high economic growth. The latest fashion was always in Tokyo, people considered new things as priceless treasures rather than the historical.

After the stock market bubble collapsed, the city reflected on this, and swiftly promoted measures on pollution, environmental improvement, and disaster prevention, leading to the creation of Tokyo as a clean metropolis. Tokyo has continued to develop through repetition of disasters, reconstructions, and improvements.

History-exploring spots ②

皇居

Imperial Palace

Where Tokyo's history and nature remain

Residence of The Emperor, located on the site of Edo Castle. Visit of the East Gardens is available free of charge. There is also a public tour course requiring reservations.

Address:1-1 Chiyoda, Chiyoda-ku
TEL:03-3213-1111 (Imperial Household Agency)
Opening hours:9:00 - 16:00 for the East Gardens *may differ depending on seasons (last admission 30 minutes before closing time) **Closed:**Mondays and Fridays for the East Gardens (closed the following day if on public holiday) **Fee:**Free of charge **Access:**Around 5 min. walk from Tokyo Metro Otemachi Station Exit C13a

MAP P.6 A-1

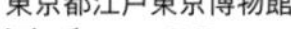
東京都江戸東京博物館

Tokyo Metropolitan Edo-Tokyo Museum

Allowing you to learn about Tokyo's history and culture

A museum transmitting the history and culture of "Edo" and "Tokyo". Apart from exhibits, there are also interactive materials that can actually be touched.

Address: 1-4-1 Yokoami, Sumida-ku **TEL:**03-3626-9974 (Main) **Opening hours:** 9:30-17:30, 9:30-19:30 on Saturdays (last admission 30 minutes before closing time) **Closed:**Mondays (closed the following day if on public holiday) **Fee:**600 yen
Access: Immediate access from Toei Subway Ryogoku Station Exit A3 and A4

MAP P.7 D-2

Photo provided by the Edo-Tokyo Museum

AREA 4

渋谷 SHIBUYA

In front of JR Shibuya Station Hachiko Exit, you can see the unique scenery of Shibuya ©Hit1912 / Shutterstock.com

What kind of town?

Shibuya, known for its scramble crossing, is a district that symbolizes the Tokyo of now, including fashion, music, etc. While it leads youth culture with the fashion mecca "SHIBUYA 109" and Shibuya Center-Gai, it also serves as an adult-oriented town with the commercial complex "Shibuya Hikarie" located on the east side of Shibuya Station.

In the Jinnan area surrounding Koen-dori, you can find "Shibuya MODI", which offers items of refined taste, and streets lined with select shops and outstandingly cozy cafés, making it an area where you can enjoy strolling around as well.

Shibuya, with its many nightlife spots such as clubs and music venues, continues to offer all kinds of charms.

1. "Shibuya Center Gai", continuing from the scramble crossing
2. "Shibuya MODI". The street on the left side is Koen-dori

1. The "Hachiko Statue", a symbol of Shibuya. The green train in front of it is the "Aogaeru (green frog) Tourist Information Center" 2. The "Shibuya Spain-zaka (Slope)", with an exotic atmosphere. Lined with restaurants, general stores, etc. 3. In Shibuya, you can get trendy items at an affordable price 4. The "Shibuya Niku Yokocho", a popular drinking area filled with restaurants specializing in meat

How to enjoy

In Shibuya, we recommend walking around "SHIBUYA 109" and "Shibuya Center-Gai", experience youth trends, or enjoy a stroll through "Shibuya Hikarie" and Koen-dori. On weekends, it is crowded with people, and you can feel the charms of Tokyo full of energy just by walking the streets.

In addition, partying till the wee hours in the clubs, bars and live houses, where you can enjoy the latest tunes, is a very "Shibuya-like" way to spend your time here.

The statue of Hachiko and the scramble crossing crowded with people right next to Shibuya Station Hachiko Exit are standard photo spots. Don't forget to take a commemorative photo as well.

1. "Shibuya Hikarie", a commercial complex directly connected to Shibuya Station
2. The "WOMB", is one of the many popular clubs you can find in Shibuya

Must-visit tourist spots

Gourmet

- Awajishima no Megumi Dashi-ya Shibuya Miyamasuzaka Shop →P.92
- miniyon Natural French wine & SAKE Bar →P.92
- Maguro Donya Miuramisakiko Megumi →P.93
- Ichiran Shibuya Spain-zaka Shop →P.93
- Niku CHIKA →P.93

Shopping

- Shibuya Hikarie →P.94
- SHIBUYA 109 →P.95
- Shibuya MODI →P.95

A
B
1
2
3
4
NHK Broadcasting Center
NHK Studio Park
Harajuku Station
Shibuya MODI(p.95)
H.I.S. Shibuya Tourist Information Center(p.89)
Koen-dori
Fire-dori
JR Yamanote Line
JR Saikyo Line
Inokashira-dori
Jinnan Elementary School
Shibuya Tobu Hotel
QFRONT
Starbucks Coffee SHIBUYA TSUTAYA Shop (1F/p.91)
Organ-zaka
Miyashita Park
Ichiran Shibuya Spain-zaka Shop(B1F/p.93)
Tokyu Hands
Jinnan Post Office
Chitose Kaikan
Niku CHIKA(3F/p.93)
Beam Shibuya
Shibuya Spain Slope
TOKYU DEPARTMENT STORE main store
Seibu Shibuya
Shibuya Marui
H&M
Bunkamura
Bunkamura-dori
Matsumotokiyoshi(p.172)
Don Quijote(p.172)
Shibuya Center-gai
Shibuya Tokyu REI Hotel
Yamada Denki
Matsumotokiyoshi (p.172)
109MEN'S
BIC CAMERA
6-3
3
3a
SHIBUYA 109(p.95)
7a
UNIQLO
Shibuya Station
1
4
2
Hachiko Statue
Hachiko Exit
8
9
5
Aogaeru Tourist Information Center
Tokyu Den-en-toshi Line
Miyamasuzaka Exit
Shibuya Excel Hotel Tokyu
East Exit
14
WOMB (p.113)
Dogen-zaka
Tokyu Department Store Toyoko Store
Shibuya Station
Shibuya Mark City
JR Shibuya Station
West Exit
Keio Inokashira Line
L'Occitane Café Shibuya Shop(2F&3F/p.91)
Shinsen Station
Scramble crossing(p.90)
Tamagawa-dori
Cerulean Tower Tokyu Hotel
Japanese University of Economics
N
0
100
200m

C
Meiji-dori
Tokyo Metro Fukutoshin Line
Shibuya High School
cocoti
Shibuya Ward Office (temporary government building)
13
Awajishima no Megumi Dashi-ya Shibuya Miyamasuzaka Shop(B1F/p.92)
Omotesando Station
13a
Shibuya Post Office
Aoyama-dori
11
Tokyo Metro Hanzomon Line
Tokyo Metro Ginza Line
Shibuya Hikarie(p.94)
12
Shibuya Station
Maguro Donya Miuramisakiko Megumi (6F/p.93,127)
15
Tokyu Tokyo Metro Shibuya Station Tourist Information Center(B2F/p.89)
Roppongi-dori
Shibuya Police Station
16b
miniyon Natural French wine&SAKE Bar(p.92)
Meiji-dori
New South Exit
Hotel Mets Shibuya
Tokyu Toyoko Line
Ebisu Station
C

Access from airports

Narita Airport Terminal 2·3
Keisei Line (Skyliner)
Nippori
Yamanote Line inner loop
Shibuya
¥ *2670yen*
75min

Haneda Airport International Terminal
Keikyu Line Limited Express and more
Shinagawa
Yamanote Line outer loop
Shibuya
¥ *580yen*
35min

Lines

[**JR**]
Yamanote Line *Saikyo Line*

[**Tokyo Metro**]
Ginza Line *Hanzomon Line*
Fukutoshin Line

[**Private railway**]
Keio Inokashira Line *Tokyu Den-en-toshi Line*
Tokyu Toyoko Line

Tourist information centers

Tokyu Tokyo Metro Shibuya Station Tourist Information Center

東急東京メトロ渋谷駅観光案内所

At the Information Center, an English-speaking concierge is always available, providing information on ground-level exits and tourist information. Feel free to ask.

Address: Shibuya Chikamichi B2F, 2-1-1 Dogenzaka, Shibuya-ku **TEL:**None
Opening hours:10:00 - 19:00
Closed: None **Access:** On the premises of Tokyu/Tokyo Metro Shibuya Station
HP
MAP P.89 C-3

◆ Other tourist information centers

H.I.S. Shibuya Tourist Information Center
H.I.S. 渋谷ツーリストインフォメーションセンター
MAP P.88 B-2

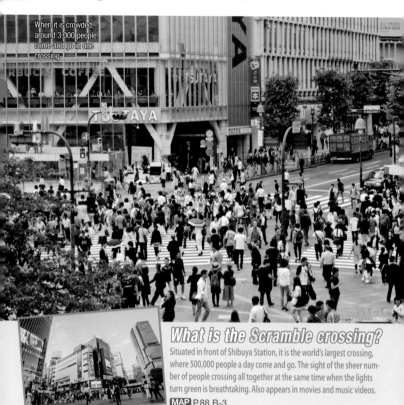

When it is crowded, around 3,000 people come and go in one crossing.

What is the Scramble crossing?

Situated in front of Shibuya Station, it is the world's largest crossing, where 500,000 people a day come and go. The sight of the sheer number of people crossing all together at the same time when the lights turn green is breathtaking. Also appears in movies and music videos.

MAP P.88 B-3

SCENE 1 Experience the flow of people from the ground!

Try actually walking through the crossing. Enjoy a feeling of presence as a rush of people come at you from the opposite side of the crossing all at once.

The view from the Shibuya Station.

People start flowing from all directions, Center-Gai, Dogenzaka, etc.

Right before the lights turn green.

While lights are red, the number of people waiting to cross grows.

Taking a commemorative photo in the scramble crossing is a must!

Near the center of the crossing.

Many people admire how so many Pedestrians can find a way to cross without bumping into each other.

1. On rainy days, the colorful umbrellas crossing by look just like a work of art
2. It looks different from the daytime at night, with the neon lights of buildings glittering
3. The crossing in the early morning. A thin crowd of pedestrians, an extraordinary atmosphere

©Lodimup / Shutterstock.com

SCENE 2 Observing while taking it slow

For those who want to see the crossing directly from above, we recommend watching it from the cafés located in the surroundings. Relax with a drink in your hand.

1. The overlook of the cityscape from the large windows offers a totally different atmosphere in daytime and nighttime
2. Crème brûlée with the scent of vanilla beans

Café L'Occitane Café 渋谷店

L'Occitane Café Shibuya Shop

A cafe where you can relax while overlooking the Scramble Crossing

A café managed by "L'Occitane", the lifestyle cosmetics brand from Provence in southern France. Many dishes using seasonal vegetables and fruits are available, and the volume is generous as well.

Address: Shibuya Eki Mae Bldg. 2F and 3F, 2-3-1 Dogenzaka, Shibuya-ku **TEL:**03-5428-1563 **Opening hours:**10:00-23:00 (last order 22:00) **Closed:**Irregular holidays **Price:**Lunch from 1,800 yen, Dinner from 2,000 yen **Access:**1 min. walk from JR Shibuya Station Hachiko Exit

MAP P.88 B-3

Café スターバックス コーヒー SHIBUYA TSUTAYA店

Starbucks Coffee SHIBUYA TSUTAYA Shop

Take a coffee break while admiring the city

The Shibuya branch boasts top sales in the world. The Frappuccino and other drinks, as well as the limited-time menus, change every one and a half to two months, are all only available in Japan, so don't hesitate to give it a try.

Address:QFRONT 1F, 21-6 Udagawacho, Shibuya-ku **TEL:**03-3770-2301 **Opening hours:**6:30 to following day 4:00 **Closed:**Irregular holidays **Price:**From 320 yen **Access:**1 min. walk from JR Shibuya Station Hachiko Exit

MAP P.88 B-3

You can also see people enjoying the popular rental karts

SCENE 3 Try to go through by car

Observe how pedestrians come and go from the car. When traffic lights turn green, you can cross the intersection with a large number of people on the sides.

→P.146

Seafood 淡路島の恵み　だしや　渋谷宮益坂店

Awajishima no Megumi Dashi-ya Shibuya Miyamasuzaka Shop

Offering all the fresh fish from Awaji Island!

This shop, with its strong network with producers on Awaji Island, provides a menu using good quality local ingredients. The rich selection of locally sake produced lets you fully enjoy the blessings of the island.

Address: Mori Bldg. B1F, 1-14-15 Shibuya, Shibuya-ku **TEL:**03-3406-7255 **Opening hours:**11:30 - 14:30 (last order 14:00), 17:00 - 23:30 (food last order 22:30, drink last order 23:00), 17:00 - 23:00 on Saturdays and public holidays (food last order 22:00, drink last order 22:30) **Closed:**Sundays, irregularly on public holidays **Price:**Lunch from 850 yen, Dinner from 4,500 yen **Access:**1 min. walk from Tokyo Metro Shibuya Station Exit 11

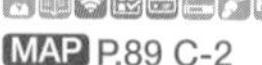

MAP P.89 C-2

1. Rice cooked with the head of a sea bream (below), and "Zarumise", the signature dish (above) 2.Spacious parlor seats that can be used even by large groups of people

For Tourists

You can eat the specialty "Zarumise" after choosing a fish you like from a bamboo basket, and have it prepared with the cooking method of your choice, for example grilled, as sashimi, etc.

1.Roast beef is served with a homemade red wine sauce and Japanese pepper. The "Fresh vegetable platter" lets you to eat seasonal vegetables produced mainly in Kimitsu, Chiba Prefecture 2.Counter on the 1st floor, and table seats on the 2nd floor

For Tourists

Happy hour between 17:00 and 18:30 from Monday through Friday. Offering good deals on beer, wine, and highballs for 324 yen a glass.

Bar ミニヨン 自然派フレンチワイン&日本酒バル

miniyon Natural French wine & SAKE Bar

Enjoying cuisine using natural ingredients together with wine

Reputed for its cuisine, which pays particular attention to the ingredients. We recommend the quiche made with roast beef from the highest rank Japanese wagyu beef and brand-name eggs. Offering only French wines, with one glass starting at 590 yen.

Address:3-14-5 Shibuya, Shibuya-ku **TEL:**03-3486-3244 **Opening hours:**17:00-24:00 (last order 23:30), 17:00 to 2:00 the following day on Fridays (last order 1:30) **Closed:**Sundays and public holidays **Price:**From 3,000 yen **Access:**10 min. walk from JR Shibuya Station East Exit

MAP P.89 C-4

*Smoking allowed on the 1st floor only

Sushi Bar まぐろ問屋 三浦三崎港 恵み

Maguro Donya Miuramisakiko Megumi

Bringing together a plentiful menu of Maguro

conveyor belt sushi shop (kaiten sushi) restaurant managed by a Maguro (tuna) wholesaler from Misaki harbor in Kanagawa Prefecture. You can taste fresh, delicious Maguro. Offers also a rich variety of Japanese sake and wine that go well with sushi.

The "Maguro san-ten-mori" (right) and "Maguro Toro Hikkaki" (left)

Address: Shibuya Hikarie 6F, 2-21-1 Shibuya, Shibuya-ku **TEL:**03-6427-7998 **Opening hours:**11:00 - 23:00 (last order 22:30) **Closed:**Corresponding with Shibuya Hikarie **Price:**Lunch from 1,900 yen, Dinner 2,450 yen **Access:**Immediate access from Tokyu Metro Shibuya Station **URL:**http://www.neo-emotion.jp

HP MAP P.89 C-3

For Tourists

The Maguro cutting show performed every month is super exciting! Check the website to know when it is held.

「ICHIRAN -Since 1960-」Classic Tonkotsu Ramen Shop

Ramen 一蘭 渋谷スペイン坂店

Ichiran Shibuya Spain-zaka Shop

A restaurant specializing only in 100% tonkotsu pork broth ramen

Offers a unique experience that allows customers to enjoy the perfect marriage of tonkotsu soup, freshly-made noodles, and secret spicy red sauce in one bowl. It is popular among people of all ages.

For Tourists

Counter booths are separated by partitions to let you concentrate on the flavor of ramen.

Address: Koyasuwan B1F, 13-7 Udagawa-cho, Shibuya-ku **TEL:**03-3464-0787 **Opening hours:**Open 24 hours **Closed:**None **Price:**From 890 yen **Access:**5 min. walk from JR Shibuya Station Hachiko Exit

HP MAP P.88 B-2

Yakiniku 肉 CHIKA

Niku CHIKA

Savor all the yakiniku (grilled meat) you want

A yakiniku restaurant located in the popular gourmet spot called "Shibuya Niku Yokocho". The all-you-can-eat yakiniku course is at an affordable price, so the shop is packed everyday. Also offers a rich side-menu with soup, rice, etc.

The 7 types of meat served in the all-you-can-eat course. Offers also a variety of sauces including garlic-shoyu (soy sauce), spicy miso, wasabi, salty green onion sauce, etc.

Address: Chitose Kaikan 3F, 13-8 Udagawa-cho, Shibuya-ku **TEL:**03-5784-0269 **Opening hours:**17:00 - 24:00 (last order 23:00) **Closed:**None **Price:**From 3,000 yen **Access:**7 min. walk from JR Shibuya Station Hachiko Exit

HP MAP P.88 B-2

*Cover charge: 500 yen per person

For Tourists

All-you-can-drink course available as well (charge separately). Since it is self-service, you can make your drink just the way you like it.

1. Bringing together shops of refined taste and much talked about restaurants
2. On the 11th floor, you can find the musical playhouse TOKYU THEATRE Orb
3. At d47 Shokudo on the 8th floor, you can enjoy a meal made from ingredients coming from all over Japan
4. At Keishindo, the series of shrimp crackers inspired by Japanese culture is quite popular
5. Papier-mache Rokuhara Hariko dolls, which are Iwate Prefecture traditional crafts, are sold at rooms Ji-Ba

Commercial Complex 渋谷ヒカリエ

Shibuya Hikarie

Where you can buy well-designed souvenirs

A high-rise commercial complex housing around 200 shops. Perfect for finding souvenirs, with shops focusing on traditional crafts and local industry from all over Japan, such as d47 design travel store, rooms Ji-Ba, and more.

Address:2-21-1 Shibuya, Shibuya-ku **TEL:**03-5468-5892
Opening hours:B3F to 5F: 10:00 - 21:00. 6F: 11:00 - 23:00. 7F: 11:00 - 23:30, 11:00 - 23:00 on Sundays. 8F: 11:00 - 20:00 *11:30 - 23:00 for some shops **Closed:**None
Access: Directly connected to Subway Shibuya Station
HP MAP P.89 C-3

For Tourists

Check the state-of-the-art women's restroom with a different atmosphere on each floor! They even come equipped with an air-shower booth to remove the dust and pollen gets on clothes.

Fashion Bldg. SHIBUYA109

SHIBUYA 109

Learn about Japan's latest fashion at a glance!

A shopping center home to about 120 shops selling brands for girls in their teens and twenties. Offers a variety of genres, from sexy to casual, and brings the latest trends.

Address:2-29-1 Dogenzaka, Shibuya-ku
TEL:03-3477-5111
Opening hours:10:00 - 21:00 *some shops may differ
Closed: None
Access:3 min. walk from JR Shibuya Station Hachiko Exit

MAP P.88 B-3

1. The bldg. on which you can see "109" written in big letters has been nicknamed "Marukyu"
2. The reasonable pricing is also a reason for its popularity

For Tourists
On the first floor entrance, a digital sign displaying information in foreign languages has been installed. Check for the shop you are searching for here.

Commercial Complex 渋谷モディ

Shibuya MODI

Shibuya's new landmark

With being an "intellectual commercial space" as its concept, this place brings together various spots to play, relax, learn, and create, in addition to food, clothing, and shelter. There is also a Tourist Information Center.

Address:1-21-3 Jinnan, Shibuya-ku
TEL:03-4336-0101
Opening hours:B1F to 4F: 11:00 - 21:00, 5F to 7F: 11:00 -23:00, 8F: 11:00 to following day 5:00, 9F: 11:00 - 23:30
Closed: Irregular holidays
Access:6 min. walk from JR Shibuya Station Hachiko Exit

MAP P.88 B-2

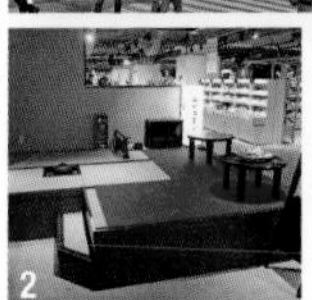

1. The plant-covered entrance serves as a landmark. There is also a Tourist Information Center on the basement floor
2. You can also have a tea ceremony experience at Café Stand Akarimado

For Tourists
The 8th floor is the karaoke floor. The interior of each room is different, and there are even rooms where you can have band performance.

“The Tokyo skyline at night is so magical Experience a moving night view”

TBS TV Producer

Hidenori Iyoda

Let’s hear about the charms of Tokyo from a hit-maker who has created several popular television dramas

Profile

Hidenori Iyoda

TV drama producer and director. Born in Aichi prefecture in 1967. After graduating from the Tokyo University of Science in 1992 and working for a company producing programs in Nagoya, he joined TBS in 1998. Since then, he has been in charge of the production of television dramas. He continues to create blockbusters such as "Hanzawa Naoki", which had a record audience rating of 42.2%, “Shitamachi Rocket”, “Akamedaka”, and others.

What made you decide to work in video production?

I aspired to become a physicist since childhood, and so I went to university. However, once I started living at the boardinghouse together with students with same aspirations, I noticed that some people were much more amazing than I was. Some of them were thinking only about physics for 24 hours a day, and others just kept on solving mathematical formulas. This is no good, I thought, and that's the reason why I decided to change my career path. I wasn't that passionate about physics. That's when I started to think and asked myself about what would make me feel happy 24 hours day, just like them. When I looked back, I realized that I still had strongly in my heart the emotion I felt when I was a kid watching movies and television dramas and thinking, "I can't believe there are such wonderful things", and now I wanted to be the one conveying that emotion, and so aspired to work in the entertainment industry. Of course I did not have the self-confidence to think I had any talent. So job hunting it was not easy. I failed at every recruitment exam I had at TV stations, I think that I failed at 50 to 60 different companies.

Through television dramas, what do you want to convey to the audience?

I think that you cannot show the appeal of something to someone if it isn't something you are interested in, or something you never found interesting, so the first thing is to enjoy it yourself. You cannot recommend some food that you don't like by saying "it might be delicious," right? It's the same thing for when you choose the subject of a drama. When something has strongly aroused my interest, for example when I am moved by a novel, attracted by the human nature of a real person, or get interested in a certain event, I want to cherish it and convey it to people through movies and television. That's why I keep in mind that I had better quit the industry once there's nothing left for me to get interested in. Fortunately, I'm in an environment that lets me still have interest in various things, so I can continue this job, but I have no idea about what may happen in the future.

Iyoda's Work 01 「Rakugoka : The way of the Comic Storyteller 赤メダカ」

A drama depicting the world of the traditional oral entertainment "Rakugo". Based on a true story, this fictional drama shows the growth of a man through joy and pain after he becomes the disciple of a genius Rakugo performer.

Iyoda's Work 02 「Women of the Red Cross レッドクロス～女たちの赤紙～」

Centered on a war nurse and her way of life after she goes to the battlefield during the Second World War. The story of a family that continues to believe in their bonds despite being at the mercy of fate and the circumstances of that period.

Iyoda's dramas depict the good old Japanese landscape and human nature

Japan's unique landscape, human nature, and customs are things that even we Japanese have fewer and fewer opportunities to feel and see. I think recording these things on video has a lot of significance, including as a way to preserve our precious culture.

Although Tokyo is known as a metropolis, there are still a lot of areas called "shitamachi" where common people live, allowing you to experience good old Japanese culture. In Ningyocho, which was used as the setting for a drama I worked on called "SHINZANMONO", the shitamachi can still be seen in the streets, and there is also this kind of old-fashioned strong relationship between people. Nowadays, especially in Tokyo, it is a common fact to not know what kind of people are living right next you. However, when I went to that district and asked someone for a favor or advice at the site where the drama was produced, 1 hour later all of a sudden about 10 people knew what I needed, and problems got resolved one after the other. I think that they really care about the community, or maybe should I say the ties they have between people. By recording and broadcasting what we are forgetting, I guess that I have the desire to make the audience feel something as well.

「SHINZANMONO
新参者」

The mystery drama series (SHINZANMONO), in which Detective Kyoichiro Kaga has to uncover the truth about a complicated murder case. Ningyocho's "shitamachi" is the main setting (location) where Kaga is working (→ P.80).

Could you tell us about a fun way to explore the "shitamachi"?

Just try to walk on your own. I recommend places that are not listed in guide books. For example, if you walked around narrow back streets or nearby small rivers, somewhere you will find landscapes that appeal to your heart. Then, by doing so, I hope you take away all those pieces of the Japanese landscape, keep them in your heart, and bring them back home. You should be able to enjoy an image of Tokyo that is different from the one of a metropolis where there are a lot of buildings.

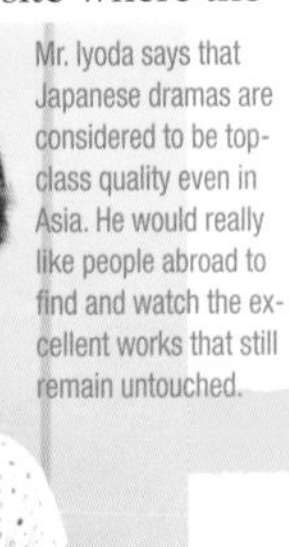

Mr. Iyoda says that Japanese dramas are considered to be top-class quality even in Asia. He would really like people abroad to find and watch the excellent works that still remain untouched.

Mr. Iyoda, after going around the locations in Tokyo used to stage your works, what spots would you recommend?

I think that Shibuya's scramble crossing is interesting. This is a human intersection between various people coming and going. Just looking at it, I feel a kind of overflowing power. In addition, there are many delicious shops in the Shibuya district, and I make new discoveries every time I visit it.

After that, I think that Tokyo Tower is beautiful. I'm not talking about climbing up the tower, but of the beauty it has as scenery itself. I have seen towers all around the world, but I think that Tokyo Tower, with the way it is lit up at night, is number one in the world. Maybe the Eiffel Tower offers more beautiful scenery during daytime (laughing).

If you want to see the night view in Tokyo, you might enjoy its beauty more by going on a night view tour rather than viewing it from one place. Since Tokyo's highway forms a ring, you can use a taxi to go around and see a night view that seems to be flowing from the car window. Tokyo Tower, Rainbow Bridge, sometimes going through tunnels, I think that you will be able to enjoy the various expressions of Tokyo.

How would you like tourists to enjoy Tokyo?

After visiting many countries, what I personally felt is the fact that Tokyo offers things that are superior in all aspects. The food is delicious, and the city offers a rich selection of entertainment. The restaurants and hotels facilities, services, and even the transportation network convenience are excellent. Even though it may seem disorderly. However, it is precisely because the city is in disorder that it gathers human power, and that it has the aura of a place where new things are created. I would be glad if tourists could feel this energy that gives you a kind of hunch as they stroll around Tokyo.

Recommended by Mr. Iyoda! ***Tokyo's Best Spots***

Scramble crossing

In front of Shibuya Station, a district with the latest of culture and fashion, this crossing splits off pedestrians and cars. Always bustling like a festival, you cannot cross here without going through a wave of people→**P.90**

Tokyo Tower

A communications tower about 333m high, completed in 1958. It can be seen from all around Tokyo, and the way it is lit up in the evening is entertaining to the eyes of the Tokyoites →**P.122**

Late Night Metropolitan Expressway Cruising

At night, try chartering a taxi and go around the metropolitan expressway for an hour. In one go, you can enjoy Tokyo's unique night view, including Tokyo Tower, skyscrapers, and more

原宿・表参道

HARAJUKU/ OMOTESANDO

Laforet Harajuku (left) and Tokyu Plaza Omotesando Harajuku (right) are the two major shopping spots in this area

What kind of town?

Harajuku, the birthplace of "Kawaii" culture, and Omotesando, lined with shops and cafés of refined taste, are areas full of energy, always creating new trends.

JR Harajuku station serves as starting point that connects Takeshita Street, which is popular among teenagers, through Takeshita Exit, to Omotesando, known to be an adult-oriented district, through the Omotesando Exit.

Omotesando is also known to be a highly competitive place for gourmet food, where famous gourmet chefs from around the world gather.

You can find shopping malls on Meiji-dori, which crosses Omotesando and has become a must-visit place in recent years, where they've been constructing many new buildings.

1. Omotesando is beautiful with its roadside trees. In winter, the street is illuminated
2. The entrance of the Takeshita Street, which is right in front of you after you leave JR Harajuku Station Takeshita Exit

1. Omotesando, with its glamorous atmosphere
2. Meiji Jingu Shrine, situated on the west side of JR Harajuku station
3. A popular street in Harajuku where young people gather
4. If you are looking for trendy items, we recommend SPINNS Harajuku Takeshita Street Shop

How to enjoy

In this area, you'll want to enjoy shopping and gourmet food. There are 3 main streets: Takeshita Street, Omotesando, and Meiji-dori.

On Takeshita Street, enjoy unique shops popular among young people as well as "one-hand gourmet" (meals you can hold in one hand), and experience the culture of young Japanese people.

On Omotesando, feel satisfied with high-brand shopping and popular gourmet restaurants where queues are inevitable.

On Meiji-dori, enjoy shopping at the two major shopping malls that bring together many unique shops. If you go further down Omotesando, the street continues to Aoyama. Since Aoyama is known as a more sophisticated district where "grown-ups" have fun, it's a good idea to check it out.

1. Cat Street is lined with classy cafés and shops
2. Unique shops gathering in Ura-Harajuku

❖ *Must-visit tourist spots*

Sightseeing

Meiji Jingu Shrine →P.104

Takeshita Street →P.108

Ura Harajuku →P.109

Gourmet

Yasaiya Mei Omotesando Hills Shop →P.107

Amenochihare Aoyama →P.110

brasserie holoholo →P.110

Shopping

Omotesando Hills →P.106

SPINNS Harajuku Takeshita Street Shop →P.108

NILE PERCH Harajuku Main Shop →P.109

A
B
1
2
3
4
Meiji Jingu Shrine(p.104)
Takeshita Street(p.108)
TOTTI CANDY FACTORY Harajuku Shop(2F/p.108)
H.I.S. Harajuku Tourist Information Center(p.103)
Takeshita Exit
JR Harajuku Station
Harajuku ALTA
Togo Shrine
Harajuku Police Station
LISTEN FLAVOR Harajuku Shop(p.31)
KAWAII MONSTER CAFE HARAJUKU(4F/p.31)
Myouen Temple
CUTE CUBE HARAJUKU
SPINNS Harajuku Takeshita Street Shop (2F/p.108)
MOSHI MOSHI BOX Harajuku Information centre
Omotesando Exit
CASCADE HARAJUKU
Ura Harajuku(p.109)
Harajuku-dori
lilLilly TOKYO(p.109)
Laforet Harajuku
Maison de Julietta (B1.5F/p.31)
Tokyu Plaza Omotesando Harajuku
NILE PERCH Harajuku Main Shop(B1F/p.109)
Meiji-Jingumae (Harajuku) Station
Onitsuka Tiger Omotesando(p.26)
Omotesando
Jingumae Elementary School
KIDDY LAND Harajuku store(p.31)
GYRE
Dojun Wing
Omotesando ROCKET(3F/p.107)
Q Plaza Harajuku
Omotesando Hills(p.106)
Yasaiya Mei Omotesando Hills Shop(3F/p.107)
Tabio Omotesando Hills(B2F/p.107)
Omotesando Hills Information Counter(1F/p.103)
Anniversaire Omotesando
oak omotesando
Omote-Sando Station
JR Yamanote Line
JR Saikyo Line
Cat Street
Tokyo Metro information desk at Omote-sando station(p.103)
Fire-dori
A0
Momotaro Jeans Aoyama Shop(2F/p.26)
Matsumotokiyoshi
United Nations University
Tokyo Metro Fukutoshin Line
cocoti
Tokyo Metro Hanzomon Line
GONBEE (p.111)
Shibuya City Office (temporary government building)
Miyashita Park
Tokyo Metro Ginza Line
Shibuya Post Office
Aoyama Gakuin University
109 MEN'S
Amenochihare Aoyama(p.110)
Shibuya Station
Shibuya Hikarie
JR Shibuya Station
Roppongi-dori
Tokyu Toyoko Line
Shibuya Police Station
Meiji-dori

表参道ヒルズ総合インフォメーション

Omotesando Hills Information Counter

The information counter on the 1st floor of Omotesando Hills. With a touch panel information that has guidance in 5 languages.

Address:4-12-10 Jingumae, Shibuya-ku **TEL:**03-3497-0310 **Opening hours:**11:00-21:00, 11:00-20:00 on Sundays **Closed:**None (closed 3 days a year) **Access:**2 min. walk from Tokyo Metro OmoteSando Station Exit A2

MAP P.102 B-2

*Support available in Chinese on Saturdays, Sundays and public holidays: 11:00-17:00

C

Aoyama-dori

Aoyama Manpuku(p.111)

brasserie holoholo(p.110)

Tokyo Metro Chiyoda Line

Seinan Elementary School

Minotti

Nezu Museum (p.175)

Taro Okamoto Memorial Museum

Choukoku-ji Temple

Sou · Sou Kyoto Aoyama Shop(p.27)

CITABRIA BAR(p.112)

Roppongi-dori

N 0 100 200m

C

Access from airports

Narita Airport Terminal 2·3	Haneda Airport International Terminal
Keisei Line (Skyliner)	*Keikyu Line Limited Express and more*
Nippori	Shinagawa
Yamanote Line inner loop	*Yamanote Line outer loop*
Harajuku	Harajuku
¥ 2670yen	¥ 580yen
70min	40min

Lines

[**JR-Harajuku Station**]

Yamanote Line

[**Tokyo Metro-Omotesando Station**]

Ginza Line *Hanzomon Line*

Chiyoda Line

[**Tokyo Metro-Meiji-jigumae (Harajuku) Station**]

Fukutoshin Line *Chiyoda Line*

Tourist information centers

H.I.S. Harajuku Tourist Information Center

H.I.S.原宿ツーリストインフォメーション

Offer services such as booking for tours and cultural experiences, Tokyo Metro Pass, Wi-Fi rental,currency exchange,luggage storage, yukata rental,etc.

Address: Harajuku Ash Bldg. 1F, 1-19-11 Jingumae, Shibuya-ku **TEL:**03-5770-5131 **Opening hours:**10:00-18:00 **Closed:**None **Access:** 1 min. walk from JR Harajuku Station Takeshita Exit

MAP P.102 A-1

◆ Other tourist information centers

Tokyo Metro information desk at Omote-sando station

東京メトロ表参道駅旅客案内所

MAP P.102 B-3

Shrine 明治神宮

Meiji Jingu Shrine

1.With a height of about 12m, the wooden Myojin Torii gate is the largest in Japan 2.The Main Shrine. Visited by many worshipers from Japan and abroad 3.You can see shrine maidens performing a service in the facilities

A beautiful shrine surrounded by greenery

A shrine with luxuriant green surroundings where around 100,000 trees donated from all parts of Japan have been planted on a site of about 700,000 m². In the precincts, you can find gardens, known as Gyoen, and the treasure museum annex Homotsu Tenjishitsu, which has exhibitions related to deities. The square in front of the treasure museum Homotsu-den is a place where you can relax.

Address:1-1 Yoyogi Kamizono-cho, Shibuya-ku **TEL:**03-3379-5511 (main) **Opening hours:**From sunrise to sunset. Gyoen: 9:00-16:00 (may vary depending on the season). Homotsu-den: 9:00-16:30 (last admission 30 minutes before closing) **Closed:**None **Fee:**Gyoen, Homotsu-den and Treasure Museum Annex (Bunkakan): 500 yen as contribution for maintenance **Access:**3 min. walk from JR Harajuku Station Omote-sando Exit

HP MAP P.102 A-1

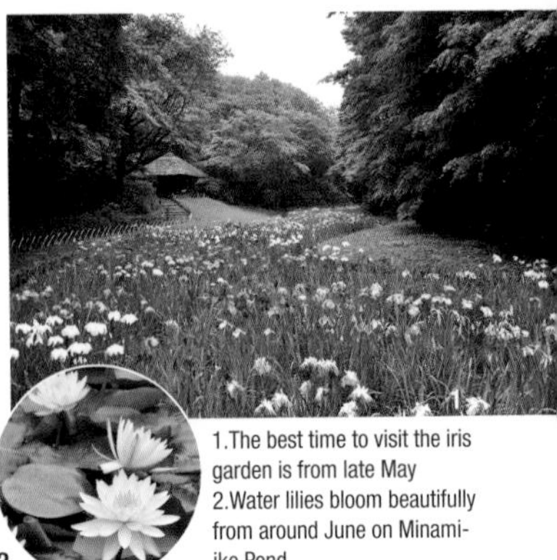

1.The best time to visit the iris garden is from late May 2.Water lilies bloom beautifully from around June on Minami-ike Pond

① Gyoen 御苑

Gyoen was originally the garden of a feudal lord during Edo period, and later became an imperial estate. Seasonal plants such as irises, water lilies and others can be seen here.

② Main Shrine 本殿

Where the souls of Emperor Meiji and Empress Shoken are enshrined. In the vicinity of the Main Shrine there are two camphor trees which were planted at the time of foundation, which are called the "camphor couple".

The shrine was rebuilt in 1958. Mind your manners when you visit here

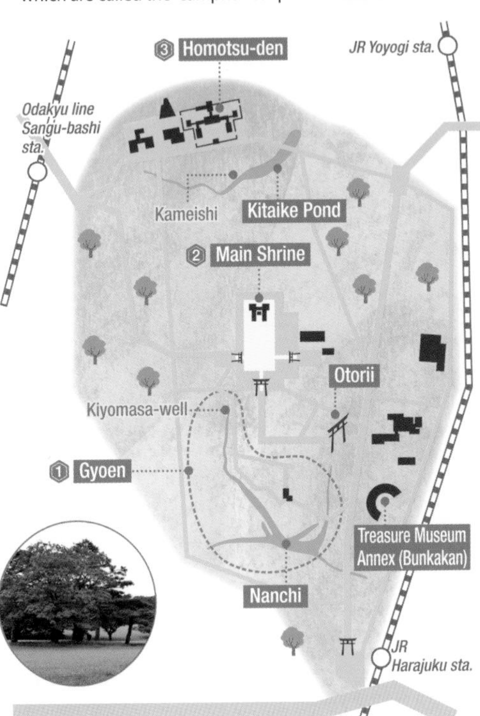

③ Homotsu-den

宝物殿

Located on the north side of the site, completed in 1921. Exhibits imperial treasures related to deities.

One of the first concrete buildings built in Japan, a National Important Cultural Property

Column

A Spiritual Place

In Meiji Jingu Shrine, there are two spots considered to be places that are particularly powerful. Kiyomasa-well, located within Gyoen, and Kameishi, in the vicinity of the Kitaike pond. Try to feel their mystical powers.

Kiyomasa-well

A spring water well, which is quite rare in Tokyo. It is said to have a purifying effect.

Kameishi

A stone in the shape of a turtle. Lie down on top of the stone and try to feel its power.

1. The center of the Main Building is an atrium with a sense of open space stretching over 6 floors
2. In the Dojun Wing, you can find cafés and a gallery space
3. Events are held sometimes at the gathering space in the Main Building on B3 floor

Commercial Complex 表参道ヒルズ

Omotesando Hills

Epicenter of the latest fashion and culture

A cultural and commercial facility built on the site of the old Dojunkai Aoyama Apartments. Composed of three buildings, the West Wing, Main Building, and Dojun Wing, Omotesando Hills is lined with high-brand shops and restaurants.

Address:4-12-10 Jingumae, Shibuya-ku **TEL:**03-3497-0310 **Opening hours:**11:00-21:00, 11:00-20:00 on Sundays. Restaurants: 11:00-23:30 (last order 22:30), 11:00-22:30 (last order 21:30) on Sundays. Cafés: 11:00-22:30 (last order 21:30), 11:00-21:30 (last order 20:30) on Sundays *may vary depending on shop **Closed:**None (closed 3 days a year) **Access:**2 min. walk from Tokyo Metro Omote-sando Station Exit A2

HP MAP P.102 B-2

For Tourists

Some shops will give you a 10% discount, a free drink, and other perks when you show your passport.

"Mei Gozen" looks good as well. You can eat plenty of seasonal vegetables

Vegetable dish やさい家めい 表参道ヒルズ店

Yasaiya Mei Omotesando Hills Shop

Enjoy their vaunted vegetable dishes

A restaurant specializing in dishes using Japanese vegetables. You can enjoy fresh vegetables delivered every morning from contract farmers located all around Japan cooked in a variety of different ways. They also hold events during which seasonal vegetables are used in the main dishes.

Address: Omotesando Hills Main Bldg. 3F **TEL:**03-5785-0606 **Opening hours:**11:00-16:00 (last order 15:30), 17:00-23:30 (last order 22:30), 11:00-23:30 (Lunch last order 16:00, Dinner last order 22:30) on Saturdays and public holidays, 11:00-22:30 (Lunch last order 16:00, Dinner last order 21:30) on Sundays **Closed:**None (closed 3 days a years) **Price:**Lunch from 1,250 yen, dinner from 5,000 yen

MAP P.102 B-2

For Tourists
The "Noen Bagna Cauda" and "Curry Combo with plenty of vegetables" are famous specialities that let you eat several kinds of vegetables at once.

From simple plain socks, to a variety of patterned socks with cute, or Japanese-style patterns and designs

For Tourists
Get your initials (up to 3 letters) embroidered for free, when you buy selected socks on offer.

Socks タビオ 表参道ヒルズ

Tabio Omotesando Hills

Socks made-in-Japan in a variety of exquisite designs

These socks are knitted by the 'Knitters (manufacturers)' who seek nothing but fine quality. Truly an artwork of Japanese craftsmanship. The store has the largest collection of Tabio's variety of socks from men's, women's to kids', in several choice of sizes.

Address: Omotesando Hills Main Bldg. B2F **TEL:**03-5785-0561 **Opening hours:**11:00-21:00, 11:00-20:00 on Sundays and public holidays **Closed:**Irregular holidays

MAP P.102 B-2

Gallery 表参道 ROCKET

Omotesando ROCKET

Spreading "new fun"!

A gallery based on the theme of "mode". Exhibition and pop-up shops held for one to two weeks by creators and brands from Japan and abroad.

Address: Omotesando Hills Dojun Wing 3F **TEL:**03-6434-9059 **Opening hours:**11:00-21:00, 11:00-18:00 on Wednesdays, 11:00-20:00 on Sundays **Closed:**Thursdays

MAP P.102 B-2

Gallery space. It has become a place of expression for many kinds of creators

For Tourists
Depending on the exhibition, there may be items on sale, so you might find something you can buy only here.

1.The arch at the entrance of Takeshita Street. Balloon art changes regularly
2.Enjoy eating crepes and other delicious food while walking, and take a look at the large-scale facilities that have been opening up in recent years!
3.Rows of colorful, wacky items

Takeshita Street

A fashion street born in 1974. Extending over a distance of about 350m from JR Harajuku Station to Meiji-dori. Lined with shops selling fashion items, miscellaneous goods, and gourmet food for young people. MAP P.102 A-1

Cotton Candy TOTTI CANDY FACTORY原宿店

TOTTI CANDY FACTORY Harajuku Shop

"KAWAII" candy with a huge impact

With a diameter of about 40cm , this huge and colorful cotton candy is very popular . It is made right in front of your eyes, so you can eat it fresh. Cotton candy from 600 yen . Other sweets also sold by weight.

Address:RYU Apartment 2F, 1-16-5 Jingumae, Shibuya-ku **TEL:**03-3403-7007 **Opening hours:**10:30-20:00 (10:30-19:00 between November and January), 9:30-20:00 on Saturdays, Sundays and public holidays **Closed:**Irregular holidays **Access:**3 min. walk from JR Harajuku Station Takeshita Exit

MAP P.102 A-1

The "TOTTI 4-color Cotton Candy". White is sugar, purple is grape flavored, orange is lemon flavored, and blue is soda pop flavored

1,2. Pleated skirts and T-shirts are classic items of SPINNS

Fashion スピンズ 原宿竹下通り店

SPINNS Harajuku Takeshita Street Shop

A shop leading Harajuku fashion

Popular apparel shop that often appears in fashion magazines for young people. Offering men's and women's items, letting you to get trendy products at an affordable price.

Address:CUTE CUBE HARAJUKU 2F, 1-7-1 Jingumae, Shibuya-ku **TEL:**0120-011-984 **Opening hours:**10:00-20:00 **Closed:**Irregular holidays **Access:**5 min. walk from JR Harajuku Station Takeshita Exit

MAP P.102 A-1

Ura Harajuku

Birthplace of the unique fashion style "Urahara-kei" popular in the 1980s. Located on the east side of Meiji-dori, near Harajuku Street. This area brings together apparel shops and trendy cafés. MAP P.102 B-1

1.Many shops are offering items of a refined sense
2.A street of a calm atmosphere. Enjoy strolling around a vast area!
3.The "NILE PERCH Harajuku Main Shop" offers also a rich variety of miscellaneous goods in pastel colors

Fashion lilLilly TOKYO

lilLilly TOKYO

Real clothes for classy girls

With "clothes that can be worn only by girls" as concept, this store is lined with clothes that use materials such as lace and fur. It also offers items from its sister brand LILICIOUS.

Address:4-27-6 Jingumae, Shibuya-ku
TEL:03-6721-1527
Opening hours:12:00-20:00
Closed: Irregular holidays
Access:6 min. walk from Tokyo Metro Meiji-Jingumae (Harajuku) Station Exit 5
MAP P.102 B-2

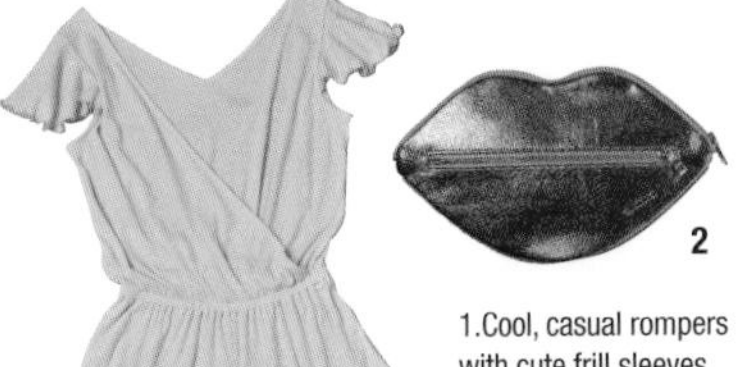

1.Cool, casual rompers with cute frill sleeves
2.Lip-shaped bag from the accessory brand LILICIOUS

Dresses from 17,500 yen. Size: one-size only

Fashion NILE PERCH原宿本店

NILE PERCH Harajuku Main Shop

If you're looking for fancy items, they're here!

Rows of cute items in a store in pastel colors. All products are original and handmade at the main shop. Customization is also possible, including a change of color and decoration, etc.

Address: Harajuku Y's Bldg. B1F, 4-26-27 Jingumae, Shibuya-ku **TEL:**03-3408-1993
Opening hours:11:00-20:00, 11:00-19:30 on Sundays and public holidays **Closed:**None
Access:6 min. walk from Tokyo Metro Meiji-Jingumae (Harajuku) Station Exit 5
MAP P.102 B-2

Kaiseki Cuisine 雨後晴 青山

Amenochihare Aoyama

Kaiseki restaurant nestled in a residential area

Characterized by its way of serving dishes on large plates, this restaurant lets you taste and share Japanese cuisine. We recommend dishes that use fresh seafood sent directly from fishing ports every day. Offers a selection of Japanese sake that go well with the food as well.

Address:2-2-17 Shibuya, Shibuya-ku **TEL:**03-6427-9216 **Opening hours:**11:30-14:30, 18:00-23:30 (last order 22:30) ,17:00-23:30 (last order 22:30) on Saturdays **Closed:**Sundays and public holidays **Price:**Lunch from 1,200 yen, Dinner from 9,000 yen **Access:**9 min. walk from Tokyo Metro Omote-Sando Station Exit B1

MAP P.102 B-4

*Dress code is smart casual. Note that cancellation fees may apply for same day cancellations

1. Courses include sashimi (front), appetizers (background left), boiled fish (background right) and more, letting you eat dishes made with seasonal ingredients 2. In front of the counter seats, tableware collected from all over Japan is arranged and used according to the dishes

For Tourists

You can enjoy authentic green tea at the end of the course. It is also possible to make the tea by yourself if you wish to do so.

1. The homemade sausage and smoked salmon and vegetable platter are classic dishes. The salmon is smoked at the restaurant 2. An interior inspired by the image of small French restaurant

For Tourists

The cuisine using guinea fowl, bought from the only guinea fowl farmer in Japan in Iwate Prefecture, is a must-eat dish.

Brasserie brasserie holoholo

brasserie holoholo

Exquisite French cuisine for which no effort is spared

Enjoy French cuisine using Japanese ingredients in an at-home atmosphere. Dishes here have a reputation the time and effort taken during their preparation, making it a popular restaurant that can be fully booked for days. Wine: One glass from 900 yen.

Address: From Five 1F, 3-17-1 Minami-Aoyama, Minato-ku **TEL:**03-6804-1136 **Opening hours:**18:00 to following day 2:00 (last order 1:00), 17:00-24:00 (last order 23:00) on Saturdays, Sundays and public holidays **Closed:**Mondays and on first Sunday of the month **Price:**From 8,000 yen **Access:**3 min. walk from Tokyo Metro Omote-Sando Station Exit A4

MAP P.103 C-3

*Wi-Fi requires password
*For a vegetarian menu, ask at the time of reservation

Yakiniku 青山まんぷく

Aoyama Manpuku

High-quality Japanese Black beef in a cozy space

A yakiniku (grilled meat) restaurant where you can eat high-quality Japanese Black beef. Among the many dishes, we highly recommend the "Tokusen Beef Platter" in which you get to taste rare parts of the beef, and the "Salty Tongue" generously topped with shredded green onions.

Address:1F, 3-14-2 Minami-Aoyama, Minato-ku **TEL:**03-5413-5529 **Opening hours:**17:00-24:00 (last order 23:00), 12:00-15:00 (last order 14:30), 17:00-24:00 (last order 23:00) on Saturdays, Sundays and public holidays **Closed:**None **Price:**Lunch from 1,500 yen, Dinner from 6,000 yen **Access:**6 min. walk from Tokyo Metro Omote-Sando Station Exit A4

HP

MAP P.103 C-2

*Full-time Chinese staff working every weekend evening

1. "Tokusen Wagyu Platter" (front), and the specialty "Salty Tongue" (back) 2. Although you have to take your shoes off, the sunken kotatsu (Japanese foot warmer) seats allow you to bend your legs

For Tourists

The yukke (beef tartare) is reputed for its freshness and a texture that melts in your mouth. Tare (sauce), salty green onions, and other seasonings available.

1. The "Seiro" (bamboo steamer) with its vaunted homemade noodles and dashi remaining unchanged since the time of establishment 2. The Japanese house-style interior. Small tatami rooms, table seats, and more available

For Tourists

At night, it offers plenty of side dishes that go well with sake, such as tempura, a la carte, etc. Taste them together with sake and shochu.

Soba / Udon 権兵エ

GONBEE

Soba Izakaya recognizable with its blue shop curtain

Taste freshly made soba using buckwheat flour produced in Japan. We recommend the "Ni-Hachi Soba", which lets you fully enjoy the taste of buckwheat. It is also possible to choose handmade Udon from the menu.

Address: Dai-ichi Minami-Aoyama Bldg. 1F, 5-9-3 Minami-Aoyama, Minato-ku
TEL:03-3406-5733
Opening hours:11:30-22:00 **Closed:**None
Price: From 700 yen **Access:**1 min. walk from Tokyo Metro Omote-Sando Station Exit B1

HP

MAP P.102 B-3

Have a blast even at night!

Tokyo Nightlife

Tokyo is home to Asia's largest entertainment district, so there are lots of ways to enjoy the night! Here are some of the standard recommended night spots, such as bars, izakaya, clubs, and more.

1. "Ochoko-don San-ko Set" (left), and the most popular dish ""truffle and egg over rice" (right)
2. Walls lined with alcohol

Izakaya 十番右京

Juban Ukyo

The largest selection of Japanese alcohol!

Enjoy Japanese alcohol, such as sake and shochu along with creative Japanese cuisine. Offers a wide variety of alcohol at all time with more than 250 brands, and the unique cups are also fun. Although it is a popular place, try to visit it on weekdays around 23:00. Han-gō (about 90cc) of Japanese sake from 510 yen.

Address:2-6-3 Azabu-Juban, Minato-ku **TEL:**03-6804-6646 **Opening hours:**18:00 to following day 4:00 (last order 3:00), 17:00 to following day 4:00 on Saturdays (last order 3:00), 17:00-24:00 on Sundays (last order 23:00) **Closed:**None **Price:**From 6,000 yen **Access:**5 min. walk from Tokyo Metro Azabu-Juban Station Exit 7

MAP P.116 B-3

Wine Bar ケンゾーエステイトワイナリー六本木ヒルズ店

Kenzo Estate Roppongi Hills

Enjoy wines that captivate the world

Restaurant managed by the luxury wine brand company, Kenzo Estate. Taste popular wines together with creative fusions of Japanese and French cuisine. A glass of wine starts from 1,000 yen.

Address: Roppongi Hills Residence D Block 1F and 2F, 6-12-4 Roppongi, Minato-ku **TEL:**03-3408-1215 **Opening hours:**1F: 11:00 to following day 4:00 (last order 3:00). 2F: 17:00-23:00 (last order 22:00) **Closed:**1F None. 2F closed on Sundays **Price:**Lunch from 1,000 yen, Dinner from 8,000 yen (course)

Access:8 min.walk from Tokyo Metro Roppongi Station Exit 1b

MAP P.116 B-2

Enjoy a casual tasting on the 1st floor

Bar

CITABRIA BAR

CITABRIA BAR

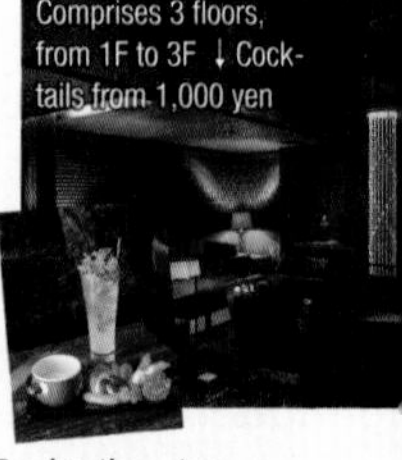

Comprises 3 floors, from 1F to 3F ↓ Cocktails from 1,000 yen

House bar nestled in a residential area

A relaxing and welcoming bar with a sophisticated atmosphere. Cocktails using seasonal fruit are recommended. There is no signboard, and a secret code number is required so ask at the time of reservation.

Address:2-26-4 Nishi-Azabu, Minato-ku **TEL:**03-5469-5777 **Opening hours:**20:00 to following 5:00 (last order 4:00) **Closed:**On Sundays and public holidays **Fee:**From 5,000 yen **Access:**16 min. walk from Tokyo Metro Omote-Sando Station Exit B1

MAP P.103 C-4

*Cover charge:1,000 yen

1. Distance between the stage and audience is close, letting you see the powerful show up close
2. A robot horse also appears
3. Dancer doing Japanese drum performance

Restaurant with a show ロボットレストラン

Robot Restaurant

The only robot show in the world

A show restaurant where reservations are required. The show performed by robots and female dancers is reputed to be gorgeous and impressive. The show is held 3 to 4 times a day.

Address: Shinjuku Robot Bldg. B2F, 1-7-1 Kabukicho, Shinjuku-ku **TEL:**03-3200-5500
Opening hours: Show held three times a day at 17:55, 19:50 and 21:45. 4 Shows a day with an extra show at 16:00 on Saturdays, Sundays and public holidays
Closed: Irregular holidays **Fee:**8,000 yen
Access:6 min. walk from JR Shinjuku Station East Exit

MAP P.39 C-1

club WOMB

WOMB

Shibuya's popular club where music lovers gather

Reputed for its sound system, lights, and smoke effects. Offers more space compared to others clubs in Shibuya, and is open even on weekdays. On weekends, you can enjoy performances by world-class foreign artists.

Address:2-16 Maruyama-cho, Shibuya-ku
TEL:03-5459-0039
Opening hours/Closed/ Price: May differ depending on events
Access:11 min. walk from JR Shibuya Station Hachiko Exit

MAP P.88 A-3

4-story building with 3 dance floors. VIP seats also available

Enjoy a powerful stage performance and the meal

Restaurant with a show 六本木金魚

ROPPONGI KINGYO

A gorgeous show unfolding every night

Restaurant theater where you can enjoy a powerful show performed by male, female, and new-half (transgender) dancers. Its avant-garde performances and phantasmagoric stage sets are very appealing. Two shows performed at 18:00 and 21:00.

Address: Taisho Bldg., 3-14-17 Roppongi, Minato-ku
TEL:03-3478-3000 **Opening hours:**18:00-24:00
Closed: Mondays **Fee:**From 6000 yen **Access:**5 min. walk from Tokyo Metro / Toei Subway Roppongi Station Exit 3

MAP P.116 B-2

ROPPONGI/ AZABU/ SHIBA-KŌEN

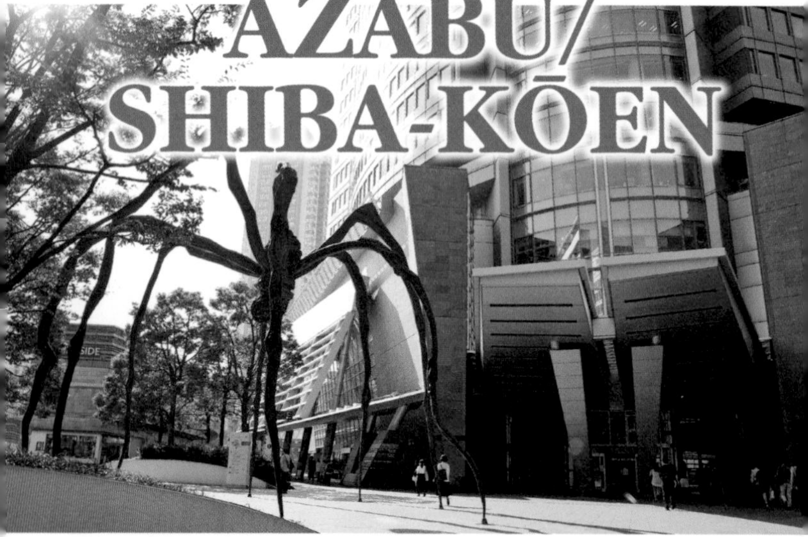

On the plaza of Roppongi Hills, there is a huge spider object called "Maman"

LOUISE BOURGEOLS«MAMAN»
2002(1999) bronze,stainless steel,marble
9.27×8.91×10.23(h)m

What kind of town?

Roppongi is a stylish area dotted with facilities geared toward adults. It is known as an international city where you can find the embassies of many different countries, and many foreign nationals working for foreign companies.

There are two large commercial complexes near Roppongi Station, Roppongi Hills and Tokyo Midtown, and also the National Art Center, Tokyo which is the largest exhibition site in Japan.

On the east side of Roppongi Station, there is the Shiba Park area with Tokyo Tower, the symbol of Tokyo, and Zojo-ji Temple.

On the south side, there is the Azabu area, an upscale residential area. You can do sightseeing at both within walking distance from Roppongi.

1. The view is also good from Shiba park situated on the east side of Tokyo Tower
2. Azabu Juban shopping street crowded with locals and tourists

1. The National Art Center, Tokyo and its inverted cones containing restaurants and cafés. The view from the inside is also unique 2. The scenery from Zojo-ji Temple. Also recommended in spring when cherry blossoms are in bloom 3. Azabu Juban shopping street lined with various shops. It is fun to get something to eat as you walk around 4. Mohri Garden, with free admission, is located inside Roppongi Hills

How to enjoy

Enjoy shopping, gourmet food, and art tours in Roppongi.

Roppongi Hills and Tokyo Midtown bring together highly refined shops and much talked about restaurants from Japan and abroad. Since you can find the Mori Art Museum and Suntory Museum of Art respectively in each facility, you can do an art tour including the the National Art Center, Tokyo as well.

Although it is nice to enjoy the scenery of Tokyo from the observation deck at Tokyo Tower, we recommend taking your time to admire Tokyo Tower from Shiba Park.

In addition, since Roppongi is dotted with trendy bars, clubs and night view spots, you can have fun all night.

1. The tearoom of the Suntory Museum of Art is beautiful
2. Roppongi-dori Crossing is a standard spot for meeting up

Must-visit tourist spots

Sightseeing

The National Art Center, Tokyo →P.120

21_21 DESIGN SIGHT →P.121

Tokyo Tower →P.122

Gourmet

Edoya →P.124

Japanese Cuisine Yamazato →P.125

Sosaku Ochazuke Senmonten DAYONE. →P.125

Shopping

Roppongi Hills →P.118

Tokyo Midtown →P.119

A
B
1
2
3
Suntory Museum of Art(3F/p.121)
21_21 DESIGN SIGHT(p.121)
Nogizaka Station
Tokyo Midtown(p.119)
Tokyo Midtown Tourist Information Center(p.117)
The National Art Center,Tokyo(p.120)
Tokyo Metro Chiyoda Line
Aoyama park
Sosaku Ochazuke Senmonten DAYONE.(p.125)
Roppongi Station
Ryori-ya Mifune(p.125)
Matsumoto kiyoshi
Izumo Shrine Tokyo Bunshi
Azabu Police Station
Mori Tower
Mori Art Museum(53F/p.121)
Roppongi Hills General Information(2F/p.117)
Tokyo City View&Sky Deck
EX THEATER ROPPONGI
ROPPONGI KINGYO(p.113)
Don Quijote(p.172)
Roppongi-dori
Roppongi Hills(p.118)
Keyakisaka-dori
Zepp Blue Theater Roppongi
CITABRIA BAR(p.112)
Kenzo Estate Roppongi Hills (1F&2F/p.112)
Roppongi Hign School
International House of Japan
Embassy of the Republic of Singapore
Koryo Junior High School
Azabu Fire Station
Nanzan Elementary School
Kogai Elementary School
Matsumoto kiyoshi
Juban Ukyo(p.112)
Japanese Red Cross Medical Center
Azabu High School
Hiroo Gakuen High School
Edoya(p.124)
Seishin Women's University
Hiro-o Station
N
0 100 200m
Arisugawa-no-miya Memorial Park
Access from airports
Narita Airport Terminal 2·3
Keisei Line (Skyliner)
Keisei Ueno
6-minute walk
Ueno
Tokyo Metro Hibiya Line
Roppongi
2670yen
80min
Haneda Airport International Terminal
Tokyo Monorail
Hamama tsucho
5-minute walk
Daimon
Toei Oedo Line
Roppongi
670yen
35min
Lines
[Tokyo Metro-Roppongi Station]
Hibiya Line
[Tokyo Metro-Azabu-juban Station]
Namboku Line
[Tokyo Metro-Roppongi-Itchome Station]
Namboku Line
[Toei-Roppongi Station/Azabu-juban Station]
Toei Oedo Line

C
D

Hikawa Shrine
Hisakuni Shrine
isho-ji Temple
ANA Intercontinental Tokyo
Ark Mori Bldg.
Hotel Okura South Wing
Japanese Cuisine Yamazato(2F/p.125)
Toranomon Hills
Saiko-ji Temple
Ark Hills South Tower
Roppongi-Itchome Station
Sakurada-dori
Hotel Villa Fontaine Roppongi
NHK Broadcasting Museum
Toei Mita Line
Kamiyacho Station
The Jikei University School of Medicine
Tokyo Metro Namboku Line
Azabu elementary school
Yoshida Hochiku Memorial Hall
Tokyo Metro Hibiya Line
The Iikura Guesthouse of Ministry of Foreign Affairs
Embassy of the Kingdom of the Netherlands
Gaien-higashi-dori
Azabu Post Office
Shiba High School
Seisoku High School
Onarimon Elementary School
Onarimon Station
Embassy of the Republic of Kazakhstan
Embassy of the Republic of Maldives
Embassy of the Philippines
Tokyo Prince Hotel
*Under renovation.
Scheduled to open in April 2017
Embassy of the Russian Federation
Tokyo Tower(p.33,122)
Tokyo ONE PIECE Tower(p.123)
Embassy of the Islamic Republic of Afghanistan
Sakurada-dori
Azabu Library
Zojo-ji Temple
Azabu-Juban Station
Daimon Station
Nakanobashi Exit
Shiba Park
Toei Oedo Line
Akabanebashi Station
The Prince Park Tower Tokyo
Azabu-Juban Station
Akabanebashi Exit
Azabu Juban shopping street
Shibakoen Station
Akabane Elementary School
Mita High School
Casa Vinitalia(p.124)
Higashimachi Elementary School
Celestine Hotel

Tourist information centers

Roppongi Hills General Information

六本木ヒルズ総合インフォメーション

General Information counter located on the 2nd floor of Mori Tower. Brochures in foreign languages are available, and strollers and wheelchairs can be borrowed.

Address: Roppongi Hills Mori Tower 2F, 6-10-1 Roppongi, Minato-ku
TEL:03-6406-6000
Opening hours:11:00-21:00
Closed: None **Access:**Directly connected to Tokyo Metro Roppongi Station Exit 1c
HP MAP P.116 B-2
*Chinese support available at certain times

◆ **Other tourist information centers**

Tokyo Midtown Tourist Information Center
東京ミッドタウン観光案内所 MAP P.116 B-1

1. The 4-story high ceiling space of West Walk is a bright shopping area where natural light enters
2. Mohri Garden is known as an oasis
3. "Tokyo City View," the observation deck is located on the 52nd floor of Mori Tower. You can enjoy a superb view both day and night

Commercial Complex 六本木ヒルズ

Roppongi Hills

Bringing together the newest fashion, gourmet food, and art

A commercial complex that serves as a landmark of Roppongi. Filled with plenty of attractions such as trendy shops, reputable restaurants, a museum, etc. Since the building covers a wide area, get a guide map from the information counter on the 2nd floor of Mori Tower before you look around.

Address:6-10-1 Roppongi, Minato-ku
TEL:03-6406-6000 (reception time 10:00-21:00)
Opening hours: Shops: 11:00-21:00. Restaurants: 11:00-23:00 (some shops may differ) **Closed:**None
Access: Directly connected to Tokyo Metro Roppongi Station Exit 1c
HP MAP P.116 B-2

For Tourists
On the West Walk, you can find a foreign currency exchange counter (6th floor) and shopping assistants fluent in foreign languages (no reservations required) available at all times.

1. The main shopping area, Galleria. The 4-story open ceiling space from B1F to 3F
2. The vast lawn plaza boasts a total surface of 1,880m². Also turns into an event space
3. Holds events in which you can enjoy light shows. This picture shows how it looked in the past

Commercial Complex 東京ミッドタウン

Tokyo Midtown

City complex surrounded by green

Besides the more than 130 shops, Tokyo Midtown houses hotels and restaurants, museums, and a variety of other facilities. The site is dotted with green spaces and public art. A variety of events are held throughout the year.

Address:9-7-1 Akasaka, Minato-ku
TEL:03-3475-3100 (Tokyo Midtown Call Center)
Opening hours:11:00-21:00, Restaurants: 11:00-24:00 (some shops may differ)
Closed: None
Access: Directly connected to Toei Subway / Tokyo Metro Roppongi Station Exit 8
HP MAP P.116 B-1

For Tourists
You can find staff able to speak foreign languages at the information counters situated in three locations who will give you their recommendations on shops and souvenirs.

1. Characterized by its glass curtain walls. The building itself is so beautiful that it looks like a work of art
2. How the library looks inside
3. The café, Salon de Thé ROND located on 2nd floor of the giant inverted cone
4. You can easily enjoy authentic French cuisine at the Brasserie Paul Bocuse Le Musée on the 3rd floor

Art Museum 国立新美術館

The National Art Center, Tokyo

The theme is "a museum in the forest"

A museum designed by Kisho Kurokawa, an architect who represents Japan. With an area of 14,000m^2, it is one of the largest exhibition space in Japan, and holds a variety of special exhibitions and public exhibitions.

Address: 7-22-2 Roppongi, Minato-ku **TEL:**03-5777-8600 (Hello Dial Service) **Opening hours:**10:00-18:00, 10:00-20:00 on Fridays during special exhibitions (last admission 30 minutes before closing time) **Closed:**Tuesdays (open if on public holidays, then closed on the following day) **Fee:**May differ depending on exhibition **Access:**Directly connected to Tokyo Metro Nogizaka Station Exit 6

HP MAP P.116 B-1

For Tourists

Besides restaurants, it also offers museum shops and a library. At the library, you can consult art catalogs and books for free.

Art Museum サントリー美術館

Suntory Museum of Art

A museum that brings tradition and modernity into harmony

A museum located in Tokyo Midtown. Holds exhibitions and collects works based on the theme of "Art in Life". Its collection comprises around 3,000 works.

Address: Tokyo Midtown Galleria 3F, 9-7-4 Akasaka, Minato-ku **TEL:**03-3479-8600 **Opening hours:**10:00-18:00, 10:00-20:00 on Fridays and Saturdays (last admission 30 minutes before closing time) **Closed:**On Tuesdays and during exhibition replacement periods **Fee:**May differ depending on exhibition **Access:**Directly connected to Toei Subway / Tokyo Metro Roppongi Station Exit 8

HP MAP P.116 B-1

©Keizo Kioku

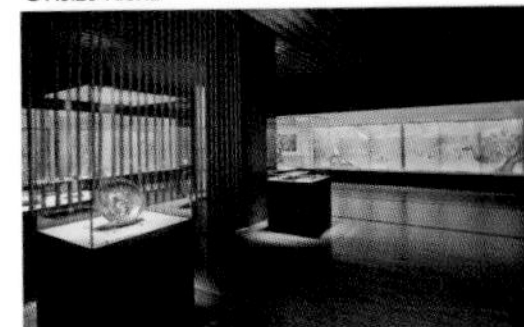

Holds exhibitions on certain occasions centered on Japanese arts such as painting, ceramics, glass, etc.

For Tourists

At the tea room Gencho-an located on the 6th floor, seats for tea ceremony are made available on specified Thursdays during the exhibitions.

53rd floor of the Roppongi Hills Mori Tower. You can enjoy the view from the observatory deck (52nd floor)

For Tourists

All the brochures and catalogs for the exhibitions have bilingual content written in Japanese and English

Art Museum 森美術館

Mori Art Museum

Experience innovative contemporary works of art

Located on the top floor of Roppongi Hills, this museum brings to the world unique exhibitions centered on contemporary art. Since it is open until 10PM, you can take your time and enjoy the exhibits.

Address: Roppongi Hills Mori Tower 53F, 6-10-1 Roppongi, Minato-ku **TEL:**03-5777-8600 (Hello Dial Service) **Opening hours:**10:00-22:00. 10:00-17:00 on Tuesdays (last admission 30 minutes before closing time) **Closed:**open everyday during exhibitions **Fee:**May differ depending on exhibition **Access:**Directly connected to Tokyo Metro Roppongi Station Exit 1c

HP MAP P.116 B-2

Exhibition Facility 21_21 DESIGN SIGHT

21_21 DESIGN SIGHT

Conveying everyday things from the perspective of design

The famous designers Issey Miyake, Taku Satoh, and Naoto Fukasawa serve as directors. You can see exhibitions that specialize in design.

Address: Tokyo Midtown Garden, 9-7-6 Akasaka, Minato-ku **TEL:**03-3475-2121 **Opening hours:**10:00-19:00 (last admission 30 minutes before closing time) **Closed:**Tuesdays **Fee:**1,100 yen **Access:**5 min. walk from Toei Subway / Tokyo Metro Roppongi Station Exit 8

HP MAP P.116 B-1

Photos: Masaya Yoshimura

The floors from B1F to 1F in the low-rise building are more spacious than one would think based on the facade

For Tourists

Participatory programs are also held, including talk shows, workshops, and other activities. Available in Japanese only.

Tower 東京タワー

Tokyo Tower

A red symbol located in the heart of Tokyo

This impressive communications tower draped in red stands out even in Tokyo. Completed in 1958, it boasts a height of 333m. Since it is located at the center of Tokyo, it gives bird's-eye view in all directions.

Address:4-2-8 Shiba-Kōen, Minato-ku **TEL:**03-3433-5111
Opening hours:9:00-23:00 (last admission 30 minutes before closing time) *may differ depending on facilities in Foot Town **Closed:**None **Fee:**From 900 yen
Access:7 min. walk from Toei Subway Akabanebashi Station Akabanebashi Exit
HP MAP P.117 C-2

Beautiful illuminations are also worth seeing!

1

1. The Diamond Veil illumination is limited to Saturdays and certain days from 20:00 to 22:00
2. The mascot characters "Nop-pon Brothers"
3. The special stage "Club 333". Located on the first floor of the Main observatory. Concerts, talks shows, and other events are held daily here

3

2

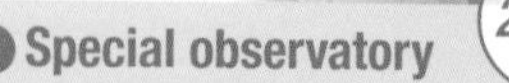

❶ Special observatory 250m

An observatory located at a height of 250m, from which you can see Mount Fuji if weather conditions are good.
*Currently undergoing renovations. Opening scheduled in summer of 2017.

❷ Main observatory

Scenery on the southwest side of the Large Observation Deck. You can see Mount Fuji when weather conditions are good

Large observatory located at a height of 150m. There a 1st and 2nd floor, complete with cafés and a special stage.

❸ Tokyo ONE PIECE Tower

The standing statues of Luffy and Chopper at the entrance. Take a commemorative photo with them

Experience the world of the popular anime ONE PIECE

You can have a variety of experiences with attractions, restaurants and other shops based on ONE PIECE characters. The "360-degree Log Theater~The World of ONE PIECE", which was opened in 2016, is also a must-see.

Address: Located in Tokyo Tower Foot Town
TEL:03-5777-5308 (Information related to the park) **Opening hours:**10:00-22:00 (last admission 1 hour before closing time) **Closed:**None
Fee:day ticket: 3,200 yen, Advance ticket: 3,000 yen
MAP P.117 C-2

Column

The Story of Tokyo Tower

About 60 years ago, Tokyo Tower was built in order to bring together as one radio towers located in different places. The design was created over a period of about three months by Tachu Naito, an architect who worked on the Tsutenkaku Tower in Osaka and other structures. Approximately 220,000 people were involved in the construction of Tokyo Tower. It was built over the short period of time of one and a half year, and amazingly the steeplejacks performed the construction manually. Tokyo Tower not only was a communication tower used for television and radio transmissions, but also played a role as a symbol of Japan. Nowadays, the number of persons who have visited Tokyo Tower exceeds the total population of Japan, and it often appears in movies and novels. It has become the tourist destination that represents Japan, and has admirably fulfilled its role.

1. A height of 300m or more was required to transmit radio waves through the Kanto area. The colors are the international orange and white that have been defined by aviation law
2. The appearance of the tower growing taller and taller excited people at that time

Western Food エドヤ

Edoya

A Western-food restaurant that was also introduced in the Michelin Guide Tokyo

A long-established restaurant founded in 1954. Try the "Omu-rice" and the "Hamburg Steak", popular dishes that have been available since the opening of the restaurant. These dishes use a sweet, rich demi-glace sauce that requires a week to be made.

Address:2-12-8 Azabu Juban, Minato-ku **TEL:**03-3452-2922 **Opening hours:**11:30-14:30 (last order 14:00), 18:00-22:00 (last order 21:30) **Closed:**On Tuesdays and every 1st and 3rd Wednesday of the month **Price:**Lunch from 2,000 yen, Dinner from 2,500 yen **Access:**3 min. walk from Tokyo Metro Azabu-Juban Station Exit 1

MAP P.116 B-3

1. The "Omu-rice" is their signature dish. With ketchup-flavored chicken rice under the eggs 2. A small restaurant offering 21 seats. From the counter facing the kitchen, you can see how the dishes are prepared

For Tourists

Since it is a popular restaurant, try to get there on weekdays rather than crowded weekends. One dish per person must be ordered.

*"Omu-rice" is not available on Saturday, Sunday, and the evenings of public holidays

1. Their signature dish Bagna Cauda is made of more than 20 different seasonal vegetables. Enjoy it with the anchovy and garlic sauce or gorgonzola cream sauce 2. Terrace seats facing the inner court. The wall is decorated with a folding screen

For Tourists

In the restaurant, you can always find Italian wines carefully selected by the sommelier, who will tell you which wine goes best with your food.

Italian Food Casa Vinitalia

Casa Vinitalia

Based on the concept of a "private home"

A cozy Italian restaurant that feels just like you were invited to a friend's house. You can enjoy cuisine that uses seasonal ingredients prepared by a chef who mastered his skills at the established Ginza restaurant Aroma Fresca.

Address:M Tower 2F, 1-7-31 Minami-Azabu, Minato-ku **TEL:**03-5439-4110 **Opening hours:**17:30 to following day 2:30 (last order 1:00), 14:30-22:30 (last order 20:30) on Sundays **Closed:**Mondays **Price:**From10,000 yen **Access:**5 min. walk from Tokyo Metro Azabu-Juban Exit 2

MAP P.117 C-3

*For a vegetarian menu, ask at the time of reservation

Japanese Food / Tempura 和食 天ぷら 山里

Japanese Cuisine Yamazato

Enjoy freshly fried piping hot tempura

A Japanese restaurant located in the long-established Hotel Okura Tokyo. Especially reputed for its tempura, this restaurant offers special counter seats from which you can see how the dishes are cooked.

Address: Hotel Okura Tokyo 2F, 2-10-4 Toranomon, Minato-ku **TEL:**03-3582-0111 **Opening hours:**7:00-9:30 (7:00-10:00 on Saturdays, Sundays and public holidays), 11:30-14:30, 17:30-21:30 **Closed:**None **Price:**Breakfast from 3,240 yen, Lunch from 4,540 yen, Dinner from 11,880 yen **Access:**10 min. walk from Tokyo Metro Kamiyacho Station Exit 4b

MAP P.117 C-1

*For a vegetarian menu, ask at the time of reservation

The "Tempura-mori" made with seasonal ingredients. You can have tempura starting from lunch

For Tourists
The breakfast, which lets you enjoy a Japanese menu with good nutritional balance, is also recommended.

Izakaya 料理屋 三船

Ryori-ya Mifune

A must-visit for fans of the world-renowned Mifune

An izakaya that expresses the world of Toshiro Mifune, a famous actor who symbolizes Japan. In this restaurant with an interior based off a movie set, taste dynamic cuisine that brings out the natural flavor of the ingredients.

Address: Utsumi Bldg. 1F, 7-18-7 Roppongi, Minato-ku **TEL:**03-6804-5548 **Opening hours:**11:30-14:00 (last order 13:30), 17:00-23:30 (last order 22:30) **Closed:**Sundays **Price:**Lunch from 900 yen, Dinner from 5,000 yen **Access:**2 min. walk from Toei Subway / Tokyo Metro Roppongi Station Exit 2

MAP P.116 B-2

The impressive sashimi platter (front) and the charcoal-grilled meat and vegetables (back), which lets you choose the ingredients

For Tourists
The menu changes monthly, letting you taste cuisine that uses seasonal ingredients. There are also cocktails that use Japanese sake.

Ochazuke 創作お茶漬け専門店 だよね。

Sosaku Ochazuke Senmonten DAYONE.

An Ochazuke specialty store that is rare even in Japan

Taste luxurious Ochazuke, which is in a dashi broth topped splendid ingredients. Particular attention is paid to the dashi as well as to the toppings, and they change depending on the dish. Only counter seats are available in the shop.

Address: Shimizu Bldg. 1F, 4-12-4 Roppongi, Minato-ku **TEL:**03-5770-5563 **Opening hours:**11:30 to following day 5:00 (last order 4:30), 11:30 to following day 6:00 (last order 5:30) on Fridays, Saturdays and days before public holidays, 11:30-24:00 (last order 23:30) on Sundays and public holidays **Closed:**None **Price:**Lunch from 630 yen, Dinner from 1,480 yen **Access:**2 min. walk from Toei Subway / Tokyo Metro Roppongi Station Exit 7

MAP P.116 B-1

The "Seafood Ochazuke with salmon and salmon roe" is topped with one slice of salmon fillet and a generous portion of salmon roe

For Tourists
This specialty store can teach you the most delicious way to eat Ochazuke. Ask cheery shopkeeper!

*Ochazuke is a dish in which hot tea or dashi broth is poured over cooked white rice

It's even more delicious when you learn about it!

The world of sushi

Check!

Sushi is already synonymous with Japanese cuisine. However, do you know about the different styles for eating sushi? Here, we introduce the origins of sushi.

What is sushi?

A probable explanation of the roots of sushi is the influence of the naturally fermented nare-zushi prepared by indigenous Southeast Asian people who used to put salted river fish on cooked rice. Nare-zushi was then brought over to Japan via China. It appears in Japanese history in records dating from around 718, at which time sushi was paid as a tax to the Imperial Court.

The iconic "Edo-mae sushi" (or Edo-style sushi) was born after the great fire of Edo in 1657. The restaurant industry flourished at this time to meet the needs of the craftsmen who gathered from all around Japan in order to work on reconstruction. In the beginning, stalls offered nori rolled sushi, but Hanaya Yohei opened his hand-formed sushi shop in 1810, and thus Edo-style sushi was born. "Edo-style" was so called because of the sea right in front of Edo, and because originally the fish and shellfish caught in the current of Tokyo Bay were used to make sushi. Although there are many types of sushi, such as oshi-zushi (pressed sushi), chirashi-zushi (scattered sushi), nowadays nigiri-zushi (hand-formed sushi) is called Edo-style sushi.

Sushi shops initially began from stalls, but since 1945 they turned into luxury restaurants with a face-to-face counter where people are able to eat sushi right after ordering. However, in 1958, a kaiten sushi (conveyor belt sushi) shop opened in Osaka. This spread all over Japan around 1980, reinstating sushi's place as a dish for common people.

Hikari-mono
❶ Maki-zushi
Shiro-mi
❷ Gunkan-maki
Kai
Ni-mono
❸ Nigiri-zushi
Aka-mi

Types of sushi

❶ **Maki-zushi** Sushi in which vinegar-flavored rice and ingredients are rolled into long sticks wrapped in seaweed, also called "nori-maki" (seaweed-roll). Ingredients generally used include cucumber, natto (fermented soybeans), negitoro (mashed tuna), etc.

❷ **Gunkan-maki** A type of rolled sushi in which vinegar-flavored rice is rolled in seaweed on the side and then topped with salmon roe, sea urchin, and other ingredients. The idea came after the shopkeeper of the restaurant Kyubey in Ginza, Tokyo, prepared sushi this way in response to a special order made by a customer. It seems that the name, literally meaning "warship" comes from the fact that it looks like a warship.

❸ **Nigiri-zushi** A sushi topping is placed on top of a small amount of vinegar-flavored rice, seared and prepared by pressing with both hands. There are difference in colors for the sushi toppings made of fish meat referred to as "aka-mi" (red flesh fish) and "shiro-mi" (white flesh fish), but also "hikari-mono", small fish with silvery shiny backs, "ni-mono" using fish meat simmered in soup after being cooked, and "kai", which uses shellfish as topping.

* The person "Hanaya Yohei" appearing here has nothing to do with the Japanese restaurant of the same name

Manners and ways to eat sushi

Basic way to eat People are free to eat sushi using chopsticks or to pick it up with their hands. Do not dip it for too long in the soy sauce. If you put it in for too long, the pressed vinegar-flavored rice may tend to fall apart easily, the taste of soy sauce will be too strong, so you will not be able to enjoy the original taste of the fish and shellfish.

Although sometimes tea is served by the waiters, in kaiten sushi restaurants, most of the time it is self-service. Tea is free of charge in almost all sushi shops.

The sweet and sour pickled ginger used as sushi garnish is referred to as "gari", and when you have some after eating a piece of sushi, it will cleanse the palate and allow you to taste the next delicious piece as well.

Is there any order to eating sushi?
In general, the eating order considered best starts with simple shiro-mi, then ni-mono, then sushi with strong flavor, and finishes with maki sushi. The reason is that if you start with fatty meat with strong flavor, some fat will remain in your mouth and dull the tastebuds. However, there is no formal rule. You can eat your sushi in any order you like.

How to use counter-seat shops
Many of the sushi shops without conveyor belts have no menu and do not list their price. If you do not understand, it is preferable to talk about your budget and the ingredients you do not wish to eat first, and then say "omakase" (I'll leave it up to you). For those who are not fans of wasabi, say "wasabi-nuki" after your order, and they will prepare sushi without wasabi. Since such sushi shops are managed by sushi chefs with many years of experience, talk to them with respect.

How to use conveyor belt sushi shops
In almost All chain stores, you will be guided to your seat once you enter. Servers will explain how to use the menu panels set for all seats and how to brew your tea. Recently, since there are menus in English and also tablet-type menus, you can look at the pictures when you order. In conveyor belt sushi shops, you can tell the price of sushi by looking at the color of plates.

Maguro Donya Miuramisakiko Megumi →P.93

PICK UP

Try! Counter-seat shop

Fully enjoy eating real sushi made by sushi chefs who have extensive knowledge of fish and seafood.

Ginza Kyubey

Well-established store with one of the best sushi in Japan

A luxury sushi restaurant founded in 1935. Even though all of the sushi are exquisite, we particularly recommend the sea urchin "Gunkan-maki" since this restaurant is also the birthplace of the "Gunkan-maki" sushi.

Address:8-7-6 Ginza, Chuo-ku **TEL:**03-3571-6523 **Opening hours:**11:30-14:00, 17:00-22:00 **Closed:**Sundays and public holidays **Price:**Lunch from 4,000 yen, Dinner from 10,000 yen **Access:**7 min. walk from Tokyo Metro Ginza Station Exit A2

MAP P.52 B-3

The Sushi Chef will teach you how to eat sushi and talk about the ingredients

Sushi Matsugen

Enjoy authentic sushi prepared right in front of your eyes

Apart from authentic Nigiri-zushi, you can taste creative dishes using seafood. In addition to the fact that sushi are offered one by one to counter seats, it is recommended since you can actually see how the sushi chefs are working.

Address: Yamanen Bldg. 2F, 2-3-13, Ebisu Minami, Shibuya-ku **TEL:**03-6452-2400 **Opening hours:**17:00-23:00 (last order 22:30) **Closed:**Sundays and public holidays **Price:**From 8,000 yen **Access:**5 min. walk from JR Ebisu Station West Exit

MAP P.7 C-4

The "Omakase Hachi-kan Nigiri-zushi" prepared with seasonal ingredients

上野

UENO

The fountain in front of Tokyo National Museum is a place of recreation and relaxation for visitors

What kind of town?

Between Ueno Park area, with its cultural facilities, and Ameyoko area, packed with a variety of retail shops, Ueno has two totally different faces.

Stretching out on the West side of Ueno Station, Ueno Onshi Park is a quiet area surrounded by greenery. Besides the museums and art galleries located in the park, there are also important cultural properties of Japan, including the Kan'ei-ji and other temples, allowing you to feel the history and culture of Japan.

On the opposite side, Ameyoko is located under the girder bridge between Ueno Station and Okachimachi Station, and densely packed with shops selling food, clothing, ornaments, etc. It is particularly crowded during the end of the year with people coming to buy ingredients for the New Year, so visiting here has become a year-end tradition.

1.Many of the foods from the shops located in the Ameyoko underpass are delicious and cheap
2.Ameyoko, crowded with many people. Offers many attractions of course on its main street, but also in the underpass

1.The surface of Shinobazu Pond is completely covered by lotus flowers. Resting spots are also available nearby
2.Shops are closely packed in the underpass of Ameyoko
3. In the JR Ueno Station Hirokoji Exit area, there is also a facility containing a shopping center and restaurants
4.Red lanterns are the symbol of bars

How to enjoy

Facilities representing Japan are concentrated in Ueno Onshi Park, such as the National Museum of Western Art, with its building designated as World Heritage Site, as well as the Tokyo National Museum, which is the oldest museum in Japan, and more. Famous as a cherry blossom spot, Ueno is visited every year by a large number of tourists during the hanami (flower viewing) season, and is filled with a festive mood.

People who want to enjoy a lively atmosphere, go to Ameyoko. You will love shopping as shopkeepers shout out energetically. Since they have everything, including food and all kind of miscellaneous goods, it is the perfect place to look for souvenirs. In addition, you can also find an area nearby where there are many popular taverns. It is also fun to do some "ladder-drinking" (pub crawl), by walking around to many different shops and drinking.

1. At the center of the "Shinobazu Pond" located in "Ueno Onshin Park", lies the hexagonal tower of "Benten-do"
2. You will see the entrance of Ameyoko after coming out from JR Ueno Station Shinobazu Exit and crossing the crosswalk

Must-visit tourist spots

Sightseeing

Ameyoko →P.132

Ueno Zoological Gardens →P.135

National Museum of Nature and Science →P.136

Tokyo National Museum →P.137

The National Museum of Western Art →P.137

Gourmet

Inshotei →P.138

Ueno Seiyoken Caferant Le Landaulet →P.139

Brasserie L'écrin →P.139

Gyukatsu AONA Okachimachi Main Restaurant →P.139

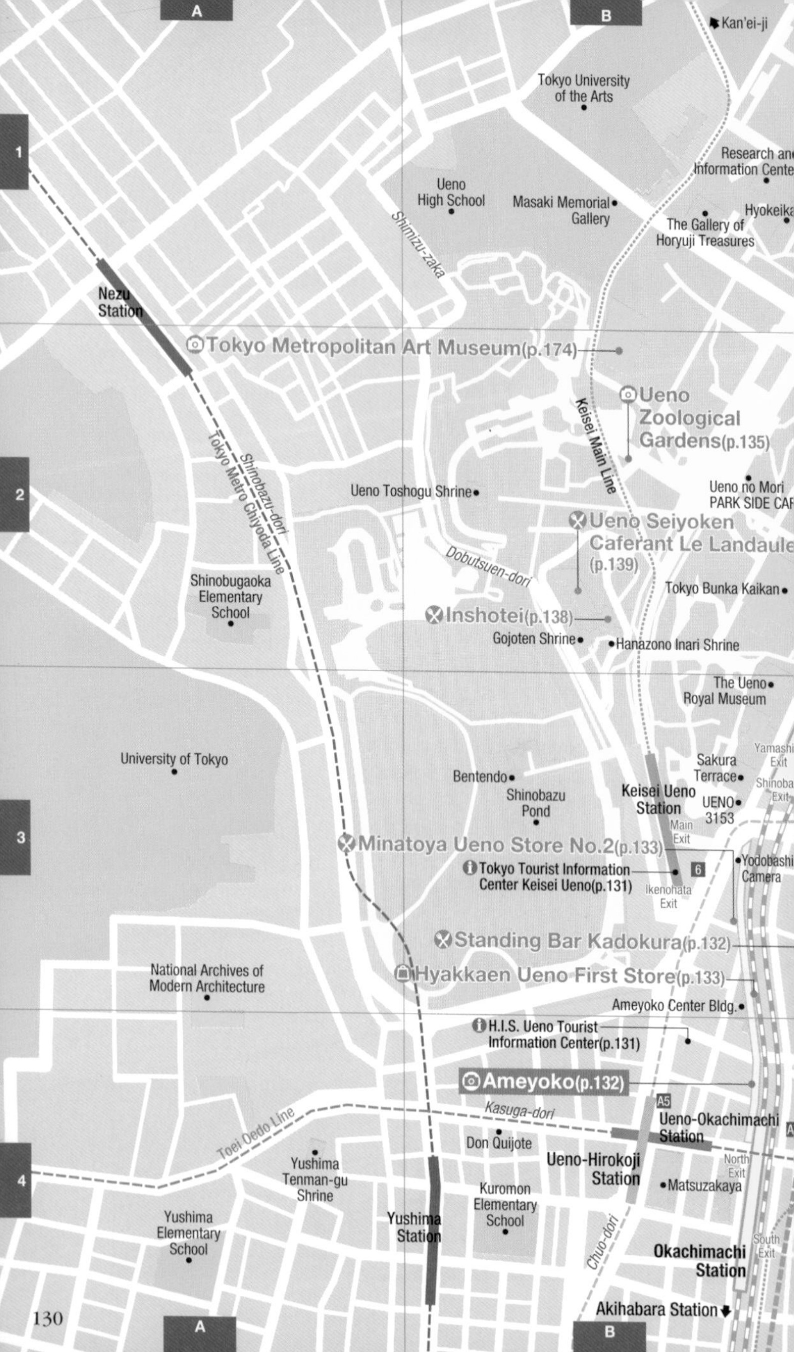
A
B
1
2
3
4
Kan'ei-ji
Tokyo University of the Arts
Research and Information Center
Hyokeikan
The Gallery of Horyuji Treasures
Ueno High School
Masaki Memorial Gallery
Shimizu-zaka
Nezu Station
Tokyo Metropolitan Art Museum(p.174)
Ueno Zoological Gardens(p.135)
Keisei Main Line
Tokyo Metro Chiyoda Line
Shinobazu-dori
Ueno Toshogu Shrine
Ueno no Mori PARK SIDE CAFE
Ueno Seiyoken Caferant Le Landaulet (p.139)
Dobutsuen-dori
Tokyo Bunka Kaikan
Inshotei(p.138)
Gojoten Shrine
Hanazono Inari Shrine
Shinobugaoka Elementary School
The Ueno Royal Museum
University of Tokyo
Bentendo
Shinobazu Pond
Sakura Terrace
Keisei Ueno Station
UENO 3153
Yamashita Exit
Shinobazu Exit
Main Exit
Minatoya Ueno Store No.2(p.133)
Tokyo Tourist Information Center Keisei Ueno(p.131)
6
Yodobashi Camera
Ikenohata Exit
Standing Bar Kadokura(p.132)
Hyakkaen Ueno First Store(p.133)
National Archives of Modern Architecture
Ameyoko Center Bldg.
H.I.S. Ueno Tourist Information Center(p.131)
Ameyoko(p.132)
A5
Kasuga-dori
Toei Oedo Line
Ueno-Okachimachi Station
Don Quijote
Ueno-Hirokoji Station
North Exit
Yushima Tenman-gu Shrine
Matsuzakaya
Kuromon Elementary School
Yushima Elementary School
Yushima Station
Chuo-dori
Okachimachi Station
South Exit
Akihabara Station

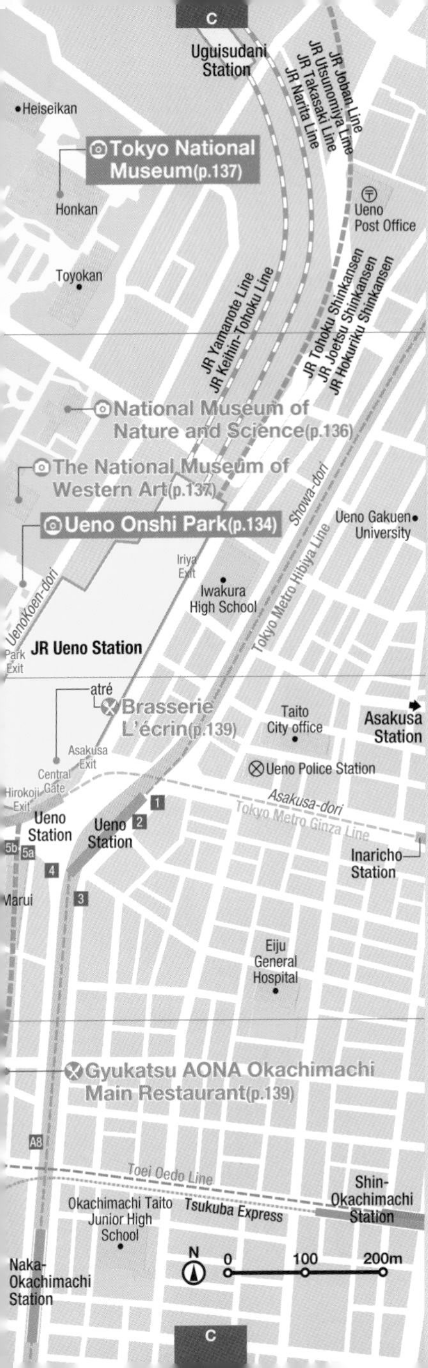

C
Uguisudani Station
JR Joban Line
JR Utsunomiya Line
JR Takasaki Line
JR Narita Line
Heiseikan
Tokyo National Museum(p.137)
Honkan
Ueno Post Office
Toyokan
JR Yamanote Line
JR Keihin-Tohoku Line
JR Tohoku Shinkansen
JR Joetsu Shinkansen
JR Hokuriku Shinkansen
National Museum of Nature and Science(p.136)
The National Museum of Western Art(p.137)
Showa-dori
Ueno Onshi Park(p.134)
Ueno Gakuen University
Iriya Exit
Iwakura High School
Tokyo Metro Hibiya Line
UenoKoen-dori
JR Ueno Station
Park Exit
atré
Brasserie L'écrin(p.139)
Taito City office
Asakusa Station
Asakusa Exit
Central Gate
Ueno Police Station
Hirokoji Exit
Asakusa-dori
Tokyo Metro Ginza Line
Ueno Station
Ueno Station
Inaricho Station
Marui
Eiju General Hospital
Gyukatsu AONA Okachimachi Main Restaurant(p.139)
Toei Oedo Line
Okachimachi Taito Junior High School
Tsukuba Express
Shin-Okachimachi Station
Naka-Okachimachi Station
N
0 100 200m
C

Access from airports

Narita Airport Terminal 2·3	Haneda Airport International Terminal
Keisei Line (Skyliner)	*Keikyu Line Limited Express and more*
	Shinagawa
	Yamanote Line inner loop
Keisei Ueno	Ueno
¥ *2470yen*	¥ *610yen*
40min	*40min*

Lines

[**JR-UENO-Station**]
- *Yamanote Line*
- *Keihin-Tohoku Line*
- *Utsunomiya Line (Ueno Tokyo Line)*
- *Takasaki Line (Ueno Tokyo Line)*
- *Jōban Line (Ueno Tokyo Line)*

[**Tokyo Metro-UENO-Station**]
- *Ginza Line*
- *Hibiya Line*

[**Toei-Ueno-Okachimachi Station**]
- *Toei Oedo Line*

[**Private railway-Keisei Ueno Station**]
- *Keisei Line*

Tourist information centers

Tokyo Tourist Information Center Keisei Ueno

東京観光情報センター 京成上野

A tourist center providing Tokyo sightseeing-related information. Offers guidance on tourist routes and transportation in four languages.

Address:1-60 Uenokoen, Taito-ku
TEL:03-3836-3471
Opening hours:9:30 -18:30
Closed: None
Access: In front of Keisei Ueno Station ticket gate

HP

MAP P.130 B-3

◆ **Other tourist information centers**

H.I.S. Ueno Tourist Information Center
H.I.S. 上野ツーリストインフォメーションセンター
MAP P.130 B-4

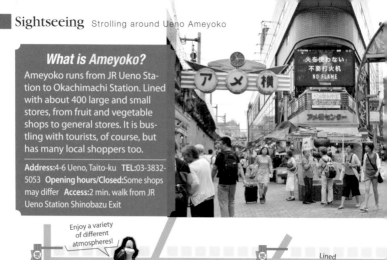

What is Ameyoko?

Ameyoko runs from JR Ueno Station to Okachimachi Station. Lined with about 400 large and small stores, from fruit and vegetable shops to general stores. It is bustling with tourists, of course, but has many local shoppers too.

Address:4-6 Ueno, Taito-ku **TEL:**03-3832-5053 **Opening hours/Closed:**Some shops may differ **Access:**2 min. walk from JR Ueno Station Shinobazu Exit

Enjoy a variety of different atmospheres!

Lined with many shops offering food!

Okachimachi Station

Standing Bar 立飲み カドクラ

Standing Bar Kadokura

Vaunted menus and drinks enjoyed in a casual way

For it is a Yakiniku company's restaurant, you can taste good-quality meat at an affordable price. There is an iron plate at the entrance in the restaurant, so you can also actually see how the meat is grilled.

Address: Forum Aji Bldg. 1F, 6-13-1 Ueno, Taito-ku **TEL:**03-3832-5335 **Opening hours:**10:00~23:30 (last order 23:00) **Closed:**None **Price:**From 500 yen **Access:**3 min. walk from JR Ueno Station Central Gate

MAP P.130 B-3

1.Pay the required amount in exchange of what you ordered
2.The "Hamkatsu"(ham cutlet) offering a perfect volume for which many layers of meat were superimposed

1,5. Ameyoko shopping street is crowded with shoppers from morning
2,3. Lined with standing bars for when you want a quick drink
4. Cosmetic shop in the underpass. Boasts a rich assortment of items.The underpass is packed with retail stores, and the streets look like a maze
6. Fresh fish is sold at the shops. The energetic shouts from the shopkeepers are entertaining

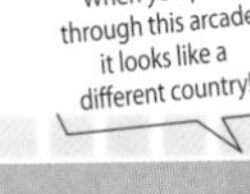

1."Toku-mori Don", 750 yen. Topped at all times with 5 types of fish, such as tuna and salmon, squid, etc. 2. A system in which you pay at the register first

B Seafood Bowl みなとや 上野2号店

Minatoya Ueno Store No.2

Enjoy a rich variety of seafood bowls

Seafood bowls are popular here, with more than 50 different types available. On weekdays, during the time service starting from 3PM, this shop offers good deals on its sashimi of octopus, tuna, squid, and more, all sold for 300 yen.

Address:4-10-17 Ueno, Taito-ku **TEL:**03-5818-5611 **Opening hours:**11:00 -19:30, 11:00 -20:00 on Saturdays, Sundays and public holidays **Closed:**None **Price:**From 500 yen **Access:**5 min. walk from JR Ueno Station Shinobazu Exit

MAP P.130 B-3

C Fruit 百果園 上野第一店

Hyakkaen Ueno First Store

Fresh fruits with perfect sugar content

Seasonal fruits gathered from all over the country, such as melon, pineapple, and strawberry, cut into bite-size pieces. Sold at an affordable price.

Address:6-10-12 Ueno, Taito-ku **TEL:**03-3832-2625 **Opening hours:**10:00-19:00 **Closed:**Wednesdays **Access:**5 min. walk from JR Ueno Station Shinobazu Exit

MAP P.130 B-3

Cut fruit is sold 100 yen per piece. Pineapple is the most popular

1.The fountain in front of Tokyo National Museum is the landmark of the park. You can also find restaurants in the surroundings 2.Lotus flowers start blooming on Shinobazu Pond starting around July and are in full bloom in August 3.The "Ueno Sakura Matsuri" (Cherry Blossom Festival) is held every year during the cherry blossom season, and the park gets crowded with tourists

Park 上野恩賜公園

Ueno Onshi Park

A park where you can enjoy the four seasons of Japan

This vast park brings together museums, a zoo, temples, and many other historic buildings. You can feel the transition between the four seasons with cherry blossoms in spring, lotus in summer, rows of ginkgo trees and red leaves in autumn, etc.

Address: Ueno-koen, Taito-ku
Opening hours:5:00-23:00
Closed: None
Fee: Free of charge
Access: Direct access from JR Ueno Station Park Exit
MAP P.131 C-2

For Tourists

Ueno Park has also been selected among "Japan's 100 best cherry blossom viewing spots". Enjoy the festive mood when the cherry blossoms are in bloom.

1. Lili, the male giant panda. We recommend you to go see it during feeding time
2,3. "Ueno Zoo" is the only place in Japan where you can see the okapi(2), the giant panda, and the pygmy hippopotamus(3), which are three of the world's rarest animals
4. Haoko the gorilla is popular with its handsome face
5. The monorail that connects the East and West gardens in the zoo. It takes about a minute and a half

Zoo 東京都恩賜上野動物園

Ueno Zoological Gardens

Go and meet lovely animals

A zoo that rears animals from all over the world. This is the only place in Japan where you can see the okapi, the giant panda, and the pygmy hippopotamus, which are three of the rarest animals in the world.

Address:9-83 Ueno-koen, Taito-ku **TEL:**03-3828-5171
Opening hours:9:30 -17:00 (last admission 1 hour before closing time) **Closed:**Mondays (closed the following day if public holiday) **Fee:**600 yen
Access:5 min. walk from JR Ueno Station Park Exit
HP MAP P.130 B-2

For Tourists

Souvenir goods featuring the giant pandas are popular among tourists visiting Japan. Includes cute stuffed animals, T-shirts, etc.

1. Navigators on History of Earth going though history, from the birth of the universe,13.8 billion years ago up to now.
2. In Global Environmental Detector, images of the Earth in quasi-real-time are projected one after another on the wall
3. Exploring the mysteries of dinosaurs with an exhibition based on the latest research

Museum 国立科学博物館

National Museum of Nature and Science

Learn about the secrets of the Earth

A science museum founded in 1877. Exhibits valuable material based on the themes of space, earth, and the evolution of organisms and mankind in an easy-to-understand way. Holds also special exhibitions and events in addition to the permanent exhibition.

Address:7-20 Ueno-koen, Taito-ku **TEL:**03-5777-8600 (Hello Dial Service) **Opening hours:**9:00 - 17:00, 9:00 - 20:00 on Fridays and Saturdays (last admission 30 minutes before closing time) **Closed:**Mondays (closed the following day if public holiday) **Fee:**620 yen **Access:**5 min. walk from JR Ueno Station Park Exit

HP MAP P.131 C-2

Pictures provided by the National Museum of Nature and Science

For Tourists

At the Japan Gallery, the evolution of Japanese people and their life in ancient times are displayed using models, etc. It is also a unique spot for taking pictures.

Museum 東京国立博物館

Tokyo National Museum

Appreciate precious Japanese fine arts

Boasting the largest collection of works in Japan, this museum preserves national treasures and more than 600 important cultural properties. When you walk around the Honkan (Japanese Gallery), the Toyokan (Asian Gallery), and the Gallery of Horyuji Treasures, you can learn about the spread of Buddhism into Japan.

Address:13-9 Ueno-koen, Taito-ku **TEL:**03-5777-8600 (Hello Dial Service) **Opening hours:**9:30 - 17:00 (last admission 30 minutes before closing time) *may vary depending on season **Closed:**Mondays (closed the following day if public holiday) **Fee:**620 yen *extra charge for special exhibitions **Access:**10 min. walk from JR Ueno Station Park Exit

MAP P.131 C-1

1.The gallery that mainly displays wooden sculpture from 10th to 13th Century (Japanese Gallery Room 11) 2. The building of the Japanese Gallery, which blends Japanese and Western styles, is an important cultural property in itself

For Tourists

There is a spectacular Japanese garden open to the public during limited periods in Spring and Autumn! The garden is also dotted with tea houses. Check the website for more details.

Pictures provided by Tokyo National Museum

1.The Main Building Permanent collection Gallery with its square and spiral shaped space. The pictures are arranged in chronological order 2.Many works of art from the 19th Century are on display in the New Wing

For Tourists

The National Museum of Western Art was listed as a World Heritage Site in July 2016 as the only architectural work designed by Le Corbusier in Japan.

Art Museum 国立西洋美術館

The National Museum of Western Art

A treasure trove of Western art

Founded on the basis of the "Matsukata Collection", comprised of works collected by Kojiro Matsukata, which were returned to Japan by the French government. This museum carries many works of Western art from the early medieval period through the late 20th century.

Address:7-7 Ueno-koen, Taito-ku **TEL:**03-5777-8600 (Hello Dial Service) **Opening hours:**9:30 -17:30, 9:30 - 20:00 on Fridays (last admission 30 minutes before closing time) *may vary depending on season **Closed:**Mondays (closed on the following day if public holiday) **Fee:**430 yen **Access:**1 min. walk from JR Ueno Station Park Exit

MAP P.131 C-2

1."Hanakagozen (Yuki)", an item on the lunch menu. A superb dish that you cannot taste anywhere else, with handmade tofu made of soy beans, tofu skin, and soy pulp 2. Seats of the 1st floor counter. Lighting is produced by Motoko Ishii, a world-renowned lighting designer who worked on Tokyo Tower and others 3. At the entrance, you can find the Japanese garden decoration "Shishi-odoshi"

Kaiseki Cuisine 韻松亭

Inshotei

Kaiseki cuisine to taste along with sceneries of the four seasons

A long-established restaurant located in Ueno Onshi Park, founded in 1875. This is one of the restaurants built by the government of the time for people visiting Ueno Onshi Park. The kaiseki course, which includes handmade tofu and the "Tori Sukiyaki" that have been made since the foundation of the restaurant, are popular dishes.

Address:4-59 Ueno-koen, Taito-ku **TEL:**03-3821-8126
Opening hours:11:00-23:00 (Lunch last order 15:00, Dinner last order 21:30), 11:00-22:00 (Dinner last order 20:30) on Sundays and public holidays **Closed:**None **Price:**Lunch from 2,600 yen and Dinner from 5,500 yen **Access:**5 min. walk from JR Ueno Station Park Exit

MAP P.130 B-2

For Tourists

Enjoy your meal along with the four seasons, with cherry blossoms in spring, fresh greenery in summer, red leaves in autumn, and more. In this two-story restaurant, parlor seats and sunken kotatsu seats are available.

Western Food 上野精養軒 カフェラン ランドーレ

Ueno Seiyoken Caferant Le Landaulet

The scenery of Ueno together with traditional western dishes

A pioneer that introduced Western cuisine to Japan, including beef stew, hashed beef with rice, and other dishes. On the seats of the terrace from where you can have bird's-eye view of Ueno Park, you will enjoy traditional taste.

"Beef Stew", which uses their vaunted demi-glace sauce generously

Address:4-58 Ueno-koen, Taito-ku **TEL:**03-3821-2181 (main) **Opening hours:**Teahouse: 10:00 - 20:00, Restaurant: 11:00 - 20:00 (last order 19:00) **Closed:**None **Price:**From 2,300 yen **Access:**5 min. walk from JR Ueno Station Park Exit

MAP P.130 B-2

For Tourists

Seiyoken, which spread "Yoshoku (Japanese-style Western dishes)". Many of the dishes have existed since the establishment of the restaurant.

*Please ask about the vegetarian menu when making a reservation

"Today's meat platter" from the a la carte menu. The photo shows a serving for 2 to 3 persons

For Tourists

The space was used as a waiting room for dignitaries at the beginning of the 20th century. You can feel the atmosphere of Japan at the time.

French ブラッスリーレカン

Brasserie L'écrin

Feel fascinated by a nostalgic space

You can enjoy casual French cuisine in a classical restaurant using the old VIP room of Ueno Station. In addition to the course meals, the a la carte menu offers a rich variety of choices.

Address:atré Ueno Retro Hall 1020, 7-1-1 Ueno, Taito-ku **TEL:**03-5826-5822 **Opening hours:**11:00 - 23:00 (last order 22:00) **Closed:**None **Price:**Lunch from 2,000 yen, Dinner from 5,500 yen **Access:**1 min. walk from JR Ueno Station Central Gate

MAP P.131 C-3

Photographer: Kenichi Takada

Gyukatsu 牛かつ あおな　御徒町本店

Gyukatsu AONA Okachimachi Main Restaurant

Proud of their carefully selected Gyukatsu (beef cutlet)

A restaurant where Gyukatsu using domestic cattle is very popular. You can enjoy an exquisitely fried beef cutlet together with fresh salad and rice. Choose between white rice or a mixture of 16 different grains.

The menu item "Na" uses marbled Japanese black beef

Address:JUN Bldg. 1F, 6-5-7 Ueno, Taito-ku **TEL:**03-6240-1979 **Opening hours:**11:00 - 23:00 (last order 22:30) **Closed:**None **Price:**From 1,500 yen **Access:**4 min. walk from JR Okachimachi Station North Exit

MAP P.131 C-4

For Tourists

Gyukatsu using marbled Japanese black beef lets you enjoy the tender texture of the meat with lots of fat marbling.

These restaurants are worth a visit!

List of well-known restaurants located in Tokyo

In Tokyo, you can find famous restaurants located outside the main areas as well. Let us introduce some of these reputed restaurants.

Kaiseki Cuisine / Sushi 白金料庭　槐樹

Shirokane Ryotei ENJU

Enjoy your meal while feeling the four seasons

A Japanese restaurant located in the Happo-en Garden. Taste dishes that change with each season as you admire a beautiful garden. Pay attention also to the interior, which was designed using Japanese traditional techniques. After the meal, take a stroll around the Happo-en Japanese garden.

Address: In the Happo-en Garden, 1-1-1 Shirokanedai, Minato-ku **TEL:** 03-3443-3125 **Opening hours:** 11:30 - 22:00 (Lunch last order: 14:30, Kaiseki Cuisine: Last order 20:00, A la carte menu: Last order 20:30, Drink: Last order 21:30) *Lunch last order at 16:00 on Saturdays, Sundays and public holidays **Closed:** Irregular holidays **Price:** Lunch from 5,400 yen, Dinner from 18,000 yen **Access:** 3min. walk from Tokyo Metro Shirokanedai Station Exit 2

MAP P.6 B-4

1. The bite-size "Hanaemi Sushi". Its name means that "you will involuntary smile" at how cute it is
2. Counter seats allow you to feel the seasons

Horse mackerel tartare in the foreground. Offers 40 to 50 different types of Japanese sake at all times

Izakaya 魚 BAR 一歩

Sakana BAR Ippo

Taste Japanese sake and dishes that use fresh fish.

A bar managed by brothers born in Sendai, Miyagi Prefecture. This restaurant's appeal is its dishes prepared with fresh fish and a special selection of Japanese sake set after visiting directly the breweries. The menu changes everyday depending on what ingredients are in stock.

Address: 1-22-10 Ebisu, Shibuya-ku **TEL:** 03-3445-8418 **Opening hours:** 18:00 to following day 3:00 (last oder 2:00) **Closed:** None **Price:** Dinner from 4,000 yen **Access:** 6 min. walk from JR Ebisu Station East Exit

MAP P.7 D-4

*The Wi-Fi requires a password

Yakiniku 旨焼もぐり　天現寺

Umayaki Moguri Tengenji

Taste sizzling roasted pork.

A restaurant specializing in roasted pork where you can eat a rare brand of pork. You can taste fresh pork in a variety of ways. We recommend the "Omakase" course in which you can enjoy small amounts of different kinds of pork.

Address: Saiwai Bldg. 1F, 4-14-3 Minami-Azabu, Minato-ku **TEL:** 03-5789-2929 **Opening hours:** 18:00 to following day 3:00 (last order 2:00), 17:00 to following day 1:00 (last order 24:00) on Saturdays, Sundays and public holidays **Closed:** None **Price:** From 3,500 yen **Access:** 11 min. walk from Tokyo Metro Hiro-o Station Exit 1

MAP P.7 D-4

The "Chateaubriand" is their signature dish. Grilled by professional cooks who have received a training on how to grill meat perfectly

Japanese Food 和味 大輔

Wami Daisuke

A hidden restaurant those who know it love it

A cozy house located in Shirokanedai in which you can find a Japanese restaurant. You can enjoy Japanese food using seasonal ingredients featured in a menu that changes every month. The Japanese sake that goes well with the cuisine is also different every month. If there are some ingredients that you don't like, tell them at the time of reservation and they will fix it for you.

Address:2-6-14 Shirokanedai, Minato-ku **TEL:**03-6408-5055 **Opening hours:**18:00 - 24:00 (Food last order: 23:00, Drink last order: 23:30) **Closed:**Irregular holidays **Price:**From 10,000 yen **Access:**11 min. walk from Tokyo Metro Shirokanedai Station Exit 2

MAP P.6 B-3

*You must contact the restaurant one week in advance for cancellation

1.The "Daisuke Omakase Course" offers a total of 9 dishes including sashimi, fried food, etc. 2.The gorgeous stained-glass windows in the private rooms on the second floor

Apart from Japanese Black Wagyu, there are also sets featuring, among others, vegetables and their famous extra thick udon.

Nabe 牛鍋アイロン

Gyunabe Iron

A wagyu hot pot that enjoyed with thick white miso soup.

Stylish renovation of a house built 80 years ago. You can taste the beef hot pot with its white miso soup in the area on the 2nd floor. There are cherry trees on the site, so we strongly recommend you to visit during spring. The 1st floor is a lounge space.

Address:5-15-10 Shirokanedai, Minato-ku **TEL:**03-5420-4551 **Opening hours:**17:00 - 24:00 (last order 23:00) **Closed:**On Mondays **Price:**From 8,000 yen **Access:** 6 min. walk from Tokyo Metro Shirokanedai Station Exit 1

MAP P.6 A-4

Yakitori 焼とり鶏梵梵

Yakitori Tori Bonbon

A yakitori restaurant often called the best in Ebisu!

For the chicken, this restaurant uses the Tottori Prefecture brand "Daisen-dori", characterized by its good crunchy texture. You can eat savory and juicy yakitori skewers. Famous for its "Chicken Cutlet Curry" topped with a large cutlet served during lunch.

Address:3-15-3 Higashi, Shibuya-ku **TEL:**03-6427-3890 **Opening hours:**11:30 - 15:00 (last order 14:30), 18:00 - 23:00 (Food last order: 22:00, Drink last order: 22:30) **Closed:**On Sundays **Price:**Lunch from 800 yen, Dinner from 3,500 yen **Access:**9 min. walk from JR Ebisu Station West Exit

MAP P.7 C-3

*Smoking allowed only during dinner time

You can enjoy rare parts of the chicken, such as yakitori skewers called "chochin", "Azuki" and others as well

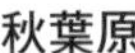

AKIHABARA

Streets lined with Bldg. featuring anime and game characters can only be found in Akihabara

What kind of town?

Akihabara has been known for a long time as one of the major shopping centers for household electronic goods in the world. However, it has now become the epicenter of the "otaku culture", and considered the holy land of Japan's pop culture, including video games, anime, manga, and pop idol groups.

The center of tourist attractions is Chuo-dori, which runs from south to north. Akihabara turns into a "pedestrian paradise" on Sundays and public holidays, crowded with performers and tourists.

In front of Akihabara Station, you can find the "Electric Town" packed with electronic parts and PC-related stores, including large-scale home electronics retailers. The surroundings are dotted with unique shops such as a maid cafés, anime shops, etc.

1. On Sunday afternoon, Chuo-dori becomes a "pedestrian paradise"
2. There are many shops specializing in electronic parts

1. "2k540 AKI-OKA ARTISAN" is located between Akihabara and Okachimachi Stations
2. Crowded with people day and night
3. There are so many cute maids at the popular maid café @home cafe!
4. Dolls you can find at Azone Labelshop located in Akihabara Radio Kaikan

How to enjoy

In Akihabara, you'll want to enjoy the unique subcultures of Tokyo, ranging from maid cafés and cosplay to browsing character figurines.

In addition , it is also fun to shop in spaces created with good taste, such as the "mAAch ecute KANDA MANSEIBASHI", built in an old station building, and the "2k540 AKI-OKA ARTISAN" arcade, which brings together shops of young creators.

A little further is the Ochanomizu district, located on the west side of Akihabara, which is also an interesting place. There, you will want to stroll along and feel the emotions provided by shitamachi, where you can find the Kanda Myojin, known as the guardian deity of Tokyo, and many long-established restaurants open since the Edo period.

1. Many people visit the Kanda Myojin to wish for prosperous business
2. A pop idol theater and concept cafés line the streets in the JR Akihabara Station Electric Town Exit area

Must-visit tourist spots

Sightseeing

Akiba Kart →P.146

「Owl nomori」 Akihabara Forest of Owl →P.147

mAAch ecute KANDA MANSEIBASHI →P.148

Gourmet

Curry no Shimin Alba Akihabara Flagship →P.154

Roast Beef Ohno →P.154

Gohan-dokoro Adachi →P.155

Shopping

LIBRARY →P.149

Akihabara Gachapon Kaikan →P.150

2k540 AKI-OKA ARTISAN →P.152

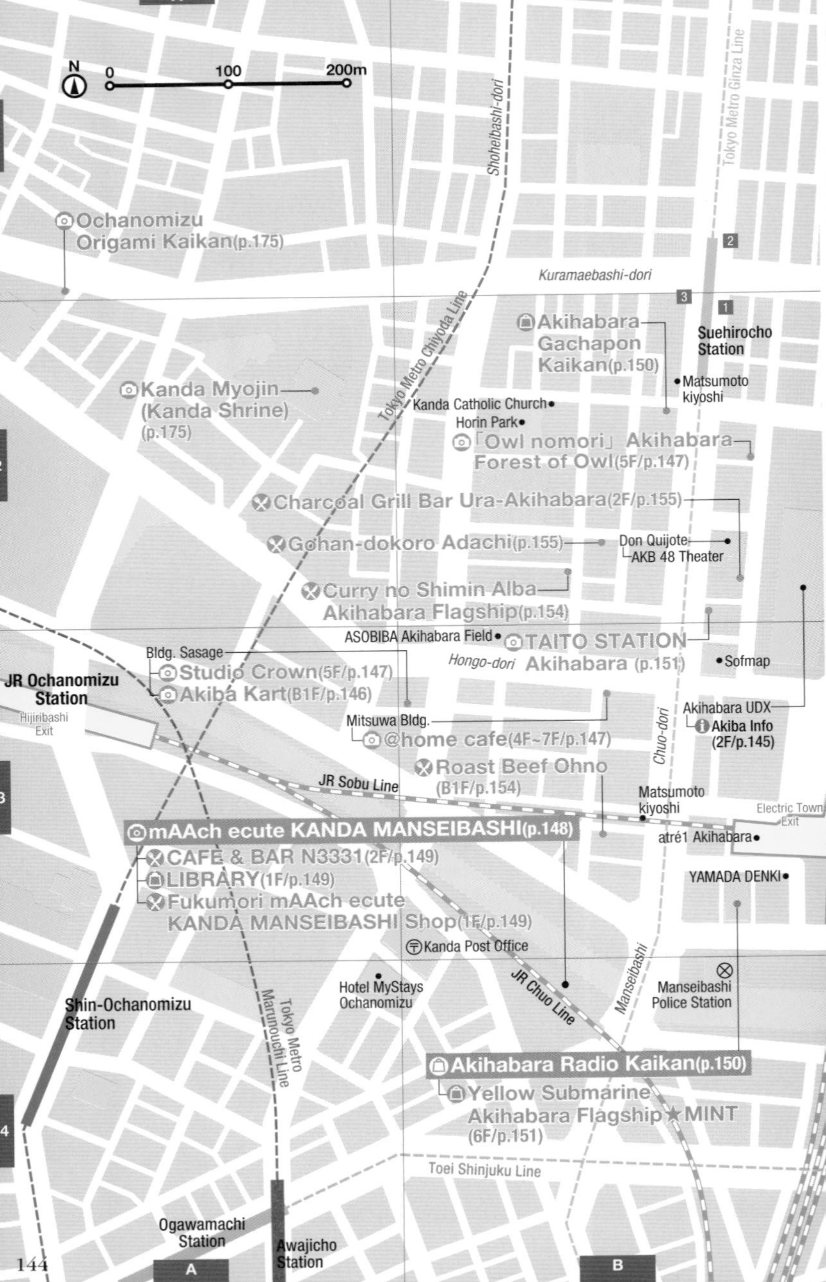
A
B
N
0
100
200m
Ochanomizu Origami Kaikan(p.175)
Shoheibashi-dori
Tokyo Metro Ginza Line
Kuramaebashi-dori
Akihabara Gachapon Kaikan(p.150)
Suehirocho Station
Matsumoto kiyoshi
Tokyo Metro Chiyoda Line
Kanda Myojin (Kanda Shrine) (p.175)
Kanda Catholic Church
Horin Park
「Owl nomori」 Akihabara Forest of Owl(5F/p.147)
Charcoal Grill Bar Ura-Akihabara(2F/p.155)
Gohan-dokoro Adachi(p.155)
Don Quijote
AKB 48 Theater
Curry no Shimin Alba Akihabara Flagship(p.154)
ASOBIBA Akihabara Field
TAITO STATION Akihabara (p.151)
Hongo-dori
Sofmap
Bldg. Sasage
Studio Crown(5F/p.147)
Akiba Kart(B1F/p.146)
JR Ochanomizu Station
Hijiribashi Exit
Mitsuwa Bldg.
@home cafe(4F~7F/p.147)
Chuo-dori
Akihabara UDX
Akiba Info (2F/p.145)
Roast Beef Ohno (B1F/p.154)
JR Sobu Line
Matsumoto kiyoshi
Electric Town Exit
atré1 Akihabara
mAAch ecute KANDA MANSEIBASHI(p.148)
CAFE & BAR N3331(2F/p.149)
LIBRARY(1F/p.149)
Fukumori mAAch ecute KANDA MANSEIBASHI Shop(1F/p.149)
YAMADA DENKI
Kanda Post Office
Hotel MyStays Ochanomizu
JR Chuo Line
Manseibashi
Manseibashi Police Station
Shin-Ochanomizu Station
Tokyo Metro Marunouchi Line
Akihabara Radio Kaikan(p.150)
Yellow Submarine Akihabara Flagship★MINT (6F/p.151)
Toei Shinjuku Line
Ogawamachi Station
Awajicho Station
1
2
3
4

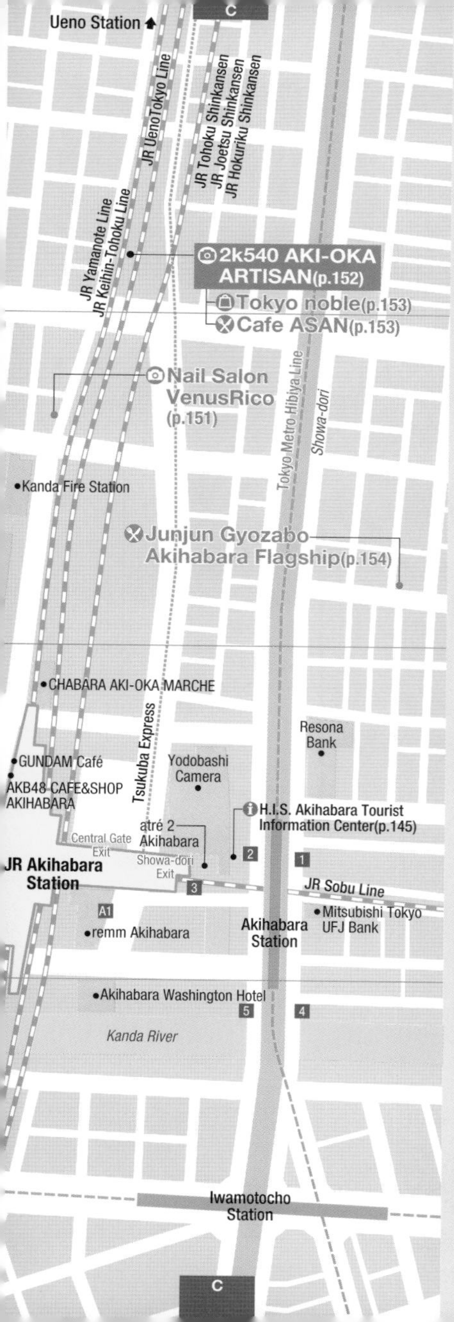

C
Ueno Station
JR UenoTokyo Line
JR Tohoku Shinkansen
JR Joetsu Shinkansen
JR Hokuriku Shinkansen
JR Yamanote Line
JR Keihin-Tohoku Line
2k540 AKI-OKA ARTISAN(p.152)
Tokyo noble(p.153)
Cafe ASAN(p.153)
Nail Salon VenusRico (p.151)
Tokyo Metro Hibiya Line
Showa-dori
Kanda Fire Station
Junjun Gyozabo Akihabara Flagship(p.154)
CHABARA AKI-OKA MARCHE
Tsukuba Express
Resona Bank
GUNDAM Café
Yodobashi Camera
AKB48 CAFE&SHOP AKIHABARA
H.I.S. Akihabara Tourist Information Center(p.145)
atré 2 Akihabara
Central Gate Exit
Showa-dori Exit
JR Akihabara Station
2
1
3
JR Sobu Line
A1
Mitsubishi Tokyo UFJ Bank
remm Akihabara
Akihabara Station
Akihabara Washington Hotel
5
4
Kanda River
Iwamotocho Station
C

Access from airports

Narita Airport Terminal 2·3	Haneda Airport International Terminal
Keisei Line (Skyliner)	*Keikyu Line*
Nippori	Shinagawa
Yamanote Line outer loop	*Yamanote Line inner loop*
Akihabara	Akihabara
¥ *1400~2630yen*	¥ *580yen*
60min	*40min*

Lines

[**JR**]

Yamanote Line
Keihin-Tohoku Line
Sobu Line
Utsunomiya Line / Takasaki Line / Joban line (Ueno Tokyo Line)

[**Tokyo Metro**]

Hibiya Line

[**Private railway**]

Tsukuba Express

Tourist information centers

Akiba Info

アキバ·インフォ

Computers are set up so you can find tourist information on your own. Free Wi-Fi can also be used if you show your passport.

Address: Akihabara UDX 2F, 4-14-1 Soto-Kanda, Chiyoda-ku
TEL: 080-3413-4800
Opening hours: 11:00-17:30
Closed: Mondays and Thursdays *Open if on public holidays, and closed the following day
Access: 3 min. walk from JR Akihabara Station Electric Town Exit

HP

MAP P.144 B-2

i
Information
TOKYO OFFICIAL SHOP AKIBA

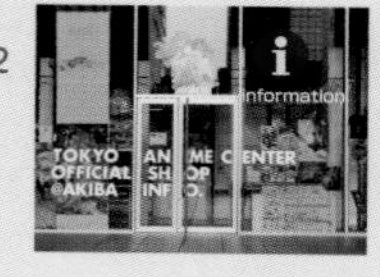

◆ Other tourist information centers

H.I.S. Akihabara Tourist Information Center

H.I.S. 秋葉原ツーリストインフォメーションセンター

MAP P.145 C-3

1.You can also rent costumes for free. Sells only secondhand game character costumes
2.Maximum speed is 60 km/h. You'll get lots of attention from passers-by, so you will feel like a star!
3.You have to fill the tank up before you return the kart if you ride it for more than an hour

Go-Kart アキバカート

Akiba Kart

Ride around Tokyo on rental karts!

This activity, in which you can ride through the streets of Tokyo on rental karts dressed up in a costume of your choice is now a hot topic in Japan. Anyone having an International Drivers Permit and a copy of their passport can try it!

Address: Bldg. Sasage B1F, 2-4-6 Soto-Kanda, Chiyoda-ku
TEL:03-6206-4752 **Opening hours:**10:00-20:00
Closed: Irregular holidays **Fee:**From 2,700 yen
Access:8 min. walk from JR Akihabara Station Electric Town Exit

HP MAP P.144 B-3

For Tourists

There is also a course with an add-on for a driver riding a kart and guiding you through Tokyo's famous tourist attractions. You can enjoy tourism and driving as well.

Maid Café @ほぉ〜むカフェ

@home cafe

Experience Japanese "Moe" culture

Cute maids serve you at this café filled with a playful atmosphere. Besides the dishes made with love from the maids, there are also other services, such as taking pictures with maids or playing games with them.

Address: Mitsuwa Bldg. 4F to 7F, 1-11-4 Soto-Kanda, Chiyoda-ku **TEL:**03-5207-9779 **Opening hours:**11:30-22:00 (food last order 20:50, drink last order 21:20), 10:30-22:00 on Saturdays, Sundays and public holidays (last order 20:50) **Closed:**None **Price:**From 2,000 yen **Access:**5 min. walk from JR Akihabara Station Electric Town Exit

MAP P.144 B-3

You can enjoy cute poses and chants according to the food menu

For Tourists

The "Moe Moe Janken Taikai" in which everybody is taking part to challenge and play rock-paper-scissors with the maids is the most exciting part!

Change into your favorite character with the perfect cosplay experience

For Tourists

Enjoy extraordinary feelings by experiencing the professional make up performed by active cosplayers, and cosplay allowing everyone to become a different person.

Cosplay Studio スタジオクラウン

Studio Crown

Dress up in "Cosplay" and take a commemorative photo

A studio where you can easily take professional level cosplay photos. Divided into 3 booths: "white", "modern and gothic" and "futuristic", you can enjoy your photo shoot based on your concept.

Address: Bldg. Sasage East 5F B block, 2-4-6 Soto-Kanda, Chiyoda-ku **TEL:**03-5577-5995 **Opening hours:**10:00-22:00 **Closed:**Irregular holidays **Fee:**From 4,000 yen **Access:**8 min. walk from JR Akihabara Station Electric Town Exit

MAP P.144 B-3

Animal Café アウルの森 秋葉原本店

「Owl nomori」 Akihabara Forest of Owl

Relax with cute owls

A café with an interior decoration that looks just like a forest where you get to pet owls big and small. These owls, which are used to people, will perch on your arm and shoulder.

Address: Matsukou Shoji Bldg. 5F, 4-5-8 Soto-Kanda, Chiyoda-ku **TEL:**03-3254-6366 **Opening hours:**12:00-22:00, 16:00-22:00 on Wednesdays, 12:00-23:00 on Saturdays, Sundays and public holidays **Closed:**None **Fee:**From 890 yen **Access:** 8 min. walk from JR Akihabara Station Electric Town Exit

MAP P.144 B-2

Please ask the staff if you want to perch the owls on your hand and shoulder

For Tourists

Home of largest number of owls in Tokyo metropolitan area. You can also have an encounter with the world's smallest owl.

1. The open deck overlooking the gently flowing Kanda River is perfect for a walk. 2.A café deck with a fine view where you can see trains coming and going on the JR Chuo Line
3.The stairway that was actually used, built in 1912 at the time of the station opening

Commercial Complex マーチエキュート神田万世橋

mAAch ecute KANDA MANSEIBASHI

A retro and stylish viaduct space

The old Manseibashi Station has been renovated into a stylish space. Housing a handful of shops with good taste such as general stores, restaurants, etc, it is full of attractions, including the stairways, which were previously used to access the train platform, and an observation deck where you can see trains coming and going!

Address:1-25-4 Kandasudacho, Chiyoda-ku **TEL:**03-3257-8910 (main phone reception hours: 9:30-18:00) **Opening hours:**Goods sales: 11:00-21:00, 11:00-20:00 on Sundays and public holidays. Restaurants: 11:00-23:00, 11:00-21:00 on Sundays and public holidays *Some shops may differ **Closed:**Irregular holidays **Access:**6 min. walk from JR Akihabara Station Electric Town Exit

HP MAP P.144 B-4

For Tourists

The red brick viaduct and the remains of the old Manseibashi Station are a great photo spots. Turning into a romantic atmosphere at night.

Café & Bar CAFE &和酒 N3331

CAFE & BAR N3331

An old train platform transformed into a café

A café & bar using the remains of a station platform. Based on the philosophy of "spreading Japanese sake to the world", it offers a rich variety of local sake. The Café menu is also recommended.

Address:mAAch ecute KANDA MANSEIBASHI 2F **TEL:**03-5295-2788 **Opening hours:**11:00-23:00 (food last order 22:00, drink last order 22:30), 11:00-21:00 on Sundays and public holidays (food last order 20:00, drink last order 20:30)
Closed: Irregular holidays **Price:**Lunch from 1,300 yen, Dinner from 3,000 yen

HP MAP P.144 B-4

The "Hakkaisan Draft Beer" is a noble draft beer produced in a Japanese sake brewery

For Tourists
An unusual location for you can see trains coming and going by a short distance.

The diorama showing Manseibashi Station surroundings 100 years ago will make you feel the bustle of those days

For Tourists
Offers books conveying the charms of walking around Tokyo, as well as Tokyo brand products, original goods, etc.

Gallery and Miscellaneous Goods LIBRARY

LIBRARY

Be moved by the elaborate Manseibashi Station diorama

A gallery and shop that passes the historical background of the Manseibashi Station surroundings down to the present day. A 1/150 scale model reproducing the appearance of the old Manseibashi Station is on display.

Address:mAAch ecute KANDA MANSEIBASHI 1F
TEL:03-3257-8910 **Opening hours:**11:00-21:00, 11:00-20:00 on Sundays and public holidays
Closed: Irregular holidays

HP MAP P.144 B-4

Café & Restaurant フクモリ マーチエキュート神田万世橋店

Fukumori mAAch ecute KANDA MANSEIBASHI Shop

Enjoy the gastronomy of Yamagata

A café and restaurant serving regional cuisine using ingredients produced in Yamagata Prefecture. With cooking methods learned from long-established ryokan (inns) located in Yamagata, it passes on the delicious taste of local ingredients.

Address:mAAch ecute KANDA MANSEIBASHI 1F **TEL:**03-6206-8381
Opening hours:11:00-23:00 (food last order 22:00, drink last order 22:30), 11:00-21:00 on Sundays and public holidays (food last order 20:00, drink last order 20:30) **Closed:**Irregular holidays
Price: Lunch from 1,000 yen, Dinner from 3,000 yen

HP MAP P.144 B-4

Set meal using seasonal fish. You can get the taste of Yamagata while in Tokyo

For Tourists
The shop placed right next to the café is selling folkcraft goods and groceries from the Tohoku region including from Yamagata.

Commercial Complex 秋葉原ラジオ会館

Akihabara Radio Kaikan

Bringing together Japanese sub-cultures!

A complex with a famous neon sign on its building. There's a lineup of various shops mainly related to comics, anime and games, and even stores selling audio equipment and security goods for professionals.

Address:1-15-16 Soto-Kanda, Chiyoda-ku
TEL:03-5807-7787
Opening hours:10:00-20:00 *Some shops may differ
Closed: Irregular holidays
Access: Immediate access from JR Akihabara Station Electric Town Exit

MAP P.144 B-3

1. Continues to diffuse subculture with figurines, trading cards, etc.
2. Contains 31 shops from B1F to 10F. There are many "maniac-level" specialized shops

For Tourists
At the "AZONE Labelshop" specialized in dolls on 7F, you can find parts to customize your favorite doll.

1. Offers a rich variety, from popular anime series up to unique lucky charms
2. The very popular series "Cup no Fuchiko-san", which you can put on the edge of a cup

For Tourists
The "Gacha-Gacha" is a machine selling different type of capsule toys. You can enjoy a feeling of excitement as you don't know what is going to come out of it.

Gacha-Gacha 秋葉原ガチャポン会館

Akihabara Gachapon Kaikan

Find your favorite "Gacha-Gacha"

Japan's largest shop specialized in "Gacha-Gacha" capsule toys, with around 500 "Gacha-Gacha" machines lined up. New fun is always waiting, since the machines are changed every 2 to 3 weeks. Antique-style machines are also popular.

Address:3-15-5 Soto-Kanda, Chiyoda-ku
TEL:03-5209-6020 **Opening hours:**11:00-20:00, 11:00-22:00 on Fridays and Saturdays, 11:00-19:00 on Sundays and public holidays **Closed:**None **Access:**9 min. walk from JR Akihabara Station Electric Town Exit

MAP P.144 B-2

Miscellaneous Goods イエローサブマリン秋葉原本店★ミント

Yellow Submarine Akihabara Flagship ★MINT

Enthralling for both adults and children!

More than 10,000 hobby-related items are available in the shop, including fighting cards, plastic models, board games, Gacha-Gacha, and more. Also offers coveted rare items for maniacs.

Address: Akihabara Radio Kaikan 6F, 1-15-16 Soto-Kanda, Chiyoda-ku **TEL:**03-3526-3828 **Opening hours:**10:00-20:00 **Closed:**Irregular holidays
Access: Immediate access from JR Akihabara Station Electric Town Exit

MAP P.144 B-3

Plastic models have become popular with the anime "Mobile Suit Gundam"

For Tourists
It is also the only place in the world to sell Gundam plastic models by parts

If you bring a copy of the picture you want them to draw, they will design it in the exact same way

For Tourists
Overseas customers can have polite counselling as well with the use of the sheet in English.

Nail Salon Nail Salon VenusRico

Nail Salon VenusRico

Nails decorated with your favorite characters are now a reality

Nails decorated with anime characters and logos are becoming a hot topic. Known for reproducing the finest details by hand and for its high-quality.

Address: Akihabara ST Bldg. 1F, 4-13-6 Soto-Kanda, Chiyoda-ku **TEL:**03-3257-5223
Opening hours:10:00-20:00 **Closed:**None **Fee:**From 5,500 yen **Access:**7 min. walk from JR Akihabara Station Electric Town Exit

MAP P.145 C-2

Game Center タイトーステーション 秋葉原店

TAITO STATION Akihabara

An exciting entertainment facility

Proposing an assortment of the latest game machines, including crane games, virtual games, etc. They've also installed the "Choi KARA" machine, in which you can easily enjoy karaoke for 100 yen a song.

Address: Takami Bldg. 1F, 4-2-2 Soto-Kanda, Chiyoda-ku
TEL:03-5289-8445 **Opening hours:**10:00-24:00
Closed: None **Access:**5 min. walk from JR Akihabara Station Electric Town Exit

MAP P.144 B-2

Many of the prizes you can get from crane games are also of high-quality

For Tourists
The "Purikura (photo booth) Corner" as well is complete. Take a couple picture to commemorate the journey.

1

2

3

1. Some shops hold events, workshops, etc.
2. The facility's name comes from a railway term which means "located at distance of about 2.540km from Tokyo Station" 3. The famous "Nijiyura", produced with Chusen traditional dyeing methods, are perfect for a souvenir

Commercial Facility 2k540 AKI-OKA ARTISAN

2k540 AKI-OKA ARTISAN

An atelier space that has appeared under a girder bridge of a railway

An entire corner of an underpass has been dramatically transformed to become a "manufacturing district"! Around 50 shops, including traditional craft shops, ateliers, cafés and more, based on the concept of manufacturing coming together into a white space.

Address:5-9-23 Ueno, Taito-ku **TEL:**None **Opening hours:** 11:00-19:00 *some shops may differ **Closed:**Wednesdays (open if public holiday) *some shops may differ **Access:**3 min. walk from Tokyo Metro Suehirocho Station Exit 2

HP MAP P.145 C-1

*Some shops do not accept credit cards

For Tourists

Many shops pass down Japanese culture and craft techniques to modern days, and you can get items that let you feel tradition and history despite their classy appearance.

Umbrella Tokyo noble

Tokyo noble

You can create your own original umbrella

A shop specializing in umbrellas, with a special commitment to quality and design. In the shop, they have an array colorful umbrellas handmade at the in-house workshop. You should definitely try it for its popular customized umbrellas that can be created in 30 minutes as well.

Address:2k540 N-3, 5-9-19 Ueno, Taito-ku
TEL:03-6803-2414
Opening hours:11:00-19:00
Closed: Wednesdays *open if public holiday
Access:3 min. walk from Tokyo Metro Suehirocho Station Exit 2

MAP P.145 C-1

1. It is possible to adjust the length of the handle, so you can buy an umbrella that fits your stature 2. Lift your spirits even on rainy days with a pop yellow design!

For Tourists

The umbrella is an art work which brings together the craftsmanship of different persons, including the handle craftsmen, sewing craftsmen, coating craftsmen, etc.

1. There are 6 popular hammock seats. Relax at your leisure in a hammock 2. The "Kurumi (walnut) Custard Caramel" has a fun texture

For Tourists

You can of course use Wi-Fi and chargers, and since iPads have been set up as well, it's the perfect spot for a break and to gather information during sightseeing.

Café Cafe ASAN

Cafe ASAN

Café time while swinging in a hammock

A café famous for its thick fluffy pancakes. There are hammocks in the shop, and you can also read manga, allowing you to relax as you enjoy the freshly cooked pancakes.

Address:2k540 F-2, 5-9-9 Ueno, Taito-ku
TEL:03-6803-0502
Opening hours:11:30-19:00 (food last order 18:00, drink last order 18:30)
Closed: Wednesdays
Price: From 1,000 yen
Access:3 min. walk from Tokyo Metro Suehirocho Station Exit 2

MAP P.145 C-1

Curry カレーの市民アルバ 秋葉原本店

Curry no Shimin Alba Akihabara Flagship

An exquisite curry blending the flavors of meat and vegetables

The Akihabara branch of a curry restaurant loved for more than 45 years, with its main shop in Kanazawa, Ishikawa Prefecture. The secret curry roux recipe in which beef and onions stewed for hours has body and deep taste.

Address:3-2-9 Soto-Kanda, Chiyoda-ku **TEL:**03-3254-5686 **Opening hours:**11:00-21:30 (last order 21:00) **Closed:**None **Price:**From 800 yen **Access:**8 min. walk from JR Akihabara Station Electric Town Exit

MAP P.144 B-2

The "Home Run Curry" with its eye-catching sumptuous toppings

For Tourists

Pre-packaged curry is available for takeaway in front of the register. You can enjoy the taste of Alba after going back home as well.

The Wagyu Roast Beef uses Japanese Black beef produced in Japan

For Tourists

Although roast beef is delicious just the way it is, you can also have fun changing its taste by adding condiments such as wasabi, cream or rock salt.

Roast Beef ローストビーフ大野

Roast Beef Ohno

The roast beef tower is splendid

A shop specializing in roast beef rice bowls. The roast beef beautifully piled up by hand is tender and has a light taste. Enjoy it mixed with poached eggs.

Address: Tsuchiya Bldg. B1F, 1-2-3 Soto-Kanda, Chiyoda-ku **TEL:**03-3254-7355 **Opening hours:**11:00-23:00 (last order 22:00), 11:00-21:00 on Sundays and public holidays **Closed:**Irregular holidays **Price:**From 1,080 yen **Access:**5 min. walk from JR Akihabara Station Electric Town Exit

MAP P.144 B-3

Dumpling 順順餃子房　秋葉原本店

Junjun Gyozabo Akihabara Flagship

Authentic dumplings bursting with flavor

Their juicy dumplings combined with homemade chicken soup are popular. Besides their classic dumplings, they offer a rich variety of dumplings using shrimp, natto (fermented soybeans), shark fin, and more.

Address: Akisu Bldg. 1F, 1-7-2 Taito, Taito-ku **TEL:**03-5688-9888 **Opening hours:**11:00-23:00 (last order 22:30) **Closed:**None **Price:**Lunch from 500 yen, Dinner from 2,000 yen **Access:**8 min. walk from JR Akihabara Station Showa-dori Exit

MAP P.145 C-2

All dumplings are handmade. When you break into the dough, you can feel the homemade soup and gravy spreading in your mouth

For Tourists

The all-you-can-eat course of dishes including dumplings, and all-you-can-drink course featuring alcoholic beverages such as Japanese sake and shochu are appealing.

Set Meal Restaurant ごはん処あだち

Gohan-dokoro Adachi

An appealing menu offering generous volume

A restaurant visited by students and local business people. Every item on the menu offers large servings, and the serving of rice is so big it comes served in a chest. Come here after making yourself hungry.

Address:3-11-6 Soto-Kanda, Chiyoda-ku
TEL:03-3253-3017 **Opening hours:**11:30-14:30, 17:30-20:30 **Closed:**festival days **Price:**From 980 yen
Access:7 min. walk from JR Akihabara Station Electric Town Exit

MAP P.144 B-2

Offers outstanding cost-performance, the "Adachi Service Set" includes a large piece of deep-fried chicken

For Tourists

The "Adachi Service Set" deep-fried chicken has a strong curry taste. Also reputed for garnish such as Japanese rolled omelet.

Ramen らーめん 福籠

Ramen Fukurou

Many people are fans of its rich miso flavor!

A chef who mastered his art for more than 10 years working at the famous restaurant "Sumire" located in Sapporo, Hokkaido, has opened a shop in Tokyo. The thick soup inherited from "Sumire" is quite addictive.

Address: Niwa Bldg. 1F, 1-13-4 Yanagibashi, Taito-ku
TEL:03-5829-6358 **Opening hours:**11:00-15:00 (last order 14:30), 18:00-22:00 (last order 21:30) **Closed:**Sundays, and some temporary closures **Price:**From 720 yen **Access:**1 min. walk from Toei Subway Asakusabashi Station Exit A1

MAP P.7 C-2

"Miso Ramen". The sweetness of sautéed vegetables penetrates the soup

For Tourists

For the noodles, special "Asakusa Kaikarou" curled noodles are used. There are many fans of their sticky texture.

Izakaya 炭グリルバー 裏秋葉原

Charcoal Grill Bar Ura-Akihabara

Gives you a taste of yakitori in a casual way

A new type of izakaya where you taste yakitori with wine. Reputed of course for its yakitori, this shop is also known for the creative cuisine prepared by a chef who accumulated experience in restaurants of various genres.

Address: Kurihara Bldg. 2F, 4-3-11 Soto-Kanda, Chiyoda-ku **TEL:**03-3526-3556 **Opening hours:**11:30-15:00 (last order 14:00), 18:00-23:00 (last order 22:00) **Closed:**Saturdays, Sundays, and public holidays **Price:**Lunch from 900 yen, Dinner from 3,000 yen **Access:**5 min. walk from JR Akihabara Station Electric Town Exit

MAP P.144 B-2

Yakitori skewers from 190 yen/1pc. Also offers full-fledged desserts

For Tourists

A good-value set menu including yakitori skewers, a drink and more is available.

*Service charge: 500 yen. Credit cards not accepted during lunch

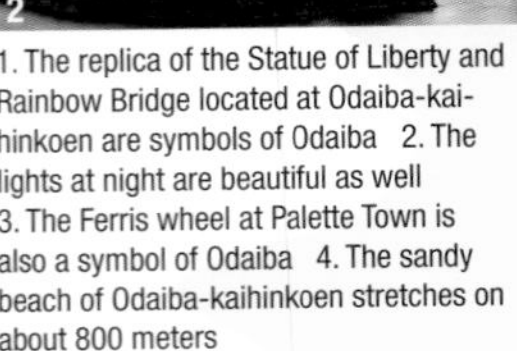

2

1. The replica of the Statue of Liberty and Rainbow Bridge located at Odaiba-kai-hinkoen are symbols of Odaiba 2. The lights at night are beautiful as well 3. The Ferris wheel at Palette Town is also a symbol of Odaiba 4. The sandy beach of Odaiba-kaihinkoen stretches on about 800 meters

4

Venture a little further! 2

Odaiba

3

Odaiba is a sightseeing destination opened on the waterfront. You can experience everything, including amusement, shopping, and gourmet food. The large scale commercial complexes: DECKS Tokyo Beach, DiverCity Tokyo Plaza, and Palette Town offer all of these.

Since it is surrounded by the sea on all sides, you can also take a cruise on a ship. We recommend the "TOKYO CRUISE" operated by Odaiba Line. You can also enjoy the night view with Rainbow Bridge and the skyscrapers lit up at night.

After fully enjoying sightseeing, ease your fatigue at the ODAIBA TOKYO OOEDO-ONSEN MONOGATARI. Odaiba is an entertainment town where you can have fun all day.

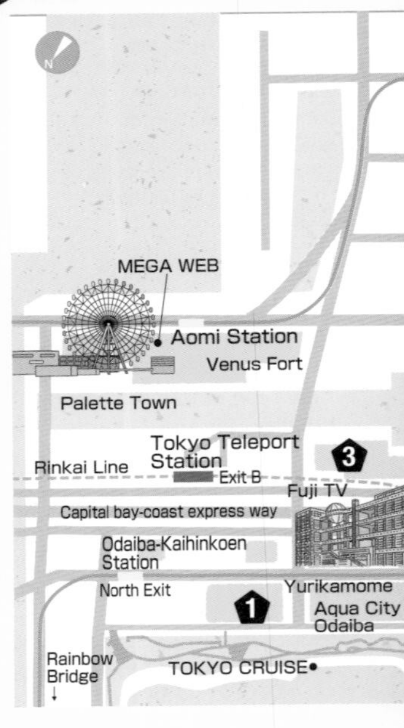

| Spots to visit |

デックス東京ビーチ

DECKS Tokyo Beach

Full of entertainment facilities

A shopping mall complex that features six different entertainment zones where you can have fun. There is also a food court where you'll find a number of takoyaki shops, so you can enjoy dining and shopping. There are illuminations all year round.

Address:1-6-1 Daiba, Minato-ku
TEL:03-3599-6500
Opening hours: 11:00-21:00. Restaurants: 11:00-23:00. *Some shops may differ
Closed: Irregular holidays **Access:**3 min. walk from Yurikamome Odaiba-Kaihinkoen Station North Exit

*There are four smoking areas within the facility

東京ジョイポリス

TOKYO JOYPOLIS

1. Japan's largest indoor amusement park
2. The "Halfpipe Tokyo" a realistic digital attraction that can be played in pairs

マダム・タッソー東京

Madame Tussauds TOKYO

1. Strike a pose with Michael Jackson and take a picture 2. Among the more than 60 figures, you can find the figure of your favorite star

Miraikan - The National Museum of Emerging Science and Innovation 日本科学未来館

Experience state-of-the-art sciences

A science museum where you can experience Japan's advanced technologies, such as the globe-like display "Geo-Cosmos", robots, and more. All of the exhibits have English descriptions, and part of the narration and audio guidance is also in English.

Address: 2-3-6 Aomi, Koto-ku **TEL:**03-3570-9151 (Main)
Opening hours: 10:00-17:00 (last admission 30 minutes before closing time) **Closed:**Tuesdays (open if on public holidays). May sometimes be temporarily closed **Fee:**620 yen **Access:**6 min. walk from Yurikamome Telecom Center Station North Exit

The humanoid robot "ASIMO"

© Miraikan

ダイバーシティ東京 プラザ

DiverCity Tokyo Plaza

Odaiba's iconic commercial complex

Offering plenty of gourmet food, with its food court featuring an order-taking system specially for foreign tourists and a rooftop BBQ space "Tokai no Noen" (that can be used from April to November).

Address: 1-1-10 Aomi, Koto-ku **TEL:**03-6380-7800 **Opening hours:** 10:00-21:00. Food Court: 10:00-22:00. Restaurants: 11:00-23:00 *Some shops may differ
Closed: Irregular holidays **Access:**5 min. walk from Rinkai Line Tokyo Teleport Station Exit B

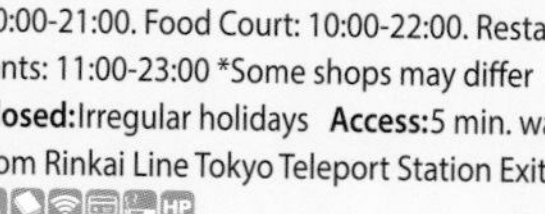

*Smoking rooms available on each floor from 2F to 6F

ODAIBA TOKYO OOEDO-ONSEN MONOGATARI(P.177)
South Exit
North Exit
Telecom Center Station
Yurikamome Line
Fune-no-kagakukan Station
Fune-no-kagakukan
Daiba Station
The Statue of Liberty

"TV and movies. Going beyond that framework, I could express myself more freely"

Artist, NAKED Inc. CEO

Ryotaro Muramatsu

Hear about the secrets of creation and the charms of Tokyo from a creator of avant-garde art representing Tokyo.

Profile

Ryotaro Muramatsu

A creator who has played an active part in TV, advertising, music video, and more, regardless of genre. He has been nominated for a total of 48 awards in international film festivals for his feature-length and short films. His major works include the Tokyo Station 3D projection mapping "TOKYO HIKARI VISION". Recently, he is working not only on video but on a restaurant (9STORIES **URL**: www.nine-stories.jp) and the production of entire spaces.

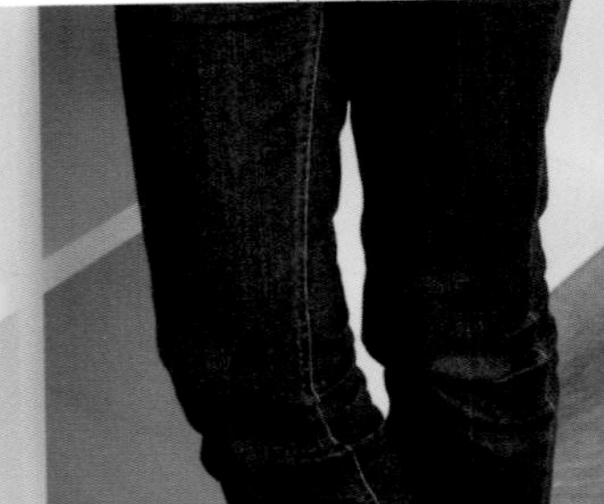

What form of expression is projection mapping?

Projection mapping is an art in which video and sound break free from the screen or the TV frame and are projected on the surface of buildings and structures. When you walk around the streets and see a building that was always familiar to you suddenly start to shine, it stops you in your tracks and you can't take your eyes away. And once the short projection is over, you go back to your day-to-day life just like nothing happened. I thought that it would be nice to have people watching experience an illusion that makes them think, "Was I dreaming?"

Projection mapping is produced by mixing expression from different fields such as design, narrative, digital technology, and music, and when these different things are mixed together, it creates something very powerful. Using that power, you can go beyond the existing framework of entertainment and create a new form of expression, which is the essence of projection mapping.

I was moved by the "TOKYO HIKARI VISION" in 2012

"TOKYO HIKARI VISION" is my first performance of projection mapping. I projected images using the entire red brick structure of Tokyo Station, and changed the station into a train or made goldfish swim on it. Although Tokyo Station is a symbolic building with a long history, I had a lot of fun without feeling restrained by that aspect.

Originally, I performed as an actor and movie director, but after finishing the recording of my 4th film, I felt I was at an impasse. In addition to the fact that nowadays in Japan there are no movies having magnificent and profound themes like what you can find in the "Godfather", which is a movie that I like, the format of Japanese movies has now turned into a kind of routine, so it seemed impossible for me to really create the movies I wanted to. I was lucky to receive the request for the unknown and undeveloped "TOKYO HIKARI VISION" right when I was worrying about how I could express myself more freely.

"TOKYO HIKARI VISION" projected splendid images on Tokyo Station. 230,000 people came to see the projection over 3 days at the end of December 2012, in the cheery year-end atmosphere.

Tokyo Michiterasu 2012 / TOKYO HIKARI VISION
Organizer: Tokyo Michiterasu 2012 Executive Committee

Projection mapping using the full scale Gundam statue (height of about 18m) standing in Odaiba.* With electricity running through its armor, it just looks like it is about to move.

TOKYO Gundam Project 2014 Gundam Projection Mapping "Industrial Revolution"-to the future- Organizer: TOKYO Gundam Project 2014 Executive Committee © SOTSU Sunrise

*Scheduled to be removed in March 2017

How about the work projecting the "Rakuchu Rakugai-zu"(scenes inside and around Kyoto) performed at the Tokyo National Museum?

It was a work I learned a lot from. "Rakuchu Rakugai-zu" is a huge folding screen picture of a Japanese painting made during the Edo era depicting the customs in Kyoto at that time. Peeking into the town from behind the golden clouds are over 1,000 people of the capital. When you look at this gorgeous folding screen, which could be considered unconventional, you can see how the painters of the Edo era had an avant-garde mind indeed. I also inherited this mind, and by trying to fuse tradition and innovation, I created a video in which the people in the folding screen are running around the walls of the museum freely.

Muramatsu "Since I want people to watch and feel it naturally, and to follow their intuitions, so when I work on a projection, I try as much as possible to not give any explanation in advance."

The projection mapping "SAGA Night of Light by NAKED" at the Saga Prefectural Government Observation hall. It fused the Saga Castle and other structures with the night view.
"Art After Dark" in SAGA SAGA Night of Light by NAKED
Organizer: Saga Prefecture

Please tell us what you feel when you come in contact with traditional Japanese forms of expression.

Tradition conjures the image of "ancient values" and "immutable beauty" but that is not always necessarily correct.

Once, when I met a person who does Kyo Yuzen dyeing, Living National Treasure, I was told that "tradition always takes in new things and keeps on living throughout the ages because it continues to innovate". A way of creating something new by mixing what exists with something different, that's exactly what I do. And this is how the energy contained in new creations can easily go beyond conservative thinking.

For example, I used projection mapping to make flowers bloom on the huge Gundam object in Odaiba. Gundam is very popular, and a performance offering something quite different from the original animation can sometimes be a double-edged sword. However, after trying the projection, it was a success, and in the end my concerns were unfounded.

Recently I am also working on spatial production using flower arrangement, but in the future I would like to work more and more on collaborations with worlds I don't know yet.

If you had to guide a foreign friend in a place in Tokyo that you personally love, where would you go?

If I had to name just one place I like in Tokyo, I would say the Park Hyatt Tokyo. The wide open reception area on the 41st floor and the three-dimensional structure going from there up to the restaurant "Girandole" are very sophisticated and puts you in a very good mood. You don't need to be on your guard because it's too classy. Since this hotel has a mysterious resort-like atmosphere that doesn't feel overeager to guests, it is perfect for curing fatigue from a long journey.

Apart from that, I recommend Meiji Shrine. The contrast of this broad forest of lush greenery wedged between Harajuku, the center of the "kawaii" culture, and the insipid buildings of Shinjuku, is very interesting. And I cannot explain why, but when I walk in the forest of Meiji Shrine, I get the impression that I am in nature while being in Tokyo. It is certainly a special place where you can feel the forest as a concept.

Seeing it from your own eyes, into what kind of city Tokyo is reflected?

Tokyo is a funny town. This city separates the facts and true meaning from all things, prising only the superficial. It's something like the incarnation of fashion, an inevitable plastic feeling, creating a kind of pop. However, this doesn't mean that it is cold, there is the warmth of diversity, as it brings together the people and things of Japan, and all the people working in shops bow politely, and the level of hospitality is high. I think that with these contradictory features mixed together, Tokyo has become a curious and charming city.

Recommended by Mr. Muramatsu! ***Tokyo's Best Spots***

Park Hyatt Tokyo
A luxury hotel situated in Nishi-Shinjuku, referred to as an urban oasis by Mr. Muramatsu. All colors have been coordinated with green, healing you with a unique calmness that cannot be found anywhere else.

Meiji Jingu Shrine
A Shinto shrine dedicated to the Emperor Meiji and Empress Shoken. About 90 years ago, it was a wild land filled with bushes and swamps, but trees planted by the hands of people grew, and it has now become a vast forest. →**P.104**

Venus Fort
An enclosed-type shopping mall located in Odaiba. It has everything, including brand shops, bookstores and restaurants. Mr. Muramatsu and his team worked on the arch-shaped ceiling decoration.

AREA 9

池袋

IKEBUKURO

The East side, where you can find major department stores, shopping buildings, and the popular commercial area Sunshine 60 dori

What kind of town?

Ikebukuro is an area filled with recreational places, from amusement parks and department stores to entertainment halls where you can watch Rakugo (traditional comic storytelling), and more.

Ikebukuro Station is divided between East and West Exit. On the West Exit are the "Tokyo Metropolitan Theatre", the "Ikebukuro Engeijo", and other spots giving to the area an air of culture. There are also shopping centers and stores where you can enjoy shopping.

On the opposite side, the East Exit is centered on the huge entertainment spot "Sunshine City", and is filled with a wide variety of places to have fun. With the "Otome Road" offering anime goods targeting women, it is getting attention as a new area for subcultures as well.

1. The entertainment and shopping complex Sunshine City is a spot you can't miss in Ikebukuro
2. Various objects can be seen in front of the Tokyo Metropolitan Theatre

1. Sunshine 60 dori is lined with restaurants, shops, and all kinds of stores
2. The SKY CIRCUS Sunshine 60 Observation, is the place where you can take unique photos
3. Toshima Ward Minami Ikebukuro Park, reopened in 2016 after renovation
4. The owl, a symbol of Ikebukuro, can be found in various places around the area

How to enjoy

Sunshine City, along with being a landmark of Ikebukuro, is a commercial complex where you can have fun all day long. In the building, there's a theme park, an aquarium, an observation deck, a planetarium, and other attractions that you can enjoy even on rainy days.

Those interested in anime should look for their favorite anime goods on Otome Road. If you go up to the Animate Ikebukuro main shop, you can be sure to find the item you are looking for.

In addition, concept cafés are very popular right now in Ikebukuro. It is home to unique cafés, such as ones where you can pet animals, detective cafés, etc. You may encounter with a world you've never seen before.

1. Otome Road, popular among female otaku
2. In the outdoor area of Sunshine Aquarium, you can enjoy performances from sea lions and penguins at a close distance

Must-visit tourist spots

Sightseeing

Otome Road →P.166
Sunshine City →P.168
Detective Café PROGRESS →P.170
Royal Afilia Grand Lodge →P.170
Cat Café MoCHA Lounge Ikebukuro East Exit Store →P.171
Usa Café mimi →P.171

Shopping

Animate Ikebukuro Main Store →P.167

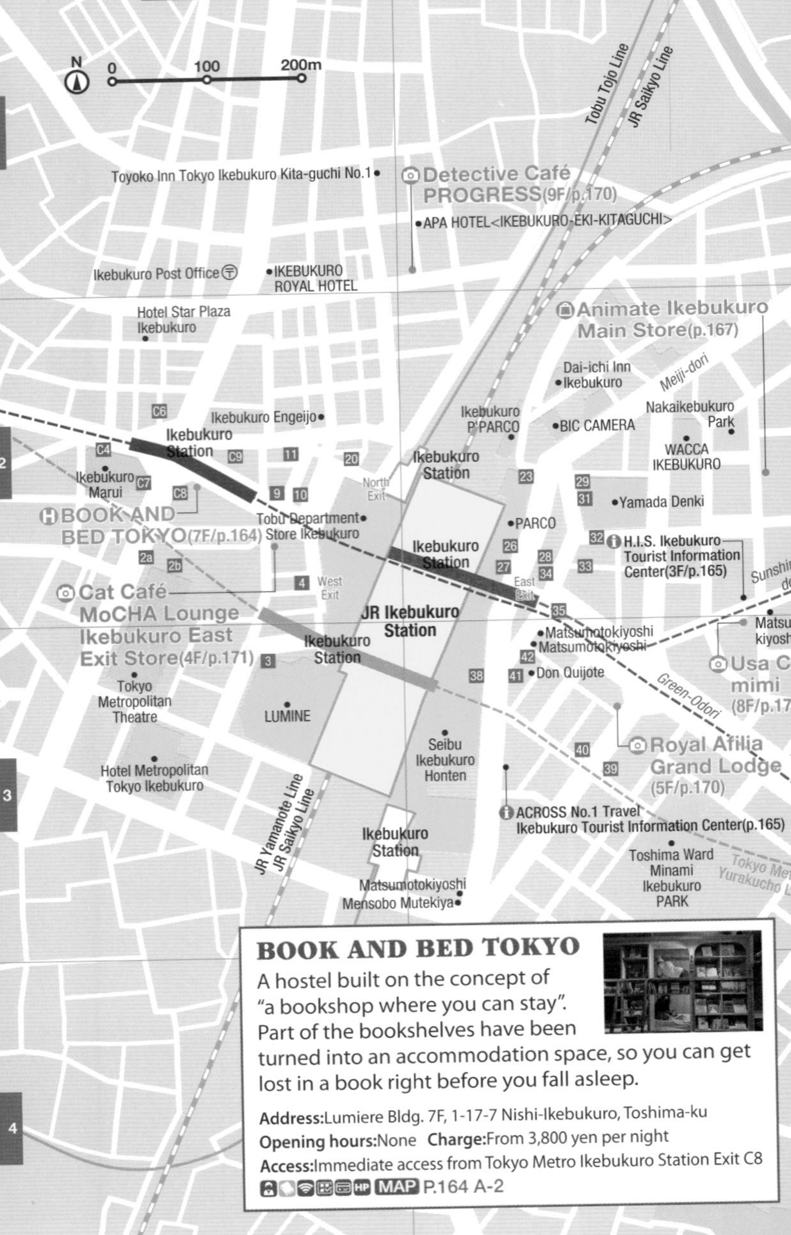

BOOK AND BED TOKYO

A hostel built on the concept of "a bookshop where you can stay". Part of the bookshelves have been turned into an accommodation space, so you can get lost in a book right before you fall asleep.

Address: Lumiere Bldg. 7F, 1-17-7 Nishi-Ikebukuro, Toshima-ku
Opening hours: None **Charge:** From 3,800 yen per night
Access: Immediate access from Tokyo Metro Ikebukuro Station Exit C8
MAP P.164 A-2

C

JR Yamanote Line
JR Syonan-Shinjuku Line

Teikyo Heisei University

Otome Road(p.166)

Sunshine60
SKY CIRCUS Sunshine 60 Observation (60F/p.169)

Higashi-Ikebukuro Park

HOTEL Grand City

Ark Hotel Tokyo Ikebukuro

Kasuga-dori

Tokyo Metro Marunouchi Line

Animate Sunshine

Tokyu Hands

Higashi-Ikebukuro Central Park

Sunshine City Prince Hotel

Toshima Post Office

Sunshine City(p.168)

World Import Mart Bldg.
J-WORLD TOKYO(3F/p.167)
Sunshine Aquarium(p.168)
Konica Minolta Planetarium "MANTEN" in Sunshine City(p.169)

Toshima Ward Central Library

1 2 6 7

Toshima Ward Office

Higashi-Ikebukuro Station

Taishoken

Honkyo-ji Temple

4 3 5

Higashi-Ikebukuro-Yonchome Station

Toden Arakawa Line

Tokyo Metro Fukutoshin Line

Toden-Zoshigaya Station

C

Access from airports

Narita Airport Terminal 2·3	Haneda Airport International Terminal
Keisei Line (Skyliner)	*Keikyu Line Limited Express and more*
Nippori	Shinagawa
Yamanote Line inner loop	*Yamanote Line outer loop*
Ikebukuro	Ikebukuro
¥ *2640yen*	¥ *670yen*
60min	*50min*

Lines

[JR]

Yamanote Line *Saikyo Line*
Shonan-Shinjuku Line

[Tokyo Metro]

Marunouchi Line *Fukutoshin Line*
Yurakucho Line

[Private railway]

Seibu Ikebukuro Line *Tobu Tojo Line*

Tourist information centers

H.I.S. Ikebukuro Tourist Information Center

H.I.S. 池袋ツーリストインフォメーションセンター

Offer services such as booking for tours and cultural experiences, Tokyo Metro Pass, Wi-Fi rental, luggage storage, etc.

Address: Oak Higashi-Ikebukuro Bldg. 3F, 1-11-1 Higashi-Ikebukuro, Toshima-ku
TEL:03-5992-9731
Opening hours:11:00-20:00
Closed: None
Access:5 min. walk from JR Ikebukuro East Exit

HP

MAP P.164 B-2

◆ **Other tourist information centers**

ACROSS No.1 Travel Ikebukuro Tourist Information Center

アクロス·No.1トラベル池袋　ツーリストインフォメーションセンター MAP P.164 B-3

1. Male characters drawn on shop advertisements catch the eyes of the women passing by
2. Many of the women walking on the streets are wearing items featuring their favorite characters
3. Row of Gacha-Gacha toy capsule machines for women

Street 乙女ロード

Otome Road

Where female anime lovers gather

Otome Road is the street located on the west side of Sunshine City. Lined with shops offering manga, anime novels, character goods, and other items targetting female consumers. In the surroundings, there are also concepts cafés such as butler cafés and more.

Address: Higashi-Ikebukuro, Toshima-ku

Access:10 min. walk from JR Ikebukuro Station East Exit

MAP P.165 C-2

For Tourists

Many of the women are after magazines published by fans mainly featuring works derived from anime. Low-priced issues can be purchased from around 200 yen.

Manga / Anime Goods アニメイト池袋本店

Animate Ikebukuro Main Store

Japan's largest animation shop

Boasts the top number of items related to anime in Japan, such as manga, Blu-rays, DVDs, character goods, etc. On the 1st floor you will find all kinds of sweets featuring illustrations of characters. Also recommended for souvenirs.

Address:1-20-7 Higashi-Ikebukuro, Toshima-ku
TEL:03-3988-1351
Opening hours:10:00 - 21:00
Closed: None
Access:5 min. walk from JR Ikebukuro Station East Exit

MAP P.164 B-2

1. You can get the latest anime goods
2. Filled with anime and game character goods

For Tourists

Sales and exhibitions of goods that specialize in animation and games are held periodically on the Only Shop Floor on the 8th floor.

1. In the "Shoot! Kamehameha!!" corner, you can shoot a Kamehameha in 3D
2. A strawberry shortcake decorated with the hats of Luffy and Chopper from the popular anime "One Piece"

For Tourists

In the food corner, you can enjoy dishes featured in manga and menu inspired by characters.

Amusement Facility J-WORLD TOKYO

J-WORLD TOKYO

Experience the world of "JUMP".

An amusement facility where you can experience the world of anime from works of the manga magazine "JUMP". Feel like a hero as you play games or take pictures in a place where both adults and kids can have a good time.

Address: Sunshine City World Import Mart Bldg. 3F, 3-1-3 Higashi-Ikebukuro, Toshima-ku
TEL:03-5950-2181
Opening hours:10:00 - 22:00 (last admission 1 hour before closing time)
Closed: None **Fee:** 800 yen
Access:5 min. walk from Tokyo Metro Higashi-Ikebukuro Station Exit 6 and 7

MAP P.165 C-3

Commercial Complex サンシャインシティ

Sunshine City

Offering plenty of indoor theme parks

This building brings together many kinds of amusement, including among others the J-World Tokyo and Namja Town, as well as restaurants and shops, letting you enjoy the place the entire day.

Address:3-1 Higashi-Ikebukuro, Toshima-ku
TEL:03-3989-3331
Opening hours: Some facilities may differ
Closed: None
Access:5 min. walk from Tokyo Metro Higashi-Ikebukuro Station Exit 6 and 7

MAP P.165 C-3

1. In the Fountain Square, water fountain spouts up every 30 minutes, and you can enjoy 3 types of performance using music and video (may be stopped sometimes) 2. There is an information board at the entrance which features facility information in foreign languages, too

For Tourists

If you want to have a meal, we recommend the Sunshine 60 Sky Restaurant. You can get a bird's-eye view of the Ikebukuro streets.

1. The doughnut-shaped tank where sea lions and penguins swim high in the sky
2. There is also a water show performance in which you can watch scuba divers petting and feeding the fish

For Tourists

For tourists visiting Japan, there is a multilingual guide service using QR codes. Enjoy the aquarium regardless of your nationality.

Aquarium サンシャイン水族館

Sunshine Aquarium

A sky-high aquarium appearing at 40m above ground

Meet cute creatures in a blue and green space reminiscent of a tropical country. The enchanting exhibitions, such as the "Fuwarium", a tunnel in which jellyfish appear to be floating in water like magic, are very popular.

Address: Sunshine City World Import Mart Bldg. Rooftop, 3-1 Higashi-Ikebukuro, Toshima-ku **TEL:**03-3989-3466 **Opening hours:**From April to October: 10:00 - 20:00, from November to March: 10:00 - 18:00 (last admission 1 hour before closing time) **Closed:**None **Fee:**2000 yen **Access:**5 min. walk from Tokyo Metro Higashi-Ikebukuro Station Exit 6 and 7

MAP P.165 C-3

Observatory Deck SKY CIRCUS サンシャイン60展望台

SKY CIRCUS Sunshine 60 Observation

An interactive observation deck filled with entertainment

You will not only enjoy the view, but also have fun with gadgets using the latest technologies. Some of these include content that lets you experience a feeling of floating in a virtual world, and will provide you all kinds of surprises!

Address: Sunshine City Sunshine 60 Bldg. 60F, 3-1 Higashi-Ikebukuro, Toshima-ku **TEL:**03-3989-3457 **Opening hours:**10:00 - 22:00 (last admission 1 hour before closing time) **Closed:**None **Fee:**1800 yen **Access:**5 min. walk from Tokyo Metro Higashi-Ikebukuro Station Exit 6 and 7

MAP P.165 C-3

1. A large panorama awaits you at the Tenku 251 Area. 2. Feel as though you were flying high-speed through the Tokyo of the future on "TOKYO Bullet Flight"

For Tourists

At Infinite Scape, surrounded on all 4 sides by mirrors, videos featuring the four seasons of Japan and other scenes are projected, making you feel just like you were in a kaleidoscope.

1. In addition to the regular seats, "Lawn Seats", which let you lie down as you watch, and "Cloud Seats", designed to look like clouds, are also available 2. The color and brightness of the stars are reflected in this planetarium, which uses ultra-high luminance LED

For Tourists

The Healing Planetarium allows you to enjoy the starry sky along with the aromas that match the performance. Fee: From 1,500 yen.

Planetarium コニカミノルタプラネタリウム"満天" in Sunshine City

Konica Minolta Planetarium "MANTEN" in Sunshine City

Experience a 360-degree view of a starry sky with the latest technology

See a clear, endless view of the starry night sky projected in all directions at the world's most advanced optical planetarium. They've also implemented a collaboration program with musical compositions created by Japanese artists.

Address: Sunshine City World Import Mart Bldg. Rooftop, 3-1-3 Higashi-Ikebukuro, Toshima-ku **TEL:**03-3989-3546 **Opening hours:**11:00 - 20:00 (projections every hour) **Closed:**Irregular holidays **Fee:**From 1200 yen **Access:**10 min. walk from Tokyo Metro Higashi-Ikebukuro Station Exit 6 and 7

MAP P.165 C-3

Concept Café 探偵カフェ プログレス

Detective Café PROGRESS

Café & Bar in which the concept is "detective"

The shop staff is made up of all real detectives. You can listen to the inside stories of actual investigations while having a drink and also see reports. It is also possible to experience special makeup on days when technical staff members are present.

Address: Dai-ni Kizuna Bldg. 9F, 2-47-12 Ikebukuro, Toshima-ku **TEL:**03-6698-2263 **Opening hours:**Bar: 19:00 to following day 5:00 (last order 4:00), 19:00 - 24:00 on Sundays (last order 23:00) *Regular business hours on Mondays falling on public holidays, and open until 24:00 if Monday is a public holiday. Café: 11:30 - 17:30 (open only on Saturdays, Sundays, and public holidays) **Closed:**None **Price:**Lunch from 1,000 yen, Dinner from 2,000 yen **Access:**5 min. walk from JR Ikebukuro Station North Exit

MAP P.164 B-1

1. The shop interior, which looks like a crime scene, is the perfect spot for a commemorative photo
2. Using the criminal identification set, you can also collect fingerprints

For Tourists

They have also prepared games to make you feel like a detective. Among these, a game in which you have to look for a wiretap in the shop by using equipment actually used by detectives is popular.

*Activities during bar time only

1. Reputed for the cute costumes of the staff. You can also take a commemorative photo with them
2. Besides the table seats, there are also counter seats, creating an atmosphere similar to a bar

For Tourists

It is set up as if customers were the sempai (elders) of the staff who are apprentice witches. That is why they will call you "sempai" affectionately in the shop.

Concept Café 王立アフィリア・グランドロッジ

Royal Afilia Grand Lodge

Welcomed by cute apprentice witches

A concept café where you can spend time as if you were living in a magic kingdom. Enjoy conversations and meals with the staff, who are all apprentice witches. You can experience the unique Japanese culture of "Moe".

Address: Dai-san Kindai Bldg. 5F, 1-26-2 Minami-Ikebukuro, Toshima-ku **TEL:**03-5927-8991 **Opening hours:**11:30 - 23:00 (food last order: 22:00, drink last order: 22:30) **Closed:**None **Price:**Lunch from 1,000 yen, Dinner from 1,300 yen **Access:**4 min. walk from JR Ikebukuro Station East Exit

MAP P.164 B-3

Animal Café 猫カフェ MoCHA ラウンジ 池袋東口店

Cat Café MoCHA Lounge Ikebukuro East Exit Store

Relax together with cute cats

In a classy space that looks like a lounge, you can interact with around 30 cats. Since there is no time limit, and since there is internet and manga available in the store, you can enjoy this place at your leisure.

Address: Sankee Bldg. 4F, 1-22-5 Higashi-Ikebukuro, Toshima-ku **TEL:**03-6914-2699
Opening hours:10:00 - 22:00 (last entry 30 minutes before closing time)
Closed: None **Fee:**1800 yen
Access:7 min. walk from JR Ikebukuro Station East Exit

MAP P.164 A-2

1. There are, of course, chairs and sofas, and even beds that let you lie down together with the cats
2. You can relax in this spacious café. It is also possible to use massage chairs

For Tourists

A limited quantity of the cats' favorite treats (extra charge) has been arranged. If you give them some treats, you may get the attention of all the cats to yourself.

1. Interact as much as you want with lots of rabbits!
2. Toro the Holland Lop, which is a popular breed, has a reputation in the store for being cute

For Tourists

Since you put on an apron before you pet the rabbits, you have little chance of getting your clothes dirty. It is also possible to take a commemorative photo together with the rabbits.

Animal Café うさカフェ mimi

Usa Café mimi

Play with fluffy rabbits!

A café where about 40 rabbits live. You can choose one drink for free among a selection of 50 different drinks (for 60 minutes of use or more). Rabbit food is also included in the admission fee, so give it to your favorite rabbit.

Address: Torikoma Dai-ni Bldg. 8F, 1-13-9 Higashi-Ikebukuro, Toshima-ku
TEL:070-5079-3841
Opening hours:12:00 - 20:00, 11:00 - 20:30 on Saturdays, Sundays and public holidays
Closed: Irregular holidays
Fee:30 minutes from 800 yen
Access:6 min. walk from JR Ikebukuro Station East Exit

MAP P.164 B-3

Useful information to know!

Things about "Japanese souvenirs"

"Souvenir-buying" during your trip is a must-do activity. Here, we'll deliver useful information to know when you buy souvenirs in Japan.

Spots to buy reasonable souvenirs

Although there are various places where you can do shopping, such as department stores and specialized shops, we recommend discount stores, drugstores and supermarkets. Sweets, pharmaceutical products and other items can be purchased at an affordable price.

ドン.キホーテ

The Palace of amazing prices Don Quijote

→MAP P.39 C-1 →MAP P.88 A-2

Discount shop selling "bargain-priced" products. You can find foods, medicines, commodities and so on at low prices. Their landmark is "Donpen" as a mascot character. Ⓐ

マツモトキヨシ

Matsumotokiyoshi

→MAP P.39 C-1 →MAP P.88 B-3

A drugstore recognizable by its yellow signboard. Apart from pharmaceutical products, it sells cosmetics, daily necessities, food, and many other products. In the shop, pharmacists and beauty staff will provide assistance. Ⓑ

Japan's famous snacks makers

We will now introduce super-well-known manufacturers together with their standard products so famous that everyone in Japan knows about them.

Without doubt, you will become addicted to taste and quality!

Calbee

main products
Kappa Ebisen, Jagariko, Potato Chips

Morinaga Seika

main products
Morinaga Milk Chocolate, Choco Ball, Koeda, Hi-chew

Meiji

main products
Kinoko no Yama, Takenoko no Sato, Curl, Kajyu Gumi, Chelsea

Fujiya

main products
Milky, Country Ma'am, Home Pie

What are "limited products"?

Among Japanese snacks, there are products using seasonal ingredients and regional specialties, and also items sold only for limited time and regions. Try to look for those as you can see the "limited" mark on the package or on store's signage.

In addition, all manufacturers sell new products every month, with only a very small number of these products turning into standard items. It is the reason why new products also are precious in some way.

How to look at the "use by" date", "best-before date", and "expiration date"

❶ use by date 使用期限

使用期限 2019.03

ⓐ ⓑ

Displayed on pharmaceutical products, etc. Mentioned on medicine for which efficacy is reduced after a certain lapse of time.

❷ best-before date 賞味期限

賞味期限 2017.02.02 DM

ⓐ ⓑ ⓒ

Displayed on moderately perishable foods such as snacks and retort foods. It does not mean that they are not edible right after the expiration date.

❸ expiration date 消費期限

消費期限 17.1.16 時間 22時

ⓐ ⓑ ⓒ ⓓ

Displayed on highly perishable foods such as fresh food and bentos, stuffed bread, etc. It is better not to eat past the expiration date.

ⓐ year ⓑ month ⓒ day ⓓ time

* The limit is in all cases set before opening and for a storage following the described methods

Plenty of souvenirs to give out

In Japan, when you go on a trip, it is a custom to give out souvenirs (often snacks) to relatives, friends, and colleagues. Therefore,you can find products subdivided into small and numerous portions easy to distribute.

Souvenirs representing regional characteristics are considered as priceless treasures.

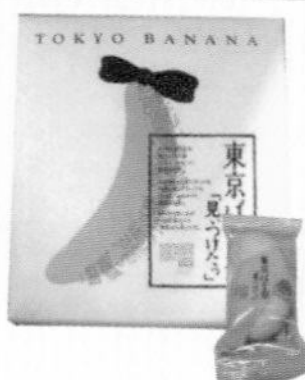

Tokyo classic souvenir "Tokyo Banana" offers many different number of pieces and tastes. There are also some products only available at the stores. Can be purchased in Tokyo Station and Shinjuku, airports, etc.

PICK UP

An introduction of popular souvenirs!

Picking-up some of the best selling items from "Don Quijote"Ⓐ and "Matsumotokiyoshi Ⓑ"

KitKat Otona no Amasa Macha ⒶⒷ
Matcha-flavored version of the classic chocolate snacks
Around 280 yen

Cororo ⒶⒷ
Popular gummy with its super soft fruit-like texture **Around 120 yen**

Perfect Whip ⒶⒷ
Facial cleanser with very dense foam
Around 450 yen

Instream Refresh Call Essence Ⓑ
Morning beauty lotion. Original product of Matsumotokiyoshi
3,800 yen

Kyusoku Jikan Ashi Sukkiri sheet ⒶⒷ
Cold sheets heal your tired legs and feet **Around 600 yen**

Heroin Make Tenmade Todoke Mascara ⒶⒷ
Mascara with excellent durability with sustaining the curl of eyelashes **Around 1,200 yen**

*Some products may not be available depending on the stores

Tokyo Sightseeing Spot Catalog

In Tokyo, there are many sightseeing spots in addition to the major areas. We will now introduce popular places, such as entertainment facilities with unique attractions, museums where fascinating exhibitions are held , and more.

Art Museum 東京都美術館

Tokyo Metropolitan Art Museum

A museum opened as a n "doorway to art"
This museum holds various exhibitions featuring famous Japanese and foreign paintings as well as calligraphy, artistic creations from contemporary creators , and more. They also hold free exhibitions.

©Tokyo Metropolitan Art Museum

Address:8-36 Ueno-koen, Taito-ku **TEL:**03-3823-6921
Opening hours:9:30 - 17:30, 9:30 - 20:00 on Fridays during special exhibitions (last admission 30 minutes before closing time) **Closed/Fee:** May differ depending on exhibition
Access:10 min. walk from JR Ueno Station Park Exit **URL:**http://www.tobikan.jp/en/index.html
MAP P.130 B-2 *Credit cards accepted only in shops

©Museo d'Arte Ghibli

Art Museum 三鷹の森ジブリ美術館

Ghibli Museum, Mitaka

Turning the world of Ghibli into reality
This Studio Ghibli museum has fans all around the world. In this museum, you can find an exhibition on film production, a theater, a café, a rooftop garden, and other attractions.

Address:1-1-83 Shimorenjaku, Mitaka-shi **TEL:**None **Opening hours:**10:00 - 18:00 **Closed:**Tuesdays *Also sometimes closed for long periods of time **Fee:**1,000 yen **Access:**21 min. walk from JR Mitaka Sation South Exit **URL:**http://www.ghibli-museum.jp/en/ MAP P.4 A-2

*Entrance to the museum requires reservations in advance. Check the website for further information

Art Museum 三菱一号館美術館

Mitsubishi Ichigokan Museum, Tokyo

A reconstructed brick building from the Meiji era
Mitsubishi Ichigokan was reconstructed and opened as an art museum in 2010. It owns a collection of Western artworks from the late 19th century. The building also houses the museum café, Café 1894.

Address:2-6-2 Marunouchi, Chiyoda-ku **TEL:**03-5777-8600 (Hello Dial Service) **Opening hours:**10:00 - 18:00, 10:00 - 20:00 on Fridays, on the second Wednesday of the month, on the final week of exhibition (last admission is 30 minutes before closing) **Closed:**Mondays (open when Monday is a national holiday or in the final week of exhibition) **Fee:**May differ depending on exhibition **Access:**8 min. walk from JR Tokyo Station Marunouchi South Exit MAP P.6 A-2

©Fujitsuka Mistumasa

Art Museum 根津美術館

Nezu Museum

Superb collection of more than 7,400 Japanese and East Asian works

The museum holds exhibitions 7 times a year on pre-modern art, such as paintings, calligraphy, Buddhist art, ceramics, lacquerware, etc. Exhibits are displayed in English as well. In the museum, you can also find a reputed garden and café.

Address:6-5-1 Minami-Aoyama, Minato-ku **TEL:**03-3400-2536 **Opening hours:**10:00 - 17:00 (last admission 30 minutes before closing time) **Closed:**Mondays (open if on public holidays and closed the following day), during exhibition installations period

Fee: From 1,100 yen **Access:**8 min. walk from Tokyo Metro Omote-sando Station Exit A5

URL:http://www.nezu-muse.or.jp/en/index.html HP MAP P.103 C-3

Kotobukizuru, folded from a piece of paper. They look like works of art

Specialty Store お茶の水 おりがみ会館

Ochanomizu Origami Kaikan

Holy land of Origami founded in 1858

A long-established store that produces dyed paper and Chiyogami paper. The mid-2nd floor is a gallery. The 3rd floor is the shop where origami sets with English translation are availble. You can visit the dyeing studio (sometimes closes without further information).

Address:1-7-14 Yushima, Bunkyo-ku **TEL:**03-3811-4025

Opening hours:9:30 - 18:00. Gallery: 10:00 - 17:30

Closed: Sundays and public holidays **Fee:**Free entrance

Access:8 min. walk from JR Ochanomizu Station Hijiribashi Exit HP MAP P.144 A-1

Shrine 神田明神（神田神社）

Kanda Myojin (Kanda Shrine)

A venerable shrine founded in 730

A traditional building that has been designated as a national important cultural asset. Offering more than 60 types of omamori (lucky charms) including some collaborations with anime and the like. There is also a museum in the precincts.

Address:2-16-2 Soto-kanda, Chiyoda-ku **TEL:**03-3254-0753 **Opening hours:**Free access to the precincts. Museum: 10:00 -16:00 on Saturdays, Sundays and public holidays **Closed:**None **Fee:** 300 yen(Museum) **Access:**9 min. walk from JR Ochanomizu Station Hijiribashi Exit

HP MAP P.144 A-2

Check!

Surprisingly, most people don't know about it...

Tokyo is a hidden city of hot springs

When you think about Japanese hot springs, called onsen, you may imagine one located in a natural environment. However, there are actually many natural onsens in the metropolis of Tokyo as well. On this page, you will learn about the right information about onsen and the fun ways to enjoy them.

What the onsen represents for Japanese people

Japan has had many volcanoes since ancient times, creating plenty of volcanic hot springs. The first time that a hot spring appeared in literature was during the Nara period (710-794). At that time, hot springs were places of religious faith, and monks opened bathing spaces at their temples for the poor and the sick. Once this practice was generalized to the public, hot springs became used by everyone for medical purposes. After that, the long-term stays for medical treatment of disease using hot springs called toji, which means "hot-spring cure", became very popular. This is how bathing in hot springs changed from an act of "faith" to an act of "fatigue recovery and health promotion" for the Japanese people. Nowadays, relaxation and leisure have also been added as reasons to go to hot springs in addition to this medical aspect.

Tokyo is actually a city of hot springs

Even in Tokyo, lined with buildings and houses, there are in fact many onsen springing forth. According to a Tokyo Metropolitan Government survey (2008), 216 permits given to sites for hot spring use. The density of hot springs (a value given per 10 square kilometers, representing how many public baths have their own hot springs, not including accommodations) found in Tokyo's 23 wards is number one in Japan. Recently in 2014, a hot spring was found in the office district of Otemachi and became a much-discussed topic.

Characteristics of Tokyo onsen

Onsen have various characteristics depending on spring quality, the color, smell, effects, and so on. For areas surrounding the coastline, such as in Ota Ward, many hot springs feature light brown and dark brown colors known as "black hot waters". They are hot springs of 25ºC or less with water that contains sodium bicarbonate and other components found in the "fossil water" coming from ancient seawaters. In the Okutama area, there are onsen that contain sulfur. You can find different spring qualities, such as simple sulfur mineral cold springs, alkaline simple sulfur spring, etc. The main effects of onsen include efficient recovery from neuralgia, joint pain, fatigue, frozen shoulder, as well as health enhancement, and so on. Check the effects at the onsen facility you are planning to use, since there is a wide range according to spring quality.

* Even if the water temperature is less than 25 degrees, it is considered an onsen if it contains designated substances

Types of bathing facilities

In Tokyo, you can take a bath in hot springs at inns, hotels, public baths, and super sento with hot springs. Super sento is a type of public bath that has been increasing in recent years, offering food as well as leisure facilities that are built centered around the hot bathing facilities. At some facilities, you can do "day-trip bathing" and use hot springs without having to stay at the inn or hotel. Public baths and super sento are facilities where you can enjoy a hot bath. Among the public baths, there are facilities for simply enjoying hot baths, so if you want to bathe in hot spring waters, check before you go.

Don'ts on how to use an onsen

First of all, avoid bathing right after eating or after drinking. Of course, do not bathe during your menstrual period, or if you are pregnant or in bad physical condition. Also, make sure to always wash your entire body in the washing area and make sure you are clean before entering the bathtub. Rinse your body with hot water using the washing buckets before entering the bathtub, which also lets your body get used to bathing temperature. When you enter the bathtub, do it quietly, and put yourself in "half-bathing" by entering hot water almost up to the solar plexus at first, and then in "full-bathing" up to the shoulders. Limit your baths to three times a day, rehydrate yourself, and take a rest after each bath.

Pictures provided by the ODAIBA TOKYO OOEDO-ONSEN MONOGATARI

PICK UP

Hot Spring spots in Tokyo

Let us introduce the popular hot spring spots.

東京お台場
大江戸温泉物語

ODAIBA TOKYO OOEDO-ONSEN MONOGATARI

Onsen theme park reproducing Edo atmosphere.

An onsen theme park that you can enjoy all day wearing a yukata, offering a natural hot spring, an open-air bath, a "Japanese Garden" themed foot bath, etc.

Address:2-6-3 Aomi, Koto-ku **TEL:**03-5500-1126 **Opening hours:**11:00 to following day 9:00 (last admission at 7:00 in the morning, exclusively on rotation system. Last admission at 21:00 once a month on maintenance day) **Closed:** Irregular holidays **Fee:** from 2,280 yen. *May differ on days of week and hours.
Access:5 min. walk from Yurikamome Telecom Center Station South Exit

MAP P.5 C-3

前野原温泉
さやの湯処

Maenohara Onsen Saya-no-yudokoro

An authentic onsen fed directly from a natural source.

Onsen facility displaying a Japanese-style building, and an impressive karesansui dry landscape garden covered with moss. There is also a restaurant where you can relish Japanese food.

Address:3-41-1 Maenocho, Itabashi-ku **TEL:**03-5916-3826 **Opening hours:**10:00 - 24:00 (closed at 25:00) **Closed:**Irregular holidays **Fee:**870 yen (1,100 yen on Saturdays, Sundays and public holidays)
Access:11 min. walk from Toei Subway Shimura-Sakaue Station Exit A2

MAP P.7 D-3

Feel relief the moment you get on board

OMOTENASHI by JAL

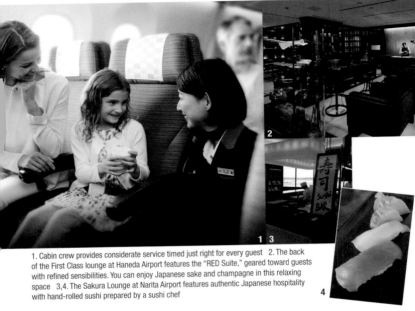

1. Cabin crew provides considerate service timed just right for every guest 2. The back of the First Class lounge at Haneda Airport features the "RED Suite," geared toward guests with refined sensibilities. You can enjoy Japanese sake and champagne in this relaxing space 3,4. The Sakura Lounge at Narita Airport features authentic Japanese hospitality with hand-rolled sushi prepared by a sushi chef

Feel Like You're in Japan before You Step On Board

In 2015, Japan Airlines (JAL) –the flag carrier of Japan–won awards for on-time performance in all three categories that it qualified for, according the data services company, FlightStats, Inc.* This marks the fifth time that JAL has been recognized as World's No. 1, exhibiting JAL's commitment to providinge professional, reliable service that is both safe and secure, without sacrificing the strong commitment to authentic Japanese hospitality renowned the world over. At both Haneda and Narita airports, JAL offers a wide range of service at their top-class lounges, and cabin crew are committed to greeting all guests one by one and providing them with an unforgettably great experience on board. In-flight meals designed by world-class Japanese chefs add to the uniquely Japanese in-flight experience.

TOPICS

World's No. 1 for On-Time Arrival Again!

Since 2009, the American company FlightStats Inc. has tracked and monitored the on-time arrival rate of airlines from around the world. In 2015, JAL was ranked as the world's best in all three categories for which it qualified, including the Major International Airlines category. This is just one more example of how JAL's operation professionals are committed to offering a worry-free journey to all its guests.

It's time for your once-in-a-lifetime journey to Japan!
Feel as if you are in Japan from the moment you step on board, and enjoy world-class Japanese hospitality before you arrive to help build the excitement you are sure to feel on your trip!

Japanese and Western in-flight meal choices available on JAL's restaurant in the sky

An in-flight meal can be one of the most critical ways in which one can enjoy a flight. With JAL First Class, we have prepared meal choices befitting of the top-class luxury you would expect, produced by top Japanese chefs. Sit back and enjoy the scenery while our knowledgeable cabin crew stand by to support your in-flight meal enjoyment.

1. Western style Business Class meals might include such offerings as Pâté of Sautéed Barracuda & Scallop with Mustard Sauce
2. Get your first taste of Japan before you land, with Business Class meal options such as Japanese Style Stewed Beef Tongue Miso-marinated Salmon

※Photos for illustrative purposes, only. Actual menu items may vary

Luxury Before Your Flight

JAL service extends beyond your in-flight experience, allowing you to experience our luxurious lounges before you step on board. The First Class Lounge at Haneda Airport features a Teppanyaki Corner, where you can enjoy a freshly baked galette in the morning and teppanyaki in the evening. At the Sakura Lounge in Narita Airport, enjoy hand-rolled sushi prepared by a sushi chef, in addition to the countless other services such as shoe polishing by the world-famous shoe brand John Lobb, and more. Spend your pre-flight time how you want to.

At the Haneda Airport First Class lounge, dining room, you can find carefully selected japanese sake, wines, and champagne

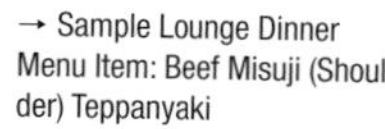

→ Sample Lounge Dinner Menu Item: Beef Misuji (Shoulder) Teppanyaki

← Sample Teppan Menu Item: Rye Galette

※Served dishes may vary

For reservations:

JAPAN AIRLINES
Japan Airlines
WEB:www.jal.com
TEL:www.jal.co.jp/en/information/inter/branch/

Venture a little further 3

Short trips from Tokyo

Since you've come all the way to Japan, there are still a few spots you'll want to visit. Here is a selection of tourist destinations only a few hours from Tokyo.

Nikko — 2 hours

Nikko is situated in Tochigi Prefecture. In this area, rich in nature and surrounded by greenery on all sides, there are many famous attractions, including Nikko Toshogu, which was registered as World Heritage, and Kegon Falls, Chuzenjiko-lake, and others. You can also find the Kinugawa Onsen nearby.

[Access]

- Shinjuku → Tobu Nikko: JR·Tobu Direct Limited Express Nikko and (Spacia) Kinugawa. (Transfer at Shimo-imaimichi along the way for (Spacia) Kinugawa) ¥4,000yen / Around 2 hours

- Asakusa → Tobu Nikko: Tobu Limited Express Kegon and Kinu (Transfer at Shimo-imaichi along the way for Kinu.) ¥2,800yen / Around 1 hour and 50 minutes (2,700 yen on weekdays)

Kamakura — 1 hour

Located in Kanagawa Prefecture adjacent to Tokyo, Kamakura is an ancient city that was the center of the Kamakura Shogunate (1185-1333), which was Japan's first military government.
In addition to the historical sites, temples, and shrines of that time, in recent years the streets are lined with refined restaurant and shops.

[Access]

- Tokyo → Kamakura: JR Yokosuka Line ¥920yen / Around 1 hour
- Ikebukuro/ Shinjuku/ Shibuya → Kamakura: JR Shonan Shinjuku Line ¥920yen / Around 1 hour

Hakone — 2 hours

©City of Angels / Shutterstock.com

Located in Kanagawa Prefecture, Hakone is one of the leading destinations in Japan for hot springs. Each of the hot springs in the area is said to have its own qualities, and together are nicknamed the "17 hot springs of Hakone." Apart from the majestic Mt. Fuji, which can be seen from the ropeway, Hakone offers beautiful seasonal landscapes, such as autumn leaves reflected on the surface of Ashinoko-lake, and more.

[Access]

- Shinjuku → Hakone-Yumoto: Odakyu Romance Car ¥2,080yen / Around 1 hour and 25 minutes
- Tokyo → Odawara → Hakone-Yumoto: JR Tokaido Line, Hakone Tozan Line ¥1,800yen / Around 1 hour and 50 minutes
- Busta Shinjuku → Hakone Glass-no-Mori: Odakyu Hakone Highway Bus ¥1,900yen / Around 2 hours

Mt. Fuji — 2 hours

An altitude of 3776m. Standing across Shizuoka Prefecture and Yamanashi Prefecture, it is the highest mountain in Japan. The distance to the summit is subdivided into 10 stages shown in units called "stations". It is possible to reach the 5th Station by bus, taxi, or with your own car. You can climb on foot only from the 5th station.

[Access]

- Shinjuku → Otsuki → Kawaguchiko: JR Chuo Line Limited Express, Fujikyuko Line Limited Express ¥4,310yen / Around 2 hours
- Tokyo → Fujisan Station: JR Bus Kanto, etc. ¥1,800yen / Around 2 hours
- Busta Shinjuku → Fujisan Station: Keio Bus, etc. ¥1,750yen / Around 1 hour and 45 minutes

BASIC INFORMATION

for Your Journey

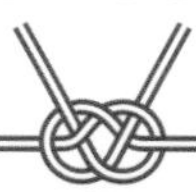

Transportation (Information from the airport to the city)

There are two airports in the suburbs of Tokyo, Narita International Airport and Haneda Airport (Tokyo International Airport). Narita Airport is around 70 km from Tokyo. Although Haneda Airport is close, located 10 km from Tokyo, it is convenient but tickets are a little more expensive. In general, Haneda is considered as good for business trips, and Narita for sightseeing trips with plenty of time to spare.

*It should be noted that since 2007, as part of counter-terrorism measures, the fingerprints and photographs of non-Japanese travelers are taken upon arrival

Check!

Narita International Airport

International airport opened in 1978 equipped with 3 terminals. The Terminal 3 for Low-Cost Carriers is separate from Terminal 1 & 2, which offer plenty of facilities such as a the Tourist Information Center (8:00-20:00) and others, so be aware. It is about 70 km from the airport to the city center. For transportation, the express train and highway bus are more convenient than taxis.

©Tooykrub / Shutterstock.com

Address: 1-1 Furugome, Narita-shi, Chiba-ken
TEL: 0476-34-8000

Train

Narita Express (JR)
URL: http://www.jreast.co.jp/e
©Sarunyu L / Shutterstock.com

Skyliner (Keisei Line)
URL: http://www.keisei.co.jp/keisei/tetudou/skyliner/us/ae_outline/index.php

Access Express (Keisei Line)
URL: http://www.keisei.co.jp/keisei/tetudou/skyliner/us/index.php

*The image features one of its iconic cars

Bus

Airport Limousine Bus
URL: http://www.limousinebus.co.jp/en

Access Guide from Narita International Airport

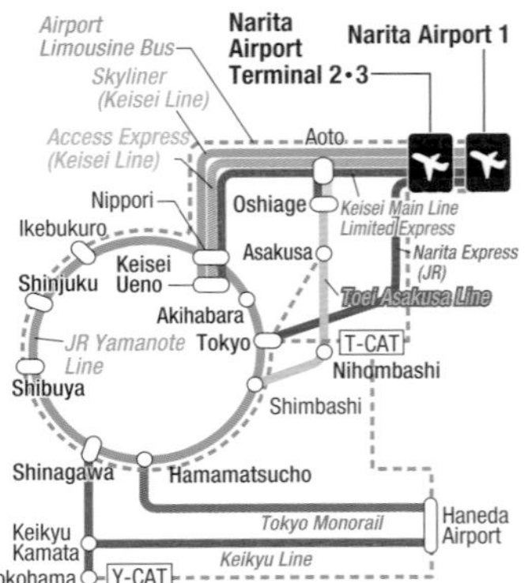

●Narita Express (JR)
Narita Airport Terminal 2・3 → Tokyo Sta.
60min ¥3,020yen

●Skyliner (Keisei Line)
Narita Airport Terminal 2・3 → Keisei Ueno Sta.
40min ¥2,470yen

●Access Express (Keisei Line)
Narita Airport Terminal 2・3 → Keisei Ueno Sta.
60min ¥1,240yen

●Airport Limousine Bus
Buses that operate in accordance with flight arrival and departure times. There are lines with access to main areas such as Shinjuku, Ginza, Tokyo, Shibuya, Roppongi, Ikebukuro, etc. Check all available stops on the website.

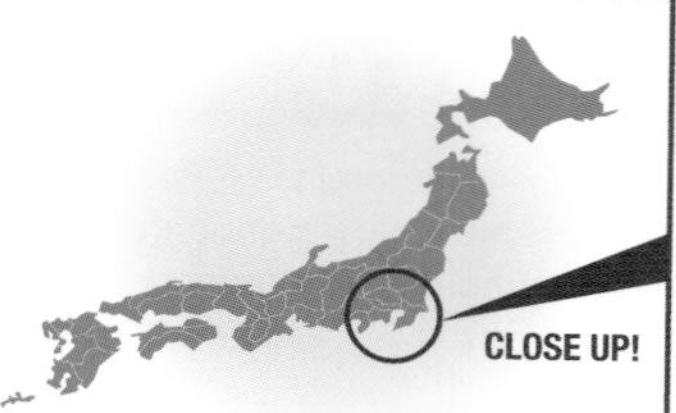

Check!

Haneda Airport

The international terminal able to run 24 hours a day opened in 2010. The biggest advantage is convenience in transportation, since it is located around 10 km from the city center. Trains (5:00-24:00) and late-night buses (5:00 to following day 2:00) are convenient means of transportation. The 2nd floor Tourist Information Center is open until 1AM, and some restaurants and cafes are open 24 hours a day.

©TIAT

Address: Haneda Airport, Ota-ku
TEL:03-6428-0888 (International Terminal)

Train

Keikyu Line

URL: http://www.haneda-tokyo-access.com/en

Tokyo Monorail

URL: http://www.tokyo-monorail.co.jp/english

Bus

Airport Limousine Bus

URL: http://www.limousine-bus.co.jp/en

Keikyu Limousine Bus

URL: http://hnd-bus.com/airport

Access Guide from Haneda Airport

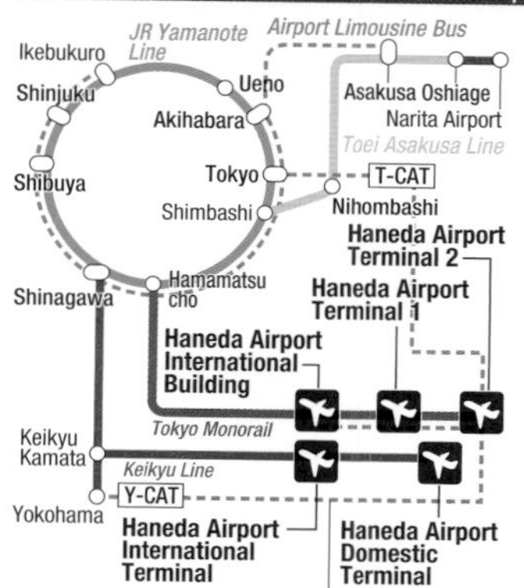

●Keikyu Line

Haneda Airport International Terminal → **Shinagawa Sta.**
11～20min
410yen

●Tokyo Monorail

Haneda Airport International Building → **Hamamatsucho Sta.**
13~21min
490yen

●Airport Limousine Bus

Buses that operate in accordance with flight arrival and departure times. There are lines with access to main areas such as Shinjuku, Ginza, Tokyo, Asakusa, Shibuya, Roppongi, Akihabara, Ikebukuro, etc. Offers sufficient late-night and early morning access. Check all available stops on the website.

●Keikyu Limousine Bus

There are routes going to Yokohama, TOKYO SKYTREE, Tokyo Disney Resort etc.

*Fares indicate the price for ticket use. Fare may vary with use of IC Card

Information on Tokyo Transportation ①

Subways and trains are two convenient ways to move around Tokyo. Public transportation is clean, safe and punctual. There are also many signboards in the stations written in English. The only thing you should be careful about is that trains stop running late at night.

Check!

Train

●JR

Japan Railway (JR) is a railway network that covers the whole country like a net. When sightseeing in Tokyo, remember two lines. One is the loop line surrounding Tokyo called Yamanote Line. The other one is the Chuo/Sobu Line that pierces through the center this loop from East to West.However, if you purchase a transfer ticket between the Tokyo Metro and the Toei Subway lines, you will get a discount of 70 yen off the total amount of each fare.

URL: http://www.jreast.co.jp
Base fare: 140 yen (ticket), 133 yen (IC card)

●Subway

There is a total of 13 subway lines in Tokyo, and they spread around the city in a complex way, just like capillaries. There are two companies in charge of management: Tokyo Metro (9 lines) and Toei Lines (4 lines), and you have to be careful since tickets are not compatible between these companies.However, if you purchase a transfer ticket between the Tokyo Metro and the Toei Subway lines, you will get a discount of 70 yen off the total amount of each fare.

Tokyo Metro
URL: http://www.tokyometro.jp/lang_en/index.html
Base fare:170 yen (ticket), 165 yen (IC card)

Toei Subway
URL: http://www.kotsu.metro.tokyo.jp/eng
Base fare:180 yen (ticket), 174 yen (IC card)

●Private Railways

Some private railways also run along the suburban areas of Tokyo, making it possible to visit quiet and fascinating areas if you take these lines. The main private railways include, among others, the Odakyu Line, which stops at stations such as Shimokitazawa and Shinjuku, and the Tokyu Toyoko Line, which stops at stations such as Daikanyama and Shibuya.

Odakyu Line
(Odakyu Odawara Line)
URL:http://www.odakyu.jp/english
Base fare:130 yen (ticket), 124 yen (IC card)

Tokyu Toyoko Line
URL: http://www.tokyu.co.jp/global/english/guide/index.html
Base fare:130 yen (ticket), 124 yen (IC card)

●How to ride the subway

How to understand Tokyo Metro line numbers

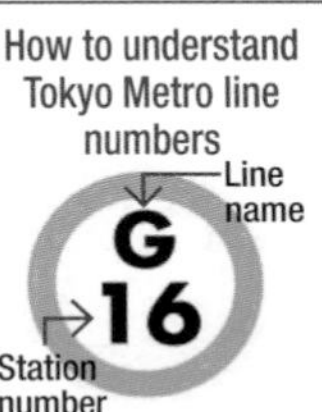

1 Look for the ticket machine

1.You can purchase tickets at the vending machines located near the ticket gate. Check the fare to your destination in advance. 2.There are also stations with a welcome board for foreigners, like in Ueno Station and others.

2 Check the fare

Check your destination and the fare on the route map right above the vending machines. Since the map is extremely complex, it might be better to ask someone at first.

3 Buy a ticket

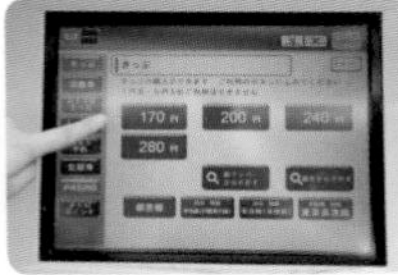

Touch the "Ticket" button on the vending machine. Then from all the fares lined up, touch the one corresponding to your destination. There is a language selection button on the upper right corner of the screen.

4 Go through the ticket gate

The automatic ticket gate will open once you insert your ticket into the ticket slot. After walking through, do not forget to pick up your ticket.

5 Go to the platforms

1.Go to the platform where the train you want to catch is arriving. Stations with multiple lines running have a complicated structure, so try to remain calm. 2.Information on destination can be found everywhere, like on walls, pillars, etc.

6 Get on the train

For safety, wait behind the yellow lines for the arrival train. Once the train has arrived, get on. Rest assure that there are announcements in English.

Check the exit nearest to your destination on the yellow information boards on platforms

[Suica & PASMO]

Prepaid cards that can be used in all railways, buses, taxis, and some convenience stores. Having one spares you the time and effort wasted checking your destination fare. Can be purchased from vending machines at the station.

COLUMN Convenient tickets

Tokyo Subway Ticket

URL:http://www.tokyometro.jp/en/ticket/value/travel/index.html

Get unlimited rides on all 9 lines of the Tokyo Metro and all 4 lines of Toei Subway. There are 3 types of tickets: 24-hour (800 yen), 48-hour (1,200 yen), and 72-hour (1,500 yen) tickets, which can be used for 24 to 72 hours after their first use within the terms of validity. Available for purchase at airports, Bic Camera, Sofmap, HIS Tourist Information Center, etc.

Tokyo Tour Ticket (1-day unlimited rides)

Lets you use JR (Rapid/ local trains of Tokyo's 23 wards), Tokyo Metro, Toei Subway, Nippori-Toneri Liner, Toden trams, and Toei buses. Available for purchase at automatic ticket machines and ticket counters at each line. Fare is 1,590 yen.

Japan Rail Pass

URL:http://www.japanrailpass.net/en/index.html

A foreign tourists-only ticket that allows use all JR lines (including express and limited-express), the Shinkansen, Tokyo Monorail and buses. In-advance application from your home country is required for use. Further information is available on the webpage.

Check!

Information on Tokyo Transportation ❷

Compared with other public transportation, taxi fare in Tokyo is expensive. It would be wiser to ride them with others rather than alone. Water buses connecting rivers to the bay area are more pleasure boats than just means of transportation, and allow you to fully enjoy sightseeing.

Taxi

The starting fare is 410 yen for up to 1.52 km, going 80 yen every 237m after that, and 80 yen every 1.30 minutes when the traveling speed is less than or equal to 10 km/h. There is an added surcharge of 20% for late night rides. It should be noted that not many drivers can speak English.

Nihon Kotsu

URL: https://www.nihon-kotsu.co.jp/en/
Starting fare: 1.52km for 410 yen

[Call a taxi from your current location!]

If you use the smartphone taxi calling app "Japan Taxi" produced by Nihon Kotsu, you can call an available taxi nearby. Since you can also specify your destination, there are no worries about language issues. You can pay online as well after pre-registering your credit card. **URL:** https://japantaxi.jp

●How to ride a taxi

How to recognize vacant or occupied taxis

Taxis are available when the board located above front passenger seat dashboard shows the red-lit characters 空車 (kuusha or "empty car").

Showing occupied taxis

1 Hail a taxi by raising your hand

Taxis will stop when you raise your hand. If you don't see any taxis, you should go to a taxi stand located at the stations.

→

2 Automatic door & climbing into the taxi

The rear door opens automatically! The back seat sits three passengers. Of course it is also possible to ride in the front passenger seat.

↓

3 Announce your destination

Sometimes drivers will not be able to understand English, and in such case you should repeat the place name or point at any map you may have.

←

4 How to understand the meter

In the front seat, there is a meter that shows the current fare. Cards can be used in most taxis, but you should carry cash just in case.

←

5 Pay the fare

Pay the fare shown on the meter. There is no need to give a tip.

Water Bus

You can go around the major sight-seeing spots along the area from the Sumida River to Tokyo Bay. This interesting experience connects Asakusa and Hamarikyu, where you can feel the traditional Japan, with the futuristic commercial facilities of Odaiba. Enjoy a journey on water that goes beyond space and time!

TOKYO CRUISE

URL: http://www.suijobus.co.jp/en/
Fare: From 410 yen

Tokyo Mizube Line

URL: https://www.tokyo-park.or.jp/waterbus/english/index.html
Fare: From 310 yen

COLUMN Sightseeing tours for foreigners

Hato Bus

Japan's long-established bus tour company that offers tours in English and Chinese. They have a variety of tours, such as half-day, one-day, gourmet food, night views, Japanese cultural experience, and more.

Hato Buses are recognizable by their yellow color. Available with reservation from 1,800 yen

Sky Bus Tokyo

The open-top double-decker bus that lets you enjoy the open view. Equipped with a voice tour guide system in English, Chinese, and Korean.

Reservation can be made. Also the ticket for today is available if there are vacant seats. From 1,600 yen

Japan's literary calendar

Whether you visit in spring, summer, autumn, or winter, Tokyo offers different atmospheres that can only be experienced during that season. This is because Japanese people, with their roots in animism, have cherished nature and its seasons since ancient times and incorporated the beauty of the four seasons into life and culture so that they can enjoy these passing seasons.

Spring (March / April / May)

©Andreas Mann / Shutterstock.com

1. The area along the Meguro River is popular cherry blossom spot in Tokyo
2. "Hina Dolls" used as decorations during Hinamatsuri (Doll's Festival)
3. The Sanja Matsuri, where you can feel the enthusiasm of the bearers
4. Koinobori (carp kites) that seem to swim in the air

Described as "so comfortable that it is impossible to wake up in the morning", spring is a special season to admire the cherry blossoms blooming in town. In the cherry blossoms blooming and falling after around 10 days all at once, Japanese people see beauty, impermanence, and wabi-sabi. Cherry blossoms fall so beautifully that they are a symbol of spirituality. In Tokyo, full-bloom is usually around the first week of April. We could say that the charm of this season is also to see ordinarily hard-working Japanese people acting without restraint under the cherry blossoms.

[Event]

Hinamatsuri (March 3) is a seasonal festival to pray for the healthy growth of girls. During the Cherry Blossom Festival (early April), people everywhere get together to admire the cherry blossoms. Children's Day (May 5) is a day to pray for boys' growth by flying koinobori, or carp kites. Sanja Matsuri (mid-May) is the most vigorous of the Asakusa Shrine festival in Tokyo, as men in Happi(Japanese festival jacket) parade around with a mikoshi (divine palanquin) on their shoulders.

COLUMN The best season to travel

Every season has distinctive features, and Tokyo being a city where you can have fun regardless of the season may be visited basically at any time. However, the period during which cherry blossoms are in full bloom starting from early April is exceptional, as the city is transformed into a world of extraordinary beauty by the cherry blossoms.

Summer (June / July / August)

4

1

1. Fireworks are a summer tradition. The Sumida River Fireworks Festival is so famous that it is broadcast live on TV 2. Unaju. It is said that you won't suffer from summer heat if you eat eel 3. Morning glory is known in Japan as a summer flower 4. Kakigori, shaved ice that you'll want when summer comes. This photo shows the "Asakusa Naniwaya(→P.79)"

Once the rainy season in June, called tsuyu, is over, in comes the hot and humid summer of Tokyo. With high temperatures of about 40°C and very high humidity, sweat keeps pouring down even you've entered the shade of a tree. Japanese people have developed many strategies to withstand this heat and humidity. Eat things such as eel for its nutrition, watch fireworks in a thin yukata, and enjoy the latest video games in a room with air conditioning during the day.

[Event]

Sanno Festival (held around mid-June), a festival of Hie Shrine, is one of the three main festivals of Edo. Tanabata (July 7), a seasonal festival during which people look at Vega and Altair across the Milky Way, and hang paper strips with their wishes written on them on bamboo leaves. The Sumida River Fireworks Festival (last Sunday of July). Koenji Awa-odori Dance (last week of August). Asakusa Samba Carnival (last week of August).

Once the severe heat of late summer has passed, the sun starts to set earlier day by day, after which comes the harvest season of autumn with its beautiful red leaves, and winter busy with preparations for the end of this year and the star of the next. There many things to see and do, including delicious foods, as well as traditional year-end and New Year events.

Autumn (September / October / November)

©MAHATHIR MOHD YASIN / Shutterstock.com

1. Meiji Jingu Gaien is a place famous for its gingko trees. They are in full bloom from mid-November
2. Jugoya is a festival held to show gratitude to the autumnal harvest
3. During Halloween, people wearing costumes parade in Shibuya

The colors of Tokyo's autumn are featuring red and yellow tones from the autumn leaves. In particular, many gingko trees line the street, and the appearance of the asphalt buried in their fallen leaves makes a deep impression. At night, a large moon floats in the clear air sky, and insects such as crickets, and suzumushi (bell-ring crickets) are singing. While admiring the autumn seasonal traditions, Japanese people eat with relish as the harvest of rich crops including the first crop rice, saury, and matsutake mushroom.

[Event]

Moon-viewing (around mid-September), an event during which moon viewing dumplings are offered to the full moon and the moon is admired. The Tokyo Game Show (around mid-September), a video game convention. The Tokyo International Film Festival (around the end of October) brings together Japanese and Western blockbusters. Tori-no-Ichi (two or three days in November), a fair featuring "rakes" for business prosperity. Tokyo's autumn leaves (around late November).

COLUMN About public holidays

There are 16 public holidays a year in Japan. Although there are important holidays, such as the Emperor's Birthday (December 23), there are also some holidays not related to history or tradition, such as Mountain Day (August 11) and others. Respect for the Aged Day (Third Monday of September), a day to honor elderly citizens and celebrate longev-ity , as well as some other public holidays, are unique events without many comparable examples around the world.

Winter (December / January / February)

1. Winter illuminations twinkle in the city, and the atmosphere becomes festive
2. It is a custom to eat the number of Setsubun beans corresponding to your age and pray for good health
3. This is how hatsumode looks. People perform the New Year's greetings to gods and buddhas

©Takashi Images / Shutterstock.com

December is also called Shiwasu (masters are running). It means that even self-possessed important people are so busy that they have to run around. Although these days people are busy enjoying Christmas, New Year's Eve, during the Edo period, December 31 was the day of the year to settle accounts, so townspeople were busy raising money . As cold winds blows around the city, people keep warm under the kotatsu at home. Even though it is the traditional way to spend winter in Japan, currently the number of houses equipped with a kotatsu has decreased.

[Event]

Ako Gishi Festival (December 14), an event held on the day when the 47 samurai struck down the enemy lord. On New Year's Eve (December 31), listen to the bells and eat soba for New Year's Eve. During the New Year holiday (January 1 to 3), Hatsumode (pay your first visit of the year to a shrine) and eat New Year's dishes purported to bring good luck, as well as Ozoni (Japanese New Year Mochi Soup). Setsubun (February 3), an exorcism ritual during which beans are thrown at demons.

＊Photos are for illustrative purpose only ＊Event schedule varies depending on the year

Travel tips

Tokyo is a city that has well-developed infrastructure and an environment safe enough that you can walk by yourself at night without any problems. However, there are still some points you should be careful about, such the Wi-Fi and ATM situation. Since you are coming all the way to Japan, enhance your journey by learning a few things in advance.

Check!

About **money**

▶ ATM

You can withdraw Japanese yen with cards issued overseas (card with credit function) if it is from Seven Bank (at 7-Eleven convenient stores) and post office ATMs. There are more and more ATMs at other banks that let you use foreign cards as well. If you are going to use a foreign card, check available ATMs and what cards are accepted in advance.

▶ Tax

Consumption tax is applied at a uniform rate of 8% on all services and products. However, recently the number of shops other than duty-free shops offering tax-free services, such as Don Quijote and others, are increasing. They are recognizable with the "TAX -FREE" mark, so keep an eye out for them.

＊Tax rate may also be subject to change due to revision of consumption tax

▶ Credit cards

Credit cards are accepted in the majority of large-scale stores such as department stores, chain stores, tax-free shops, etc. The most accepted are Visa cards. There are also stores where you can use MasterCard, American Express, Diners Club, and UnionPay cards. In many cases, the logos of cards accepted are displayed near the store entrance and cash register or on the menu, etc. However, there are many small privately run shops that accept only cash, so generally it is better to use cash.

About **emergency contacts**

▶ Hospitals

In Tokyo, there are hospitals that can perform medical examinations in foreign languages as well. For each hospital, you may want to check the "Guide for when you are feeling ill" available on the Japan National Tourism Organization website. It should also be noted that the number to call an ambulance is "119".

▶ Disasters

If a disaster or incident occurs, seek assistance from your country's embassy or consulate. For emergencies, call "119" for the fire department and "110" for the police.

About **living in Tokyo**

▶ Drinking water

You will have no problem drinking Tokyo tap water. Bureau of Waterworks Tokyo Metropolitan Government is more stringent than the national standards and continues to work on water quality management. If you are concerned about the smell, you can still buy mineral water in convenience stores.

▶ Smoking and drinking

Smoking and drinking is permitted starting at 20 years old. In regards to smoking, regulations on littering and smoking while walking differ depending on the ward. Some wards have banned street smoking completely (those caught doing so will be fined), so be careful. In recent years, the number of restaurants prohibiting smoking and with separate seating for smokers has increased as well.

▶ Business hours

Bank counters are open from 9:00 to 15:00. Standard hours for museums and other tourist attractions are from 9:00 to 17:00. Convenience stores, family restaurants, and chain restaurants such as Fuji Soba are open 24 hours a day. Public transportation, including trains and buses, run from around 4:30 in the early morning until around 1 at night.

＊Time for first train and last train may differ depending on the line

▶ Power supply and voltage

The voltage in Japan is AC100V. The voltage in many countries, such as Europe, China, and others, is AC220V, so a transformer may be required sometimes. In addition, the shape of plug sockets may be different in Japan, you should bring along a multifunctional conversion plug as well. Some hotels lend transformers and conversion plugs, too.

About **telephones and mail**

▶ Phones

In areas around stations and other public areas, you can find public phones that can be used starting from 10 yen. If you want to use your own phone, a Wi-Fi router or SIM card is recommended. Wi-Fi routers can be rented for a fee from some tourist information centers and at airports. SIM cards are available for purchase at airports, electronics stores, etc.

▶ Mail

Post offices are recommended if you want to send packages back to your country. When sending an air mail, it is the earliest to take it to the post office. Postage rate is 70 yen for postcards.

▶ Internet

Although there is little public Wi-Fi in Tokyo, many hotels and restaurants offer Wi-Fi to their customers. If you want to rent a Wi-Fi router, they can be rented conveniently at airports, as all airports have a rental booth. Even though same-day rental is possible, advance online reservation is more certain.

Manners and customs

In Japan, there is a saying that means the same as "When in Rome, do as the Romans do". This means that you should follow the rules of an unknown land when you go. Here, let us introduce the most typical Japanese manners, etiquette, and customs.

About **sightseeing**

Do not cut in line

Line up at the end of the queue when you see one in front of popular restaurants. Cutting in line is one of the manner breaches Japanese people hate the most.

Separate your garbage

The public garbage cans found in parks and others places are classified into 3 types: burnable garbage, non-burnable garbage, and cans and PET bottles. Separate your garbage properly when you throw it away.

Leave the right side of the escalator open

On escalators, people line up on the left side, leaving the right side open. The right side is used for walking by those who are in a hurry.

It is rude to point at people

Pointing at people is rude in Japan, too. It is not acceptable even with someone you are friendly with, so don't do it.

Filming and recording during shows is prohibited

Filming and recording of stage performances such as Kabuki and others are prohibited. It is also sometimes forbidden to take pictures in the main hall of temples and shrines, so be careful.

Smoke at the designated locations

Many areas in Tokyo have banned smoking in the streets, but you can find public smoking areas around parks and train stations. Also, there are restaurants that are completely non-smoking, restaurants with smoking seats, and those with smoking permitted depending on the hours, so be careful.

Walk on the right side of the sidewalk

Walking on the right side of broad sidewalks is a standard. It should be noted that if you ride a bicycle, the rule is to ride it on the left side of the road.

Pocket tissues distributed on the streets are free

No need to pay any money, because these tissues are a type of advertisement. Don't hesitate to take some.

About **restaurants**

③Mayoi-bashi:When you hesitate about which dish to eat, hence hovering the chopsticks over the dishes.
④Sashi-bashi:When you stab food with your chopsticks
⑤Nigiri-bashi:When you grab chposticks together

How to use chopsticks and chopstick taboos

You won't have any problems if you use chopsticks smoothly without useless movements, just like with fork and knife. However, sticking chopsticks into a bowl of rice, known as "tate-bashi①", or passing food from chopstick to chopstick, known as awase-bashi②", are taboos. This is because these are both customs used during funerals and considered to bring bad luck.

Hold the bowl in your hands

It is considered good manners to hold rice bowls or soup bowls in your hands. However, you must not hold plates containing the main or side dishes.

Eat without leaving anything left

Leaving food on your plate means that the food wasn't good. Even in restaurants with all-you-can-eat course, you should serve yourself only the amount you can eat.

It's OK to slurp noodles

In Japan, slurping noodles such as soba, udon, and ramen is not considered bad manners. It is said that this eating style started during the Edo period, and that slurping vigorously made it possible to eat in a short time without the noodles getting too soft (various explanations exist). Also, it is said that by slurping the noodles, the air, soup, and noodles provide a well-balanced mix, making it even tastier.

Do not place your elbows on the table when eating

Putting your elbows on the table makes you slouch, which looks bad. Dishes are tastier when they are eaten in a good mood with a beautiful posture.

Water, tea, and wet towels are free

In the almost restaurant these products are generally available as a free service provided by the restaurant. Feel free to ask when you are thirsty.

Write your name on the waiting list when it's crowded

When popular restaurants are crowded, you may have to write your name and the number of people in your group regardless of whether you are Japanese or a foreigner.

Bring your bill to the cash register for payment

In many restaurants, customers bring their bill to the register. There are also many places where you pay at the table, such as places with alcoholic beverages and fancy restaurants.

COLUMN

Japanese Cuisine

The basic form of Japanese cuisine is: "cooked rice", "main dish", "side dish", "pickles", and "soup", all served in vessels appropriate to each of them beautifully. Since the taste of the ingredients themselves is considered the most important aspect, seasoning is simple, and more than anything, attention is paid to the freshness of the ingredients. It could be said that it has a totally different philosophy from French cuisine, which is elaborated with sauces.

Characteristics of Japanese cuisine and its indispensable condiments

●Bringing out the taste of ingredients

In order to keep the taste of ingredients spices and other strong seasonings are not often used and instead condiments are there to complement flavor. Sashimi, soy sauce, and wasabi are the ultimate representation of this.

●Soy food

Soy sauce and miso, both made from soybeans, are indispensable condiments to the Japanese cuisine, and their unique saltiness is the base of seasoning for all dishes.

●Dashi and Umami

The broth that contains flavor components extracted from boiled bonito, kelp, shiitake mushrooms, and other ingredients is called dashi. This gives depth to the taste of Japanese cuisine.

●Sake

Japanese sake is an alcoholic beverage brewed using mainly rice, koji(malted rice), and water. With its extremely delicate flavor, Japanese sake and Japanese cuisine enhance each other's flavor.

About **shopping**

Ask before you try

Ask the store clerk before you try items on. To use the fitting rooms in Japan, you will have to take off your shoes first in some stores. If you are provided with a sheet or bag to cover your face when trying something on, make sure to use them.

Japanese Phrasebook→P.204

Do not touch food excessively

Especially when it comes to deli items or raw food, be considerate of other customers and avoid touching the products.

Do not drink or eat in stores

You cannot drink or eat in any store while shopping. The only exceptions are for tasting of food and drink samples.

Check with the clerk first before you take pictures of products and the inside of the store

Since there are stores where you cannot take any pictures, avoid trouble by asking permission in advance from the clerk.

🚺🚹 About **toilet**

Stand in line even when it's crowded

Lining up and waiting for your turn in any situation is part of Japanese manners. Line up near the entrance and use the next available toilet on your turn. For emergencies, ask the person waiting at the start of the line.

How to use Japanese-style toilets

Although their number have decreased in recent years, you can still find "Japanese-style" toilets (squatting toilets) in Japan. Use them by squatting down carefully.

Experience the washlet

Washlet is the toilet seat with electric bidet to wash bottom with warm water. There are functions to control water pressure and temperature, a dryer, etc. Your can operate them with buttons on one side of the seat or on the wall.

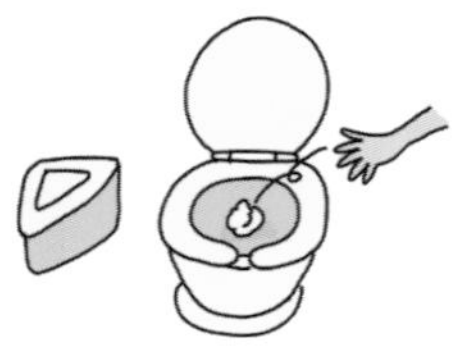

It's OK to flush the toilet paper

Flush the used toilet paper in the toilet. Even if you find a garbage can nearby, do not throw the toilet paper there.

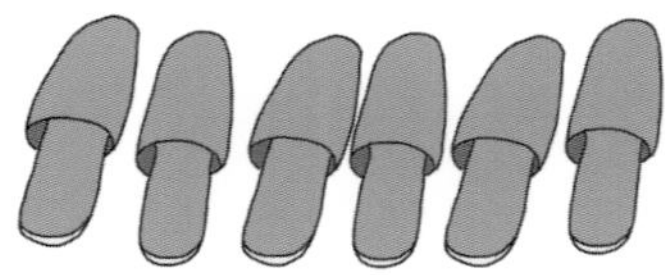

Place the slippers side by side when you leave

There are slippers for toilet use in some inns and restaurants. Align them properly for the next person once you are done.

About **public transport**

Cooperate with others during rush hours

The rush hour commute is from 9:00 to 10:00 in the morning and 17:00 to 20:00 at night. It also gets crowded around 24:00, just before the last train. You should cooperate with people getting off if you are close to the door by getting out of the train at each station to let people out.

The magic words: "Sumimasen, orimasu"

When the train is packed with people and you cannot get off, say out loud, "Sumimasen, orimasu", which means "Excuse me, I'm getting off". By saying so, people around will open the way for you.

Priority to those getting off the train

When the train arrives, don't rush in immediately. First of all, let those who are getting off do so first.

Stay quiet on the train

Talking loudly with your friends or on the phone is a breach of manners. Speaking in a volume slightly lower than your usual speaking voice is fine.

Refrain from eating and drinking when crowded

Although it is not forbidden to eat or drink on public transport, considering that it may bother other passengers, it is preferable to refrain from doing so when the train is crowded.

Go with the flow of people in the station and on platforms

In small stations, traffic often flows naturally on the left side, so go with the flow.

Be careful handling luggage on the train!

During rush hour, bulky luggage takes space on the train. Although it depends on the size, try to be considerate by keeping your luggage in front of you, using the overhead rack, etc.

At the station, "Suica" and "Pasmo" are all-purpose cards

Prepaid train cards "Suica" and "Pasmo" are super convenient items, since they are not only used for train fares, but also in vending machines and at Kiosk stores.

At the station, stay calm and look at the direction boards

Even though the stations can be complicated, inside you can find an easy-to-understand guide divided by color and information provided on direction boards available in English, too. If you stay calm and check your current location, you should be all right.

COLUMN

The useful facilities at Tokyo Station

No wonder many people use Tokyo Station, with its good access. Here we introduce some spots in Tokyo Station that you will be better off knowing.

Inside the ticket gate *A convenient service*

B1F Station Concierge Tokyo

A concierge is available at all times, and gives guidance on station information, tourist attractions, etc. Support in English is also available. The concierge is located in View Square nearby Yaesu underground central ticket gates.

Inside and outside the ticket gate

Within the premises of Tokyo Station, you can find several facilities. Since it is not easy to leave the ticket gates once you enter, know your destination first.

B1F Foreign currency exchange corner

Located next to Station Concierge Tokyo. Open from 9:00 to 20:00, it lets you exchange 33 currencies.

B1F/1F Rest areas

You can find rest spaces free of charge inside of View Square and at ecute Tokyo located near the Shinkansen Transfer Gate on the 1st floor.

B1F Tax-free counter

Available for products purchased in the Ekinaka facilities such as "Gransta", "Central Street", and others. Immediate access after going down to B1F from Shinkansen South Transfer Gate

Outside the ticket gate *Perfect for choosing a souvenir*

東京駅一番街

First Avenue Tokyo Station

Address: 1-9-1 Marunouchi, Chiyoda-ku
TEL: 03-3210-0077 **Opening hours:**Differs depending on the store **Closed:**None
Access: Immediate access from JR Yaesu Underground Central Exit ticket gates.

Tokyo Okashi Land 東京おかしランド

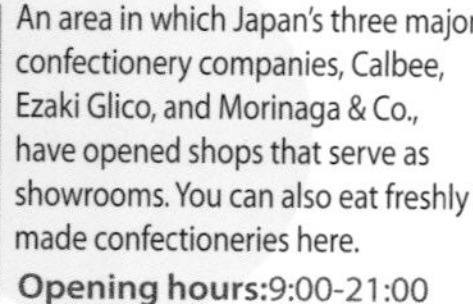

An area in which Japan's three major confectionery companies, Calbee, Ezaki Glico, and Morinaga & Co., have opened shops that serve as showrooms. You can also eat freshly made confectioneries here.

Opening hours:9:00-21:00

東京キャラクターストリート

Tokyo Character Street

Lines with the official shops of TV stations and characters. Among them, the popular are the Pokémon Store, Rilakkuma Store, and JUMP Shop.

Opening hours:10:00-20:30

Pokémon Store Tokyo Station Shop

Japanese Phrasebook

Basic Phrases

Thank you
ありがとう
a ri ga tō

Hello
こんにちは
kon ni chi wa

Good morning
おはようございます
o ha yo u go za i masu

Good night
おやすみなさい
o ya su mi na sai

Goodbye
さようなら
sa yō na ra

Excuse me
すみません
su mi ma sen

I'm sorry
ごめんなさい
go men na sai

Let's eat
いただきます
i ta da ki masu

Thank you for the meal
ごちそうさまでした
go chi sō sama de shi ta

For Sightseeing

Where am I?
ここはどこですか?
ko ko wa do ko desu ka

How much (is the admission fee)?
(入場料金)はいくらですか?
(nyū jō ryō kin) wa i ku ra desu ka ?

What time is it now?
今何時ですか?
ima nan ji desu ka

I want to go here (point to the map)
ココ(地図を指差して)に行きたいです
ko ko ni i ki ta i desu

What line should I take for ◯◯?
◯◯は何番線に乗ればいいですか?
◯ ◯ wa nanbansen ni no re ba i i de su ka

Where is the (Tourist Information Center)?
(観光案内所)はどこですか?
(kankō an nai jyo) wa do ko desu ka

For Dining

When making reservations

I'd like to make a reservation for ◯ persons at ◯ o'clock
◯時に◯名の予約をお願いします
◯ ji ni ◯mei no yo yaku o o nega i shi masu

My name is ◯◯
私の名前は◯◯です
watashi no na mae wa ◯◯ desu

I am a vegetarian
私はベジタリアンです
watashi wa be ji ta ri a n desu

Do you have vegetarian food?
ベジタリアン料理はありますか?
be ji ta ri a n ryō ri wa a ri masu ka

I am vegan. I do not eat (eggs)
私はビーガンです
watashi wa bī ga n desu
(卵)が食べられません
(tamago) ga ta be ra re ma sen

I am allergic (to soba)
私は(ソバ)アレルギーがあります
watashi wa (so ba) a re ru gī ga a ri masu

I can not eat ◯◯.
◯◯が食べられません。
◯◯ ga ta be ra re ma sen

I'd like to use a coupon
クーポンを使いたいです
kū po n o tsuka i ta i desu

When entering a restaurant

Do you have an English menu?
英語のメニューはありますか?
ei go no me nyū wa a ri masu ka

What do you recommend?
おすすめは何ですか?
o su su me wa nan desu ka

Give me ◯◯, please
◯◯をください
◯◯ o ku da sai

Cheers! (toast)
乾杯!
kan pai

Delicious!
おいしい!
o i shi i

When leaving a restaurant

Check, please
お会計をお願いします
o kai kei o o nega i shi masu

For Shopping

When entering a shop / shopping

That's cute
かわいいです
ka wa i i desu

Let me try this on
試着させてください
shi chaku sa se te ku da sai

Do you have a different color?
色違いはありますか?
iro chiga i wa a ri masu ka

Do you have a larger (smaller) size?
大きい(小さい)サイズはありますか?
ō ki i (chii sa i) sa i zu wa a ri masu ka

How much is that?
これはいくらですか?
ko re wa i ku ra desu ka

Give me (number of items) please
○個ください
○ ko ku da sai

When paying

Do you accept credit(AMEX) cards?
クレジット(AMEX)カードは使えますか?
ku re ji tto (amekkusu) kā do wa tsuka e masu ka

You gave me the wrong change
おつりが違います
o tsu ri ga chiga i masu

For Emergencies

Accident

Help!
助けて!
tasu ke te

Stop!
やめて!
ya me te

I've lost (my bag)
(鞄)を落としました
kaban o o to shimashi ta

When you feel ill

Where is (the hospital)?
(病院は)どこですか?
(byō in wa) do ko desu ka

My ○○ hurts
○○が痛いです
○○ ga ita i desu

In the event of a disaster

What happened?
何があったのですか?
nani ga a tta no desu ka

Where should I evacuate to?
どこに逃げたらいいですか?
do ko ni ni ge ta ra i i desu ka

Convenient words to know

Body Parts

Head	頭(atama)	Eyes	目(me)	Ears	耳(mimi)	Nose	鼻(hana)
Neck	首(kubi)	Arm	腕(ude)	Finger	指(yubi)	Stomach	お腹(onaka)
Knee	膝 (hiza)	Foot	足(ashi)	Back	背中(senaka)	Chest	胸(mune)

Facilities

ATM	ATM (ei thī emu)	Post office	郵便局 (yū bin kyoku)	Station	駅 (eki)
Embassy	大使館 (tai shi kan)	Consulate	領事館 (ryō ji kan)	Bank	銀行 (gin kō)
Pharmacy	薬局 (yak kyoku)	Tourist Information Center	観光案内所 (kan kō an nai jyo)	Convenience store	コンビニエンスストア (ko n bi ni e n su su to a)

Number

1	一(ichi)	2	二(ni)	3	三(san)	4	四(shi/yon)	5	五(go)
6	六(roku)	7	七(nana)	8	八(hachi)	9	九(kyū)	10	十(jū)
20	二十 (ni jū)	30	三十 (san jū)	40	四十 (yon jū)	50	五十 (go jū)	60	六十 (roku jū)
70	七十 (nana jū)	80	八十 (hachi jū)	90	九十 (kyū jū)	100	百 (hyaku)	1000	千 (sen)

INDEX

● Sightseeing ● Eating ● Shopping ● Other

* Misplaced pages and missing pages will be replaced. Please enclose the publication and paper with return address and send to the following address.
Address: Shoeisha Co., Ltd　Readers Service Center
Postal Code: 160-0006　5 Funamachi, Shinjuku-ku, Tokyo

STAFF

編集	株式会社翔泳社（昆清徳）
編集・取材・本文	アーク·コミュニケーションズ（小此木裕子、山本明佳、塚田奈菜子、早川薫子）、魚住陽向、本山光、編集室アルパカ（内山賢一）
カバー・本文デザイン	岸麻里子
カバーイラスト	武藤文昭
本文イラスト	岡本倫幸　かたおかともこ
本文 DTP	株式会社エストール
写真撮影	アーク・フォト・ワークス（清水亮一、田村裕未）、田尻陽子、野田真、花田真知子
写真協力	Shutterstock
地図製作	マップデザイン研究室
校正	株式会社聚珍社
アクセス校正	アイドマ編集室
翻訳	株式会社ビーコス
協賛	SOMPOホールディングス株式会社

SOMPO GUIDE TOKYO（ソンポ ガイド トウキョウ）

2017年2月9日 初版第1刷発行

著者	翔泳社トラベルガイド編集部
発行人	佐々木幹夫
発行所	株式会社翔泳社（http://www.shoeisha.co.jp）
印刷・製本	凸版印刷株式会社

ISBN 978-4-7981-4808-3
Printed in Japan